S0-APO-396

THE LUNGS
AND RESPIRATORY SYSTEM

YOUR BODY YOUR HEALTH

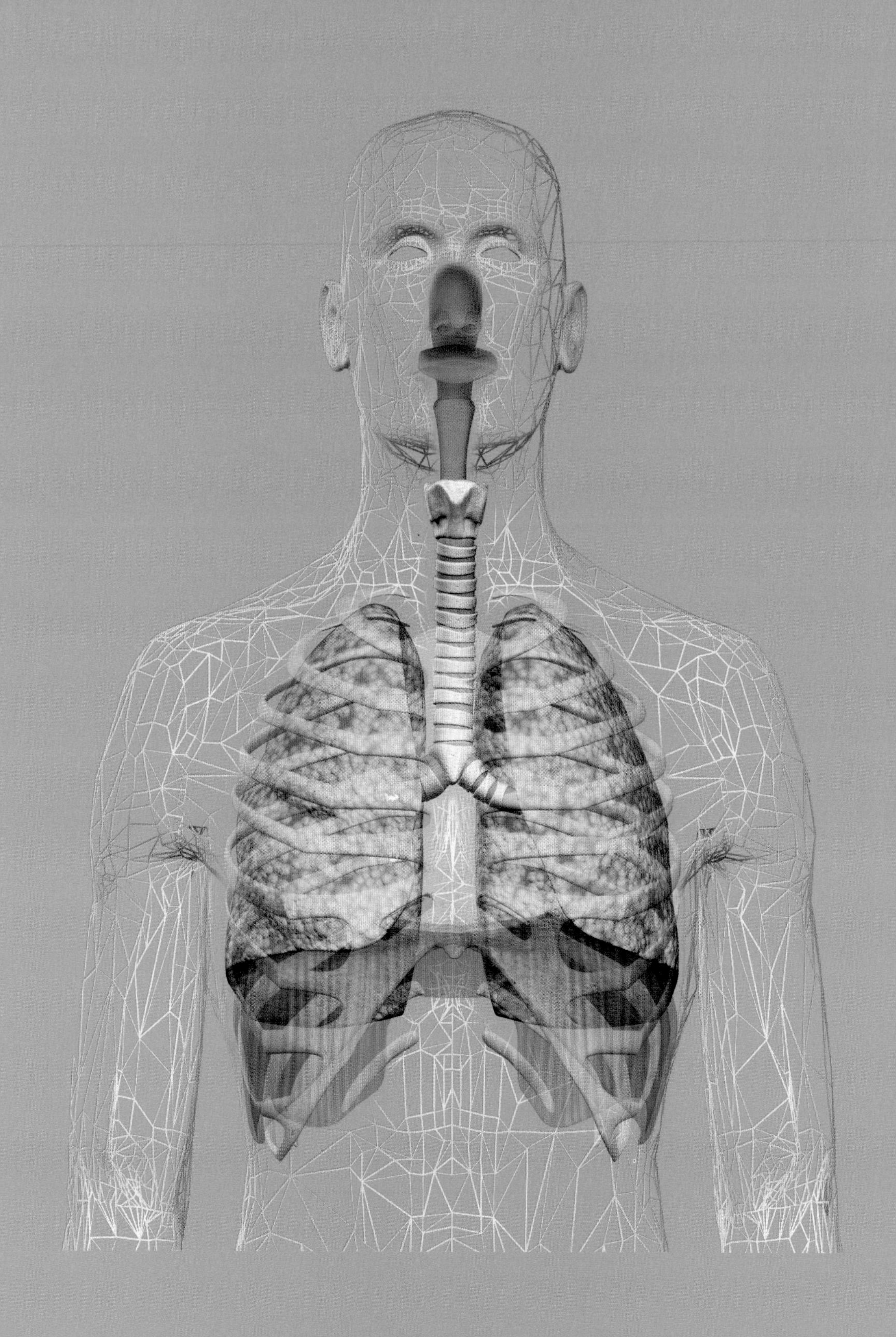

YOUR BODY YOUR HEALTH

THE LUNGS AND RESPIRATORY SYSTEM

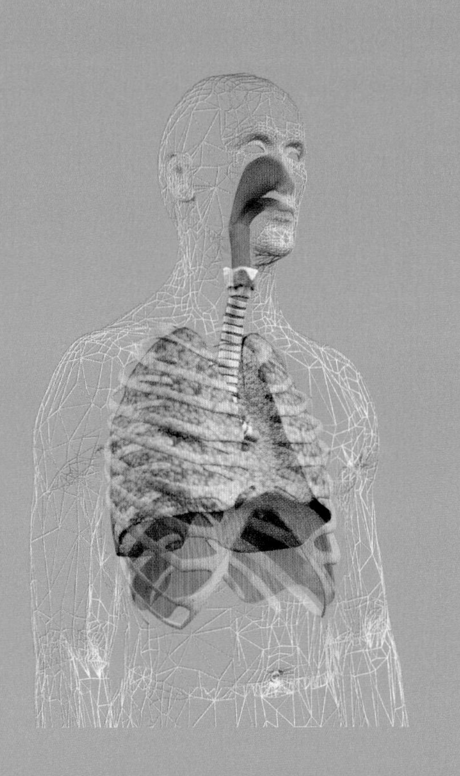
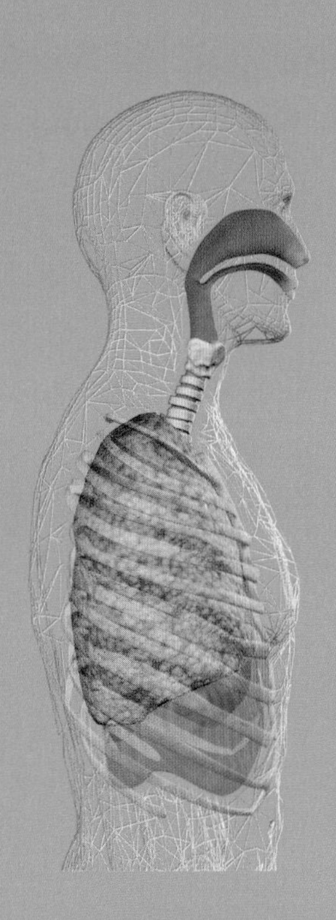
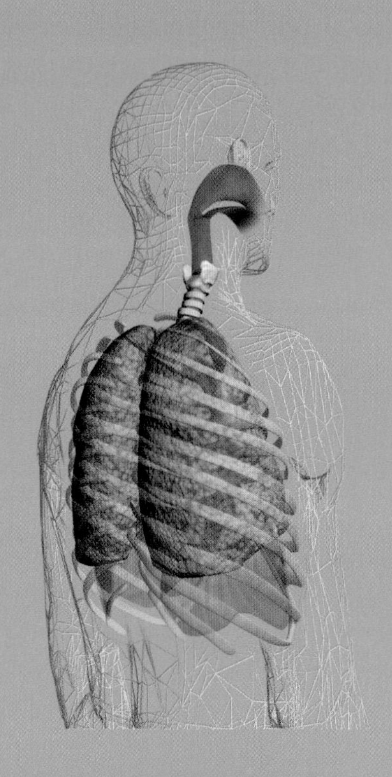

The Reader's Digest Association, Inc.

Pleasantville, New York

London Sydney Montreal

The Lungs and Respiratory System

was created and produced by
Carroll & Brown Limited
20 Lonsdale Road
London NW6 6RD

Library of Congress Cataloging-in-Publication Data has been applied for.

ISBN 0-7621-0458-9

Printed in the United States of America
1 3 5 7 9 8 6 4 2

The information in this book is for reference only; it is not intended as a substitute for a doctor's diagnosis and care. The editors urge anyone with continuing medical problems or symptoms to consult a doctor.

American Edition Produced by
NOVA Graphic Services, Inc.
2370 York Road, Suite A9A
Jamison, PA 18929 USA
(215)542-3900

President
David Davenport

Editorial Director
Robin C. Bonner

Composition Manager
Steve Magnin

Art Director
Paul Fry

Associate Project Editor
Linnea Hermanson

Pulmonary Specialist Consultant
Dr. Rohit Ahuja, MD,
Fellow, Pulmonary and Critical Care Medicine,
Thomas Jefferson University, Philadelphia

CONTRIBUTORS

Dr Saul Berkowitz, MRCP, Department of Gastroenterology, Whittington Hospital, London

Wynnie Chan, BSc, PhD, Public Health Nutritionist

Marilyn Eveleigh, BA, PGCE, RGN, SRM, RHV, NP, FWT, FRSH, Nurse Advisor in Primary Care and Public Health, East Sussex Brighton and Hove Health Authority

Katy Glynne, BSc, MRPharmS, Dip Pharmacy Practice, Clinical Services Manager, Charing Cross Hospital, London

Mr Pankaj Kumar, MA, FRCS, Department of Thoracic Surgery, Royal Brompton Hospital, London

Mr George Ladas, MD, Consultant Thoracic Surgeon, Royal Brompton Hospital, London, Honorary Senior Lecturer, Imperial College School of Medicine, London

Joel Levy, BSc, MA, Medical Writer

Dr Marcus Munafo, MA, MSc, CPsychol, Research Fellow, Imperial Cancer Research Fund General Practice Research Group, University of Oxford

Patsy Riley, BSc, CBiol, MIBiol, Medical Writer

Dr Nicoletta Scaravelli, Department of Medicine, Watford General Hospital

Dr Jenny Sutcliffe, MB BS, MCSP, Medical Writer

Karan Thomas, BSc, Physical Activity and Health Specialist

For the Reader's Digest
Editor in Chief Neil E. Wertheimer
Editorial Director Christopher Cavanaugh
Senior Designer Judith Carmel
Production Technology Manager Douglas A. Croll
Manufacturing Manager John L. Cassidy

YOUR BODY YOUR HEALTH

The Lungs and Respiratory System

Awareness of health issues and expectations of medicine are greater today than ever before. A long and healthy life has come to be looked on as not so much a matter of luck but almost as a right. However, as our knowledge of health and the causes of disease has grown, it has become increasingly clear that health is something that we can all influence, for better or worse, through choices we make in our lives. *Your Body Your Health* is designed to help you make the right choices to make the most of your health potential. Each volume in the series focuses on a different physiological system of the body, explaining what it does and how it works. There is a wealth of advice and health tips on diet, exercise, and lifestyle factors, as well as the health checks you can expect throughout life. You will find out what can go wrong and what can be done about it and learn from people's real-life experiences of diagnosis and treatment. Finally, there is a detailed A-to-Z index of the major conditions that can affect the system. The series builds into a complete user's manual for the care and maintenance of the entire body.

This volume looks at the mechanics behind breathing—the source of life itself. Follow a breath of air from the nose deep into the lungs and then into the bloodstream, which takes it to every cell in your body. See how the respiratory system filters and cleans air from the moment it enters your nostril. Discover the best ways to preserve lung health through simple lifestyle choices, like getting regular exercise. Find out how infections are spread and when self-medication is appropriate. Conquer the biggest threat to lung health—smoking—by following our 10-point plan. Read about what you can do to safeguard your lung health against the atmospheric threats like pollution and what you can do to handle asthma. Most important, find out how the respiratory system experts determine what is wrong—from simple measurement tests to sophisticated imaging techniques that allow doctors to see inside the lungs—and the wide range of treatments available.

Contents

1 How your lungs work

2 Breathing free and easy

3 What happens when things go wrong

The life story of the lungs

In cultures around the world and throughout history, from ancient Rome to the present day, the breath of life has been synonymous with the human soul; even the word *spirit* comes from the Latin *spirare*, "to breathe." According to the Bible, the divine spark that brought man to life, turning a lump of clay and dirt into a living being, was the breath of God.

The ancient Romans and Bible scholars weren't far off the mark in their beliefs—the air that you breathe does contain the vital essence on which life depends, the fuel that keeps your internal fires burning. That fuel is oxygen.

FUELING THE ENGINES OF YOUR BODY

Every cell in your body needs a constant supply of oxygen to live; that's a lot of oxygen—about a quarter of a liter every minute when you are at rest. It is the job of the lungs to supply this fuel. If you think of the cells of your body as billions of tiny engines, burning fuel to keep going, then your lungs are like an amazingly efficient biological oil refinery, ceaselessly extracting pure fuel from the air all around us. It provides this precious fuel through the blood, which passes down the amazing network of supply pipes that make up the circulation. When the cells burn oxygen to get energy, they produce carbon dioxide, a waste gas. When the blood delivers oxygen to a cell, the blood also picks up this carbon dioxide, taking it back to the lungs so that it can be breathed out.

Formal greeting
The Maoris of New Zealand share breath as part of their traditional greeting, by touching foreheads and noses.

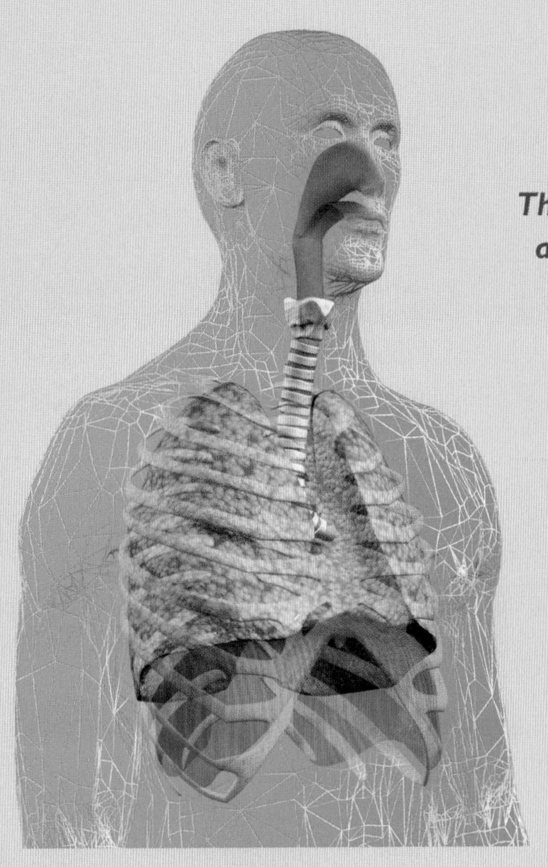

The network of airways in the lungs has more than a million branches leading to around 300 million tiny air pockets, called alveoli.

FROM THE SEA TO THE LAND

The human lung is among the most complex in the animal world, and it is possible to follow the course of its evolution by looking at the lungs of simpler animals. Humans, like birds and reptiles, descended from animals that crawled out of the sea hundreds of millions of years ago. Our marine ancestors probably had gills like today's fish, but gills are not a viable option on land because they are too exposed and would quickly dry out. The first creatures to move onto the land were probably similar to today's lungfish, a type of fish that can survive for long periods out of water. In lungfish, the top of the digestive tract is expanded and surrounded by many blood vessels, and they "swallow" air in order to breathe. Amphibians use a similar system, but when reptiles and mammals evolved, they developed more complex lungs, almost completely separated from the digestive tract, together with intricate bone and muscle arrangements for breathing. Your lungs are the culmination of more than 400 million years of evolution since the first creature crawled out onto the land.

PUMPING FOR YOUR LIFE

The human heart is celebrated for its tireless pumping and apparently boundless energy, but it is not the only organ in your body that has to keep working every minute of every hour of your life. The rate at which your body burns oxygen means that your lungs need a constant supply of fresh air to refine and the physical capability to do so. They have to deal with the mechanics of expanding and contracting several thousand times a day.

The lungs are part of the set of structures and tissues known as the respiratory system. All are highly specialized to make breathing easy so that most of the time you don't even know you're doing it. You draw at least 17,000 breaths a day, each of them involving a gulp of cold, dry, dirty air. This air has to be filtered, heated, and humidified as it travels from your nose and mouth, down a network of branching airways, to your lungs. The distance involved isn't great, but the network is fantastically complex, with branches leading to tiny air pockets where blood receives its rich cargo of oxygen. The muscles and bones of your chest surround and protect these tubes and pockets, and act like an endlessly pumping bellows.

The evolution of breathing

When the first creatures left the sea to live on the land, they probably breathed as lungfish do now, by gulping oxygen from the air.

A LIFE HISTORY OF YOUR LUNGS

The complex machinery of your lungs grows from humble beginnings, starting off as a sort of cellular "sock" in the developing embryo. The first lung tissue appears in the third week of pregnancy. By this time the digestive system is already present in a primitive form, and the lungs develop from a shallow groove in the floor of what is destined to become the pharynx (part of the throat). Within a few days the groove has lengthened and deepened, becoming a pocket of tissue that hangs down like a sock. This will become the windpipe. In week 4 the tip of the sock branches to give a pair of lung buds, which get longer, extending down inside the embryo to the level of the heart. By week 8, a membrane has formed, dividing the lungs and heart, and a space has opened up around the latter. A sheet of muscle forms underneath the growing lungs, separating them from the fetal liver.

As well as getting longer, the lung buds continue to branch repeatedly, until by the end of the sixth month of pregnancy there are more than a million branches. All around them other types of tissue develop into blood vessels and support cells that help to hold the lungs together. In the seventh month of pregnancy, hundreds of alveoli sprout up around the end of each branch of the airways, like a vine

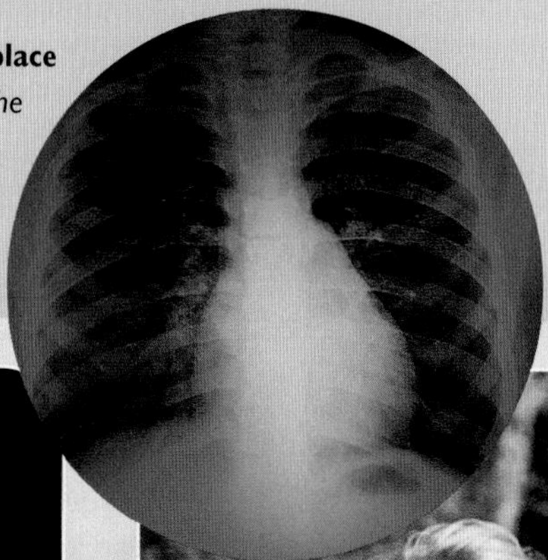

All in place
Lungs continue to develop until the age of 8, when children's lungs have their full complement of branches and alveoli.

LUNGS FOR A LIFETIME

Your lungs must work from the moment of birth until the moment of death to keep you healthy. The lungs grow and mature in childhood and face many threats to their health, but if you treat them well, they will serve you for a century or more.

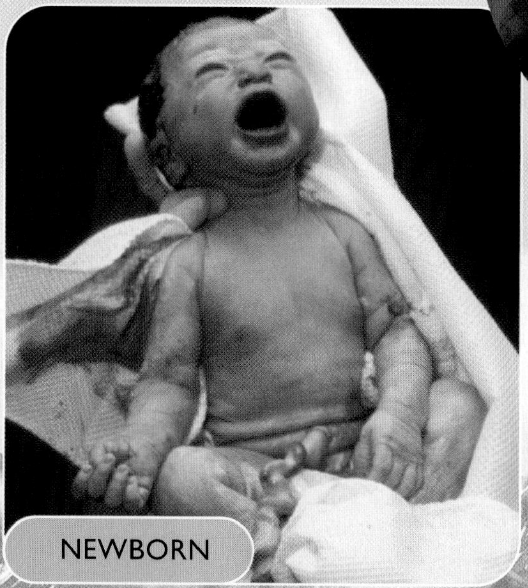

NEWBORN

CHILDHOOD

The first breath
A newborn baby takes an enormous step in drawing the first breath. This inflates the lungs and sets the respiratory system to work.

bearing bunches of grapes. Each alveolus is tiny, but collectively they have a massive surface area—opened out and laid flat, the alveoli in the adult lungs would completely cover the floor, walls, and ceiling of a small room.

The growing baby starts to practice breathing while still in the womb, sucking amniotic fluid in and out of its lungs, even though the mother is supplying all of the oxygen it needs through the umbilical cord (and breathing 20 percent harder than normal herself to keep up). The baby needs all the practice it can get—as a newborn, it will take its first breath within seconds, and by the time it is a few minutes old it will be breathing up to 80 times a minute (six times faster than an adult). As a child matures, its lungs get larger, and it can take in more air with each breath, so the rate of breathing gradually falls. By the age of 8, the alveoli have reached full size and remain this way for more than 20 years.

Like most parts of the body, the lungs are affected by aging from a relatively early age. A human male loses one square foot of the inner lining of his lungs each year after the age of 30. Fortunately, he has a lot to start with and still has 85 percent left in his mid-80s. But by the time you reach your ninth decade a host of factors may have affected your lung capacity and respiratory health.

Senior lungs
If you treat your lungs well and do not smoke, your lungs will continue to work efficiently regardless of age. Brisk exercise in the fresh air is one of the best ways to help keep your lungs in good shape.

Enjoyment of life
A healthy respiratory system allows you to live life to the fullest, taking every opportunity that presents itself.

Tree of life
This arteriograph of a healthy adult lung clearly shows the branches of the respiratory "tree."

Breathing high

A tribe of Peruvian Amerindians lives in the Andes at an altitude of 17,500 ft above sea level. They work at 19,000 ft, an altitude where most people would pass out or have seizures.

Physical characteristics, including lung capacity, vary among individuals and are determined by a mixture of hereditary and environmental factors. Elite athletes like Spanish cyclist Miguel Indurain, for example, seem almost to have been designed for physical excellence. Indurain has a lung capacity of 8 liters—33 percent more than an average athlete and 50 percent greater than a 25-year-old man of Indurain's height. Environmental conditions, too, can shape the respiratory system. Children born and raised at altitude show profound adaptations to the thin air and low oxygen levels of the environment. Such children have bigger chests and smaller bodies, making their lungs even bigger in relation to their overall size.

PROTECTING YOUR LUNGS

Ultimately, the size of your lungs is less important than what you put in them. Your lungs are exposed to damaging influences every day. Some are obvious—smoking and traffic smog, for example. Some are invisible or unexpected—they include germs floating in the air and natural radioactive gas leaking into houses from underlying rocks. Taking care of your respiratory health doesn't mean wearing a face mask at all times or moving to an unspoiled rural wilderness. It involves making informed choices about your lifestyle and taking simple steps to improve your environment. Avoiding cigarettes, adopting a healthy diet, and getting regular exercise can protect your lungs and keep them healthy. Improving your domestic and work

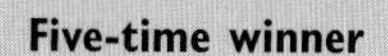

Five-time winner

A low resting heart rate and high lung capacity helped Miguel Indurain win the Tour de France, one of the world's most grueling sports events, five times in succession.

About 360,000 Americans die each year from lung diseases. Lung disease is responsible for one in seven deaths, making it the number three killer in the United States.

environments to minimize asthma triggers, air pollution, and other atmospheric irritants can also preserve and in many cases dramatically improve respiratory health.

The need to look after your lungs is becoming increasingly important—the lungs may soon replace the heart as the world's most endangered organ. Respiratory illness is already one of the world's biggest killers, but unlike many types of illness, such as cardiovascular disease, respiratory problems are on the increase in the developed world. Lung cancer, for instance, is the most common type of fatal cancer in the United States, and in Australia 25 percent of children now have asthma (that's three times more than in the mid-1980s).

The upsurge in respiratory illness has led some commentators to argue that we risk returning to early 20th-century levels of respiratory health. Then, tuberculosis was a common killer of children and adults alike, and terrible influenza pandemics spread around the globe killing millions: the Spanish flu pandemic of 1918–1919 killed 20 million people. Tuberculosis (TB) is once again on the rise in the developed world, and according to the World Health Organization there is a very real global threat from deadly new strains of influenza.

TAKING THE LUNG VIEW

Despite these emerging threats, the near eradication of diseases like TB and killer influenza has been one of the great success stories of medicine in the West; the development of antibiotics and vaccines are its greatest milestones. And medicine has continued to make strides in understanding and treating respiratory illness, with advances in drug therapy, for instance, revolutionizing the management of conditions from asthma to lung cancer. However, lung disease remains one of the hardest types of illness to treat, and it is in the future that respiratory medicine may really come into its own, in part through the emerging genetic technologies.

Vaccines for influenza are already an important public health tool, and genetic technology offers the hope of new and better vaccines for a range of respiratory illnesses. In the near future, improved understanding of the causes of asthma and the role pollution plays in its occurrence should help scientists to design better treatments or even ways to prevent the development of the disease altogether. Sprays and inhalers may be used a lot more, as delivery of genetic therapy via engineered airborne viruses becomes common. And in the imagined far future, perhaps, explorers and settlers of new planets might benefit from genetic improvements to lung capacity and other respiratory capabilities in order to cope with extreme atmospheric conditions. For most of us, however, looking after the lungs we've got—one of nature's most delicate but efficient designs—is the best way to ensure we enjoy the best of respiratory health.

Respiratory threat
The flu virus readily attaches to mucus, hence its threat to healthy lungs. In this coloured transmission electron micrograph the nucleus of the virus appears red; the green "spikes" allow the virus to attach itself to a cell.

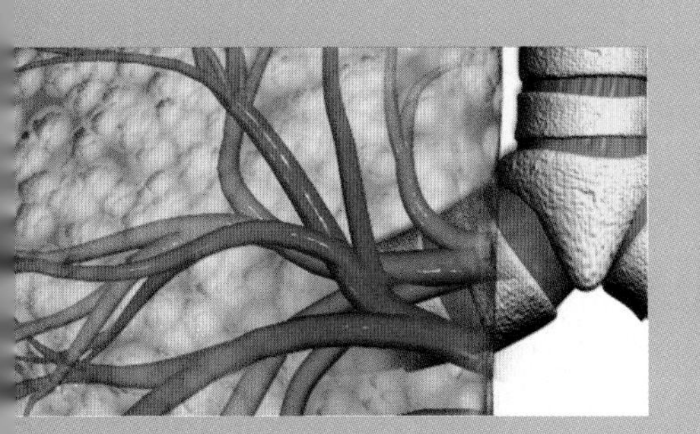

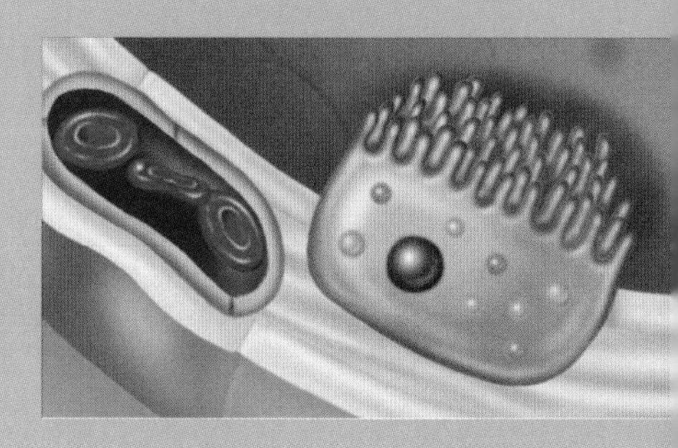

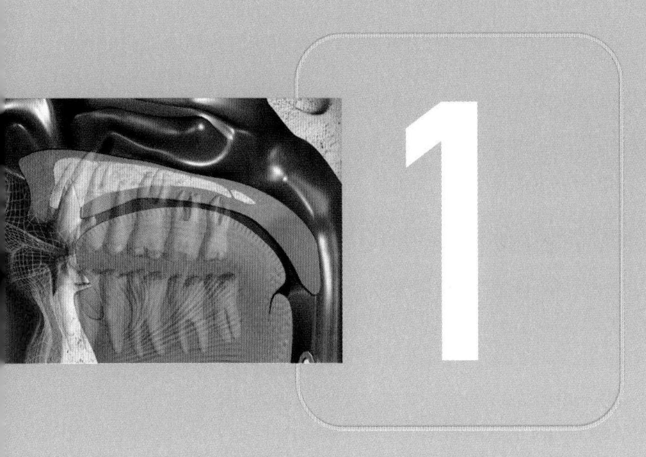

1

How your lungs work

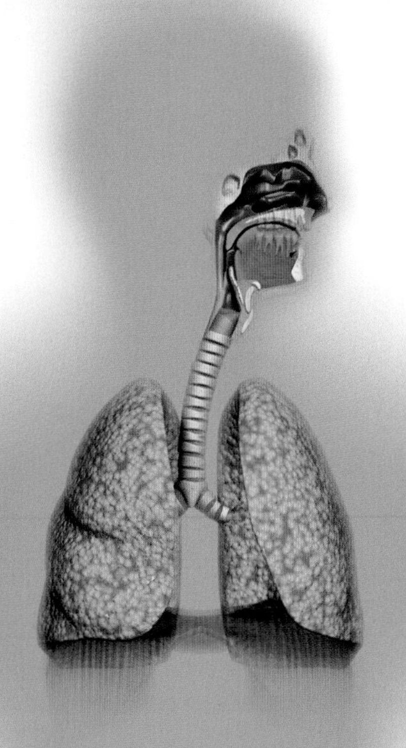

Your amazing lungs and respiratory system

Your respiratory system is an intricate network of tubes and passageways that performs the vital task of supplying your body with the oxygen it needs to survive. In the process it must defend itself against a range of harmful invaders.

BREATH OF LIFE

Your lungs are two cone-shaped organs that sit on either side of the heart. They are connected to the outside world by a system of air passages. These hollow pipes carry air from your nose and mouth, down your throat, and into a branching system of tubes, which end in millions of tiny air pockets that are surrounded by blood vessels. Here your blood can pick up oxygen and dump waste gases. This collection of pipes, passages, and spaces, together with the structures that surround them, is known as the respiratory system.

Strong but sensitive

Your respiratory system is extremely delicate and yet also robust. Its main function is, naturally, respiration—breathing in and out. On average, you take 12 breaths per minute while at rest—more than 17,000 a day. The exact volumes are carefully controlled in response to a system of sensors that monitor levels of oxygen and other gases in your blood.

Your respiratory system is one of the most vulnerable parts of your body, and to protect its delicate membranes from the germs and pollution in the air it is equipped with a range of defenses, from nostril hairs to roving killer cells.

UPSTAIRS DOWNSTAIRS

The respiratory system can be divided into two parts. The upper respiratory system includes the nostrils, the nasal cavity, the mouth, and the pharynx and larynx (the upper and lower parts of the throat). The lower system includes the trachea (also known as the windpipe), the bronchi, and all the structures of the lungs themselves.

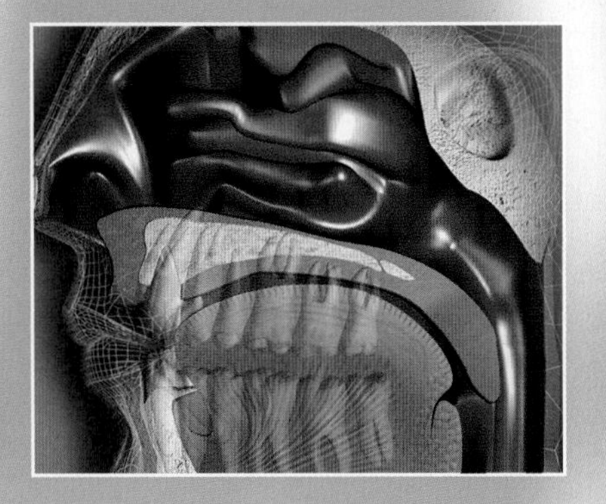

Air-conditioning
The air you take into your body in a breath is very different from the air that reaches your lungs. See how your nose and throat begin the task of conditioning this air on pages 22–23.

Lung defenses
Your respiratory tract contains millions of tiny hairs called cilia. Learn how these microscopic features make an enormous contribution to the defense of the lungs; see pages 30–31.

In a healthy adult, at least 8,500 liters of air pass in and out of the lungs every day, which is roughly enough to fill the average terraced house.

Right is left

The lungs are usually shown as if you were looking at them from the front, which means that in the images in this section, the right lung is pictured on the left and vice versa.

The trachea *connects the lungs to the nose and mouth, via the larynx, and splits to form the bronchi;* *see pages 24–25.*

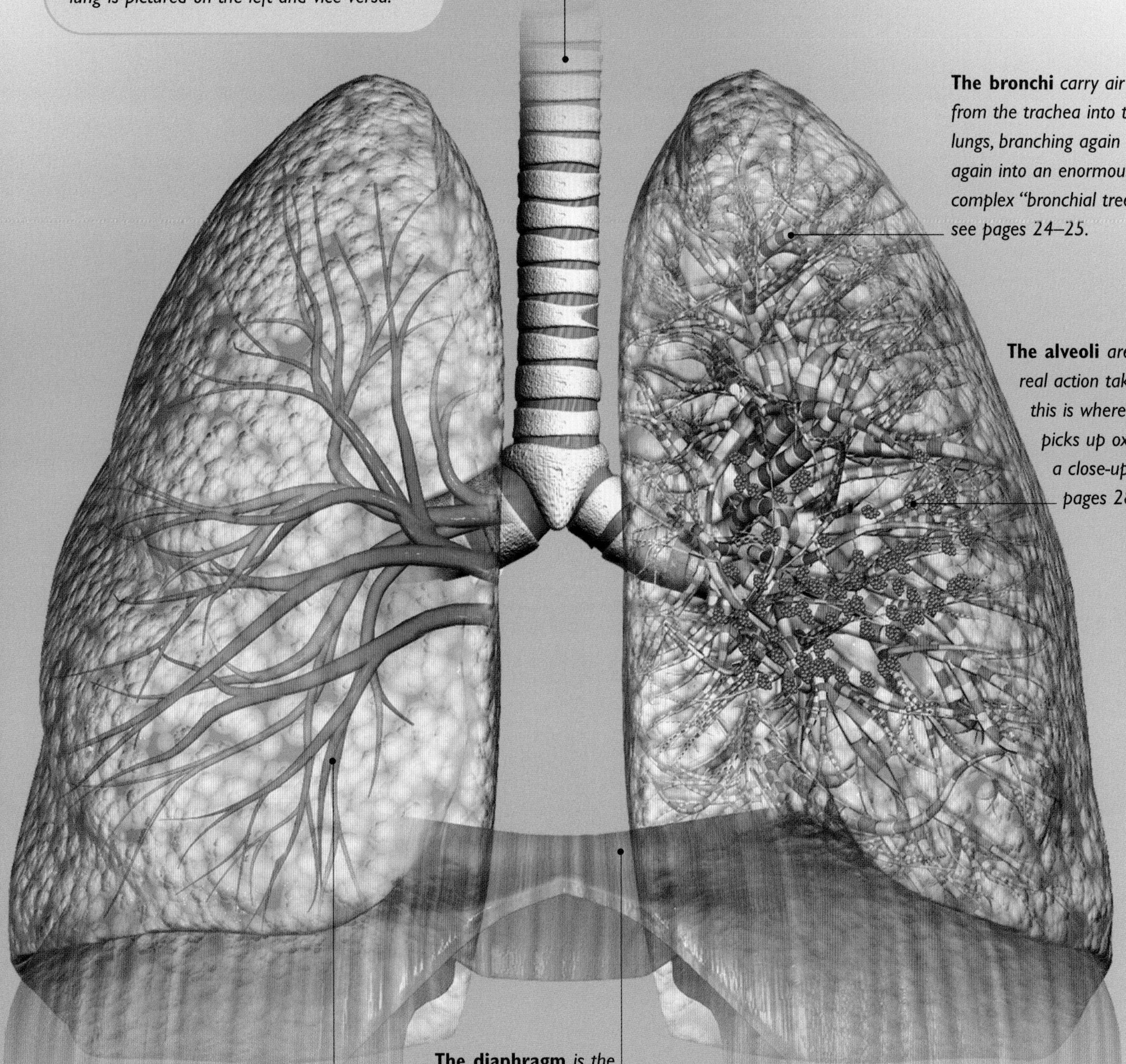

The bronchi *carry air from the trachea into the lungs, branching again and again into an enormously complex "bronchial tree";* *see pages 24–25.*

The alveoli *are where the real action takes place—this is where your blood picks up oxygen.* *Get a close-up view on pages 28–29.*

Blood vessels *leading directly from the heart bring a continuous supply of blood to the lungs for the process of gaseous exchange;* *see pages 32–33.*

The diaphragm *is the most important muscle involved in breathing. To find out how it and other muscles perform the coordinated movements required to breathe in and breathe out,* *turn to pages 20–21.*

A lung by any other name

As well as "respiratory," the lungs and their associated structures are also called the "pulmonary" system. The pulmonary arteries bring blood from the heart to the lungs, and the pulmonary veins take it back again.

Why do we need lungs?

It is no accident that the lungs are situated in proximity to the heart. The combined functions of these vital organs make sure that life-giving oxygen reaches every single cell in the body.

ALL-IMPORTANT OXYGEN

Every cell in your body needs oxygen to live. If you were as thin as a leaf or as small as an ant, you could simply absorb oxygen from the air around you. But most of the cells in your body are separated from the atmosphere by millions of other cells. They rely on your blood to deliver the oxygen they need, and your blood picks up the oxygen in the lungs—a large, carefully controlled area where air and blood come into close contact, separated only by a thin wall, which is one or two cells thick.

YOUR COZY HEART AND LUNGS

The inner faces of the lungs do not have the smooth, rounded form of the outer faces: there are grooves and hollows made by the pressure of other organs and vessels, which are packed in tightly with the lungs. The main hollow is the cardiac impression left by the heart, which is much bigger in the left lung because the heart sits to the left of your chest. There are also grooves made by the esophagus—the tube that leads from your mouth to your stomach—and the major blood vessels leading from the heart, including the aorta and the subclavian arteries.

The average person takes around 480 million breaths in a lifetime.

THE BONE CAGE

The lungs are such delicate vital organs they need all-around protection. This is provided by the thorax—a bone cage formed from your ribs, sternum (also known as the breastbone), and backbone. Within the thorax, nestled between the lungs in a space known as the mediastinum, sit the heart, the windpipe (trachea), and the nerve bundles that carry nerve signals to the lungs. The thorax is bounded at the bottom by the diaphragm; on the other side of the diaphragm are the liver and intestines.

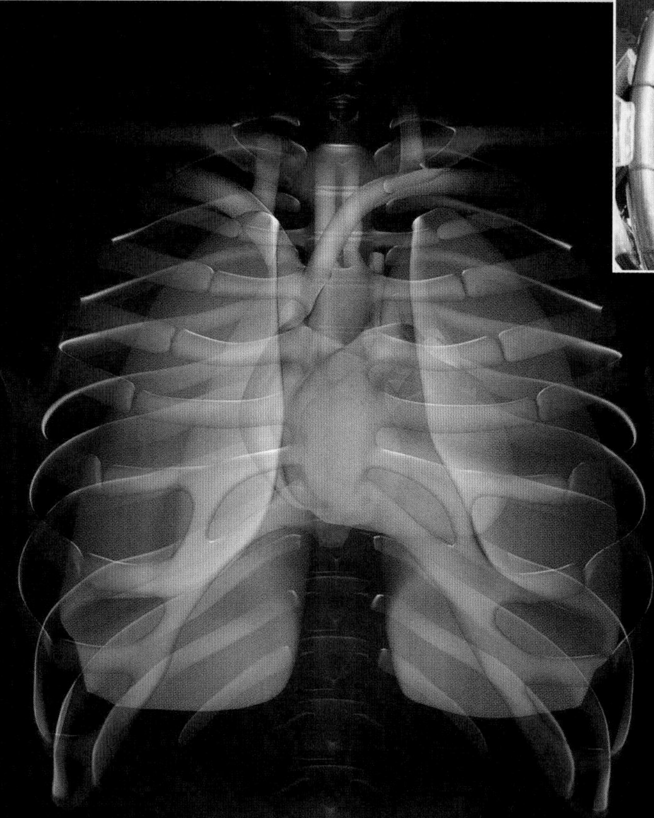

Body armor
Your ribs, sternum, and backbone together protect your lungs in much the same way that the rigid structure of a roll bar protects the occupant of a race car.

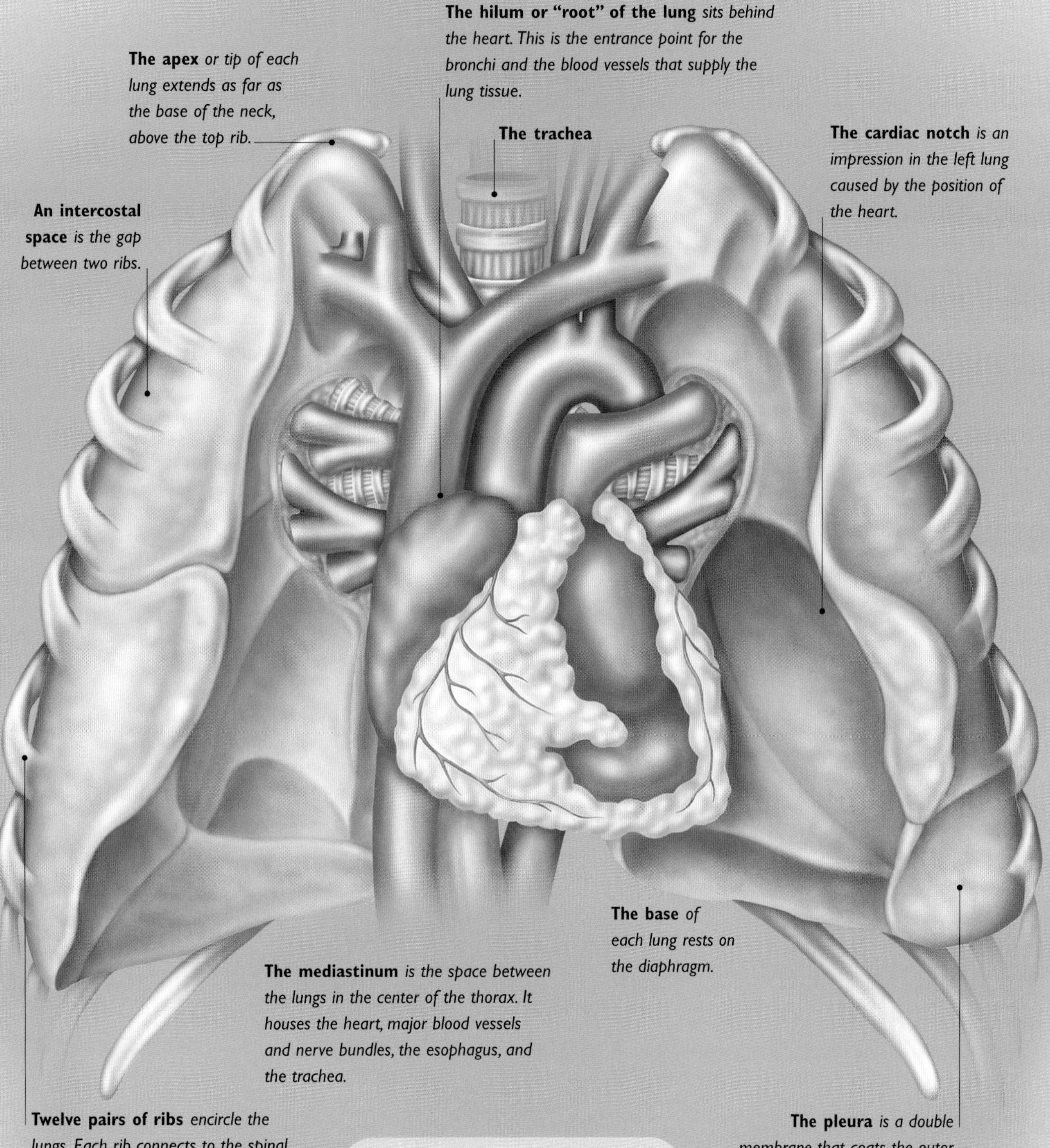

Twelve pairs of ribs *encircle the lungs. Each rib connects to the spinal vertebrae at the back. The upper seven ribs, or "true" ribs, attach to the sternum at the front. Rib pairs 8–10, the "false ribs," also attach to cartilage at the ends of the ribs above them. The final two pairs are unattached at the front and are called the "floating ribs" (not shown).*

A tight fit

In this illustration, the ribs and front sections of the lungs have been peeled back to reveal the center of the thorax. Everything is so tightly packed that these inner organs form impressions on the inner surface of the lungs that encase them.

The pleura *is a double membrane that coats the outer surface of each lung and then doubles back to coat the inside of the thorax. Fluid between the two membranes lubricates the lung's constant expansion and contraction.*

The mechanics of breathing

Like the beating of your heart, breathing is a muscular process that is essential to life—it must be maintained for every minute of every hour of your life. Your chest is designed to do this using simple mechanical principles.

THE PRESSURE PRINCIPLE

The process of breathing follows one basic concept: air flows from areas of high pressure to areas of low pressure. This means that in order to get air to flow into the lungs, the pressure in the lungs must be lower than the pressure outside (the atmospheric pressure). One way of lowering pressure is to increase volume—in other words, if you make the lungs bigger, the pressure inside them drops, and air will flow in (inspiration).

However, the lungs are not muscular organs and cannot expand themselves. Instead, they rely on the muscles that surround them, mainly the diaphragm, to expand the chest. This lowers the pressure in the chest cavity surrounding the lungs, causing them to expand in turn, drawing in air. When the diaphragm and chest muscles relax, the elastic recoil of the lung tissue contracts the lungs back to their original size, expelling the air (expiration).

The old in–out

Forced breathing is used when a higher rate and depth of breathing are required, for example, during exercise. It involves active expiration and inspiration, which calls on accessory muscles to aid the muscles used in normal, or quiet, breathing.

A LITTLE HELP FROM FRIENDS

Several parts of the body are involved when we breathe, but only the chest muscles are active in the process. These muscles increase and decrease lung volume, either directly or by moving the bones that encase the lungs.

The main force for breathing comes from the diaphragm—when the muscle fibers contract, they pull the dome-shaped diaphragm flat, increasing the size of the chest cavity and thereby lowering the pressure inside. Other breathing muscles include the intercostals, which move the ribs and sternum, and a number of accessory muscles that are used only during forced breathing.

THE ANATOMY OF BREATHING

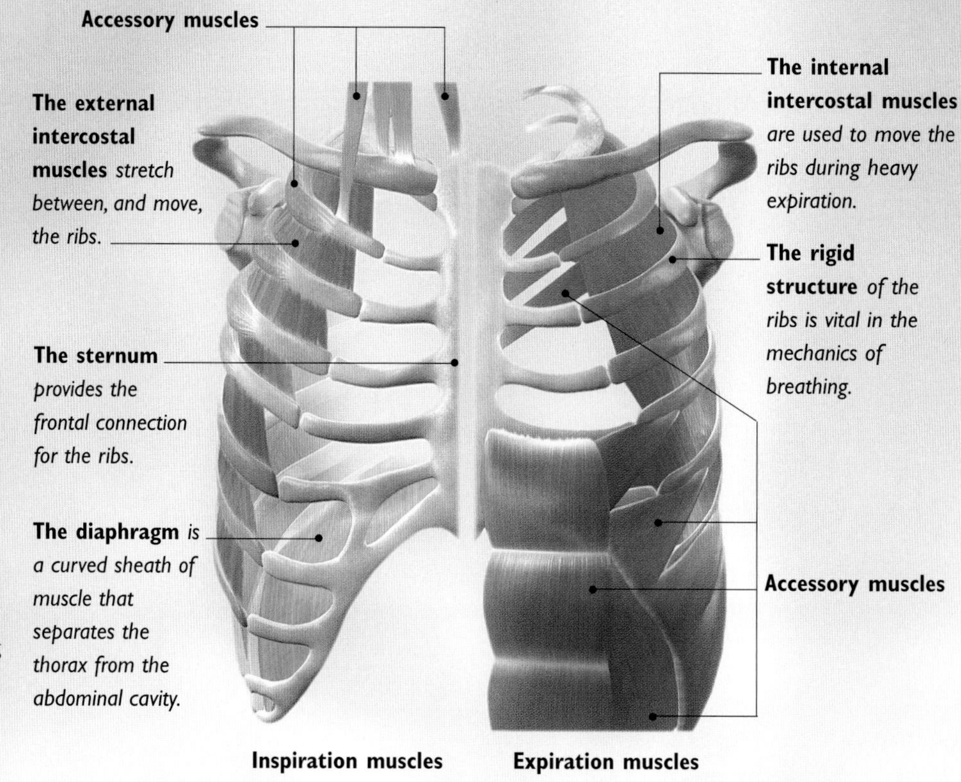

Breathing space

Your lungs do not completely fill and empty with each breath. The total volume breathed in and out in a normal breath is called tidal volume and is, in fact, only approximately 8 percent of the total lung capacity. Lung capacity can be affected by disease, however, and knowing exactly how much air is being used is an important indicator of lung health.

Lung capacity

100%

Total lung capacity is usually about 6 liters. However, you never use this total volume. You rarely use more than 4 liters, giving you plenty of reserve capacity to ensure that the lungs don't collapse.

100%

80%

60%

Functional residual capacity is the amount of air left in your lungs after a normal expiration—about 2.2 liters.

40%

40%

20%

Residual volume is the amount of air left in your lungs after you've breathed out as hard as you can—normally about 1.2 liters.

20%

0%

NORMAL BREATHING

The sternum *rises when the ribs move out and up, like a pump handle lifting the lungs.*

The ribs *are pulled outward and upward by the external intercostals during inspiration, drawing the pleura with them. During expiration these muscles relax, and the ribs drop back to their original position.*

The diaphragm *contracts to a flat position during inspiration, considerably increasing lung size and drawing air into the lungs. During expiration, it returns to its conelike resting shape.*

Breathing in
Contracting chest and diaphragm muscles increase the size of the lungs, enabling inhalation.

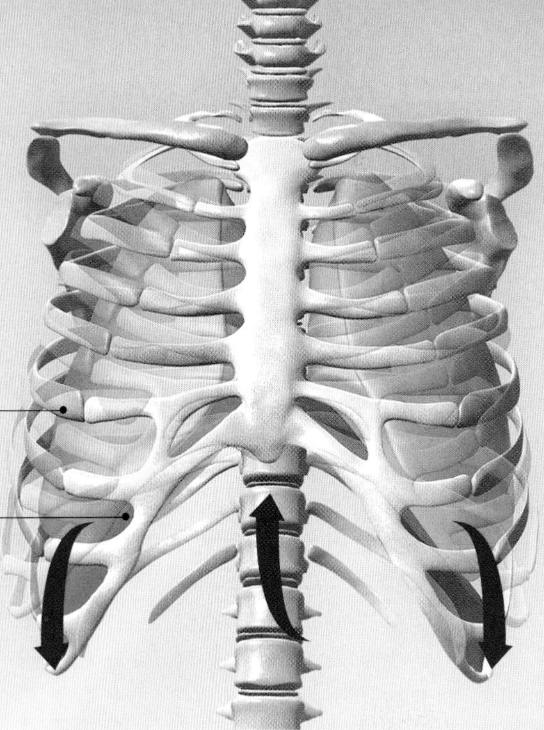

Breathing out
When all the muscles relax, the elasticity of the lungs returns them to resting size, forcing the breath out.

The upper respiratory tract

Your nose and throat have a vital role to play in the efficient working of the lungs. Without their air-conditioning and defensive abilities, your lungs would find it extremely difficult to function.

AIR-CONDITIONING UNIT

The surfaces inside your lungs are moist and delicate and could be damaged if continuously in contact with the relatively cool, dry air of the atmosphere. The upper respiratory system acts as an air-conditioner, heating and humidifying the air before it passes into the lower respiratory system. Incoming air bounces off the surfaces of the nasal cavity and nasal conchae. The turbulence created mixes and churns the air, increasing the time it is in contact with the moist, warm walls of the upper respiratory passages.

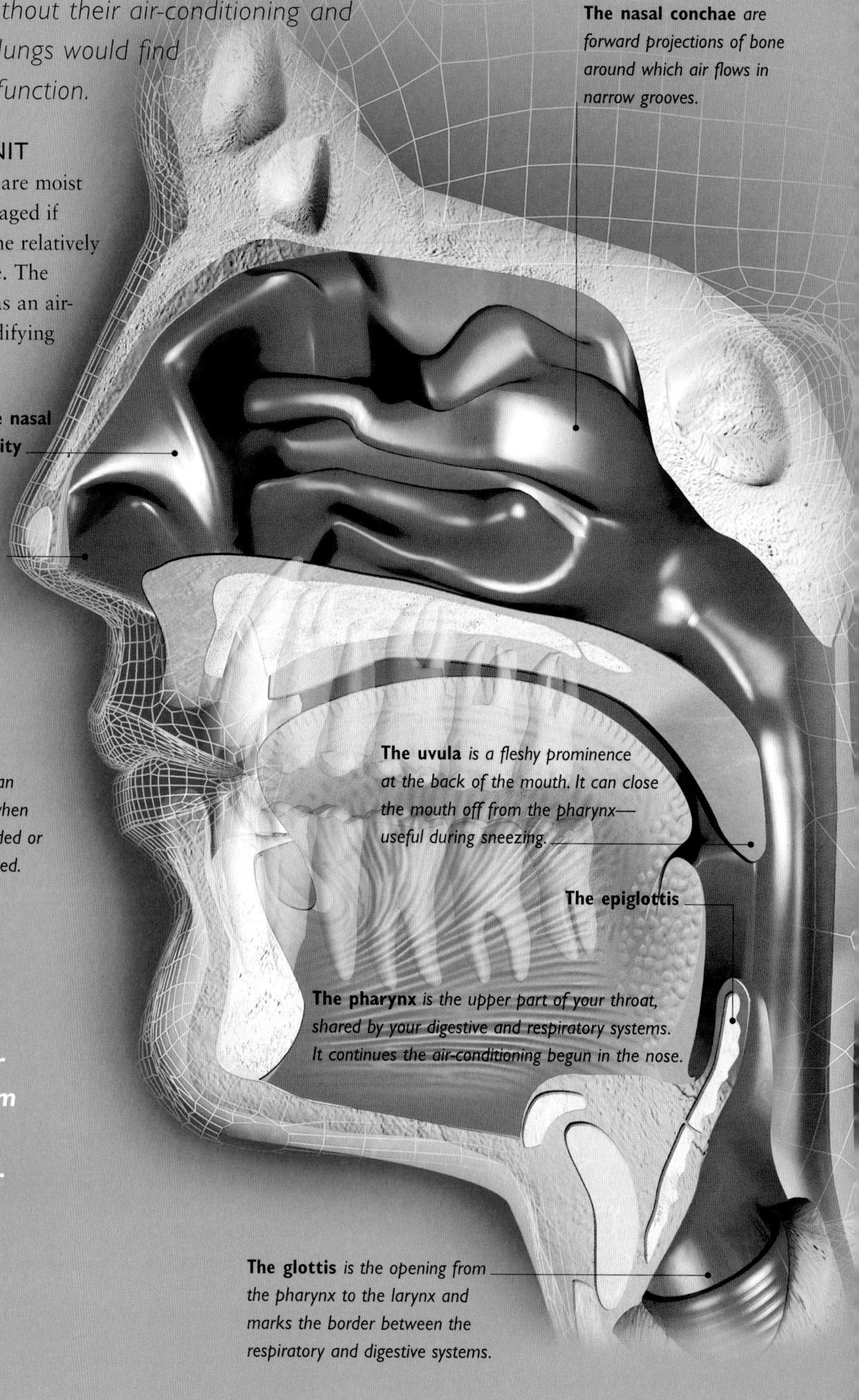

The nasal conchae *are forward projections of bone around which air flows in narrow grooves.*

The mouth *provides an alternative air intake when large volumes are needed or when the nose is blocked.*

The uvula *is a fleshy prominence at the back of the mouth. It can close the mouth off from the pharynx—useful during sneezing.*

The pharynx *is the upper part of your throat, shared by your digestive and respiratory systems. It continues the air-conditioning begun in the nose.*

During a cough, air can be expelled from the lungs at up to 160km/h (100mph).

The glottis *is the opening from the pharynx to the larynx and marks the border between the respiratory and digestive systems.*

THE LARYNX

The larynx is a 1.4–1.8-inch passage leading from the pharynx to the top of the trachea. Within its complex arrangement of ligaments and folds of flesh are the vocal cords—folds of tissue and ligament that are kept under tension so they vibrate and produce sound waves when air passes over them. Of the nine pieces of cartilage that sit in the larynx, perhaps the most important is the epiglottis, which guards the entrance to the airways.

The gatekeeper

As breathing is such a vital and constant process, the airways remain open most of the time. However, because the opening to the airways leads off the pharynx, which is used as a passage by both the digestive and respiratory systems, there is a risk that, when you swallow, food or liquid may go down the wrong way. Therefore, during swallowing the epiglottis acts like an automatic trapdoor, folding down over the glottis to close off the airway. Throat muscles and ligaments in the larynx also help to close the airway and direct foreign matter down the esophagus to the stomach.

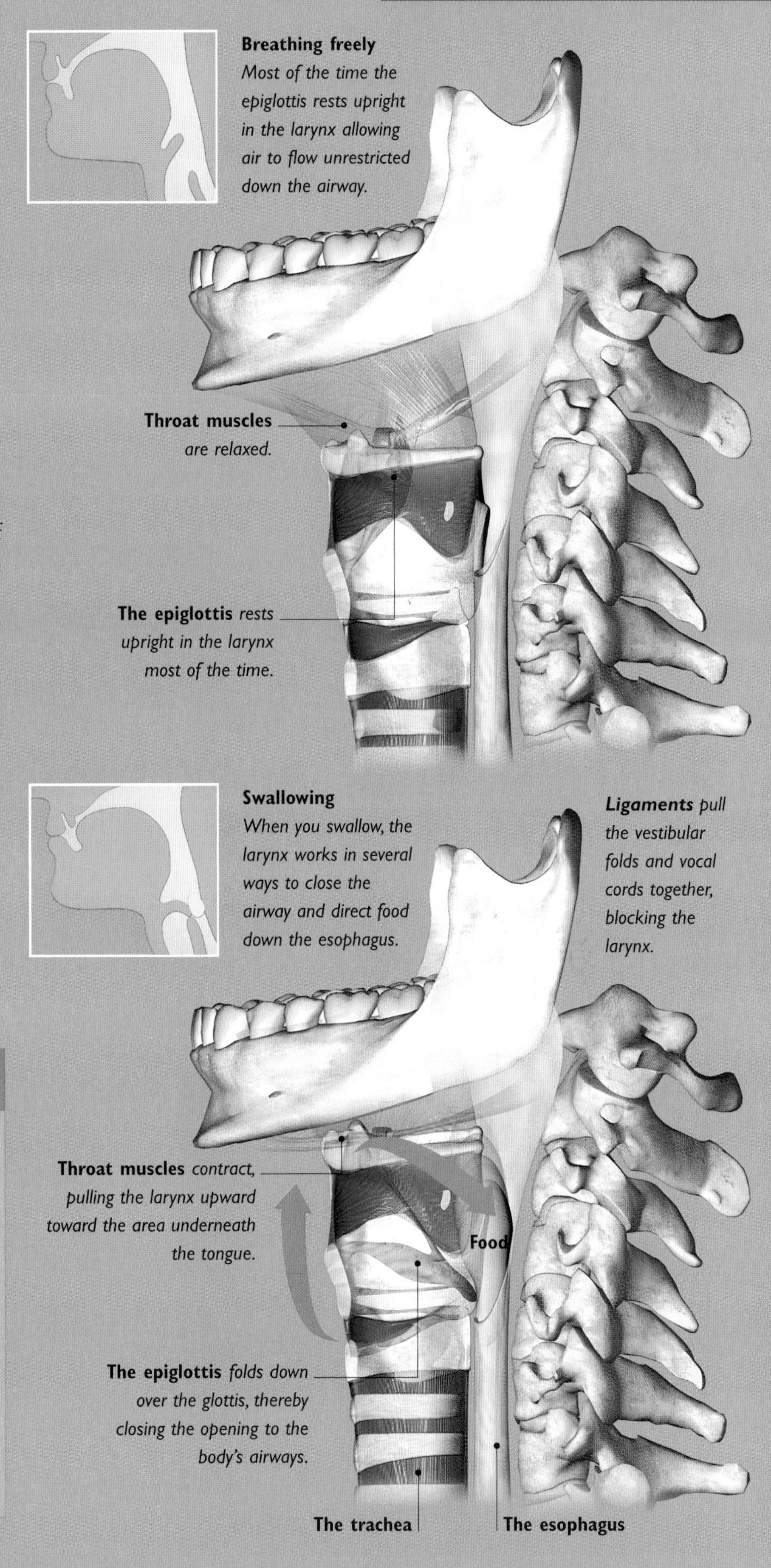

Cough reflex

A cough can be triggered by pressure on, or irritation of, the vestibular folds or vocal cords. In response, these folds come together, closing the glottis, and at the same time muscles in the chest contract, causing a buildup of air pressure in the lungs. When the vestibular folds reopen, the high pressure forces the air out in an explosive cough, blowing any foreign matter into the pharynx so that it can be swallowed.

The lower respiratory tract

To go from a single tube to a huge mass of tiny air sacs, your lower respiratory tract—the system of airways from your larynx to your lungs—traces a pattern as intricate as the most complex tree.

THE BRONCHIAL TREE

The air passages in your lower respiratory tract branch so many times that they create a sort of upside-down tree pattern, sometimes called the bronchial tree. The single "trunk" of the trachea splits into two branches called primary bronchi, which split again to give secondary (or lobar) bronchi. In turn, these split into tertiary (or segmental) bronchi, and so on. Each generation of bronchi has a narrower diameter and thinner walls.

Bronchioles

Eventually the bronchi split into bronchioles, which branch six or seven more times until they reach terminal bronchioles. The inner lining of the bronchioles is similar to that of the bronchi—with tiny hairs and mucus-producing cells working to warm, moisturize, and filter the incoming air (see pages 30–31). The final branches, the respiratory bronchioles, split from the terminal bronchioles and lead to the alveoli, where the real business of the lungs—absorption of oxygen by the blood—actually takes place.

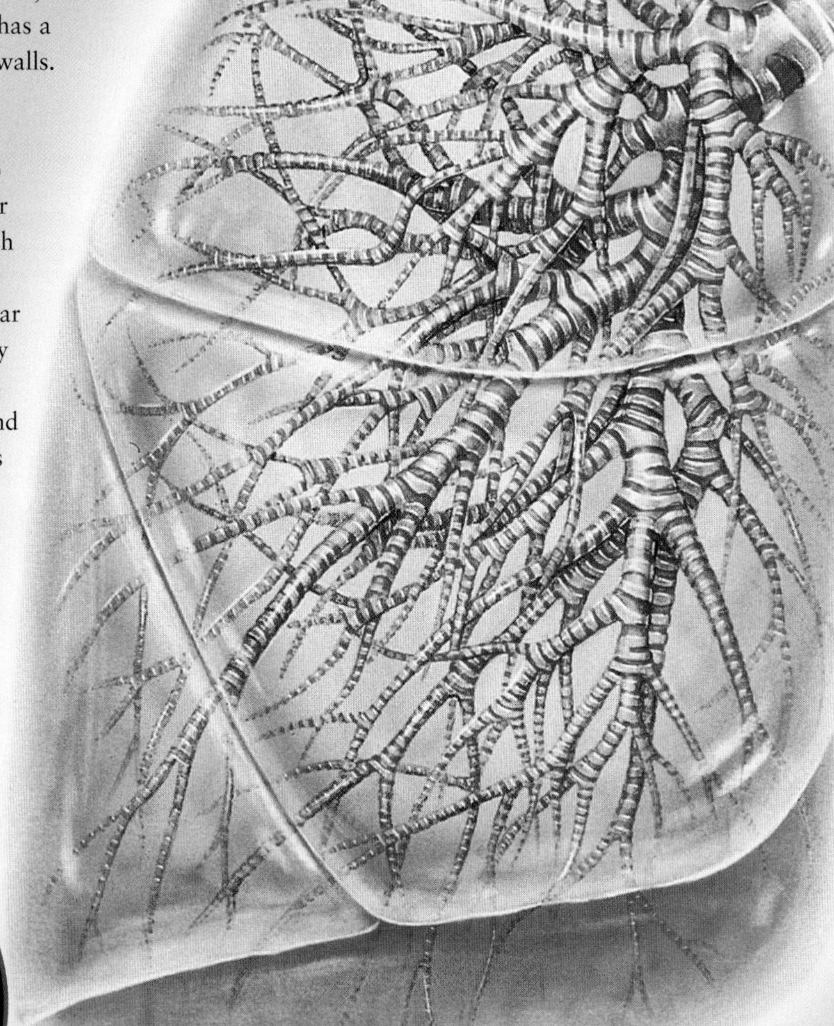

The trachea

The right primary bronchus *is steeper and wider than the left one, which means that accidentally inhaled foreign objects are more likely to end up in the right lung.*

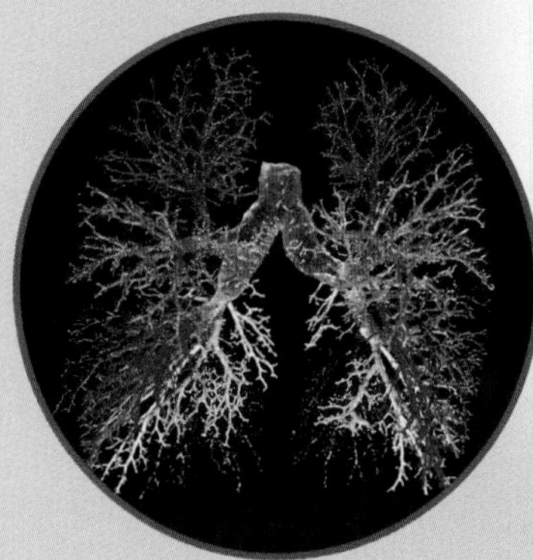

Segments of the same tree
Altogether, the lungs are divided into 20 segments, each supplied by a tertiary, or segmental, bronchus. The color-coding in this resin cast illustrates air supply to these segments.

Branching out

All incoming air travels down the trachea before it is diverted down the branches of the bronchial tree. The trachea is made of about 15–20 thick, strong, C-shaped pieces of cartilage, connected by highly elastic ring-shaped ligaments. The ends of each "C" are connected by a band of muscle and elastic ligaments.

Each segmental bronchus *supplies air to one of the 20 segments of the lungs.*

The lobar bronchi *supply air to the lobes of the lungs. The left lung is divided into two lobes, and the right into three.*

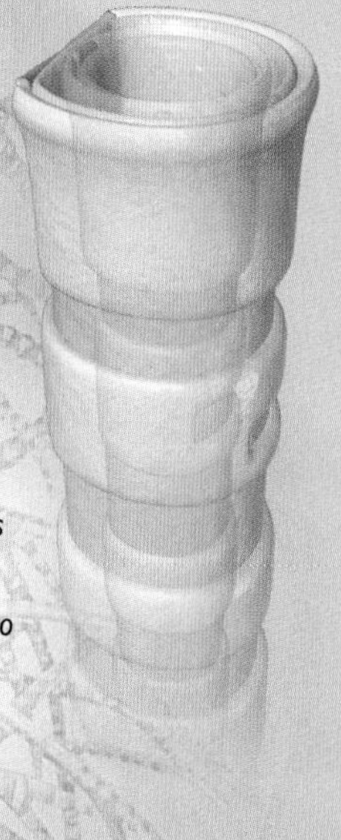

Tube control

The walls of the bronchi also contain C-shaped pieces of cartilage and muscle fibers. When these fibers contract, the airways narrow, which helps to prevent harmful substances from reaching the alveoli. However, it can also cause breathing difficulties, as in asthma. When the fibers relax, the airways widen, which helps to increase the amount of air reaching the alveoli, for instance, during exercise.

Descending generations

Each branch of the bronchial tree can be classified by its number of divisions, called its generation number. For example, the generation number of the trachea is 0 and the primary bronchi 1; the respiratory bronchioles are 18+.

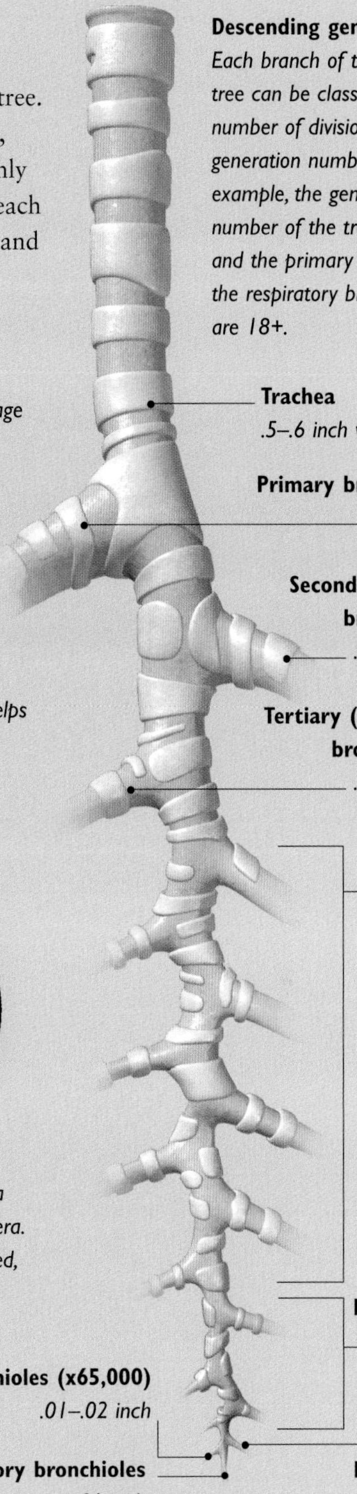

Trachea
.5–.6 inch wide

Primary bronchi (x2)
.47 inch

Secondary (lobar) bronchi (x5)
.31–.47 inch

Tertiary (segmental) bronchi (x20)
.19–.28 inch

Bronchi
.04–.19 inch

Bronchioles
.04 inch

Terminal bronchioles (x65,000)
.01–.02 inch

Respiratory bronchioles
.01 inch

Lobular bronchioles
.02 inch

Shutterlike

The respiratory airways operate a little like an iris shutter in a camera. They constrict or dilate as required, but let in more or less air, rather than light as in a camera.

The alveoli *are situated at the ends of the terminal bronchioles and are the sites for gaseous exchange;* *see pages 26–27.*

The structure of the lungs

Like a ship with bulkheads, the lungs are designed in separate compartments, increasing their ability to withstand damage or disease. If one area is damaged, the others can continue to function normally.

THE HIERARCHY OF THE LUNGS

The lungs have a hierarchical structure:

- Each lung is separated into lobes—the right lung has three lobes, the left lung only two—which are supplied with air via secondary, or lobar, bronchi.
- Each lobe is separated into segments—20 in all—that are supplied by tertiary bronchi.
- Each segment is then divided into lobules.

The lobules themselves are made up of a number of alveoli, which are arranged in clusters like bunches of grapes. A group of several of these clusters, and their associated bronchioles, is called an acinus (plural: acini), and each lobule contains 3–5 acini.

HOLDING IT TOGETHER

The lungs are like two large sponges; most of their volume is air spaces, but surrounding these spaces is connective tissue that supports and glues together other structures. The spongy connective tissue of the lungs starts at the root, or hilum, of the lungs and extends all the way through to the alveoli, providing support for blood vessels, nerve fibers, and tissues of the immune system.

It is this connective tissue that forms partitions between the air spaces. As with the bronchi, these partitions branch repeatedly, and as they do, the lungs divide into progressively smaller compartments.

Despite each one being so tiny, the alveoli are so numerous that they make up the majority of the volume of the lungs—a pair of lungs may contain up to 400 million alveoli.

LUNG DIVISION

The division of the sections of the lungs produces lobules. The great advantage of lobules is that they function independently from one another, because each is separated by a partition called an interlobular septum. This means that if one lobule or segment gets damaged, for example, by lung cancer or tuberculosis, it can be removed without impairing the function of the others.

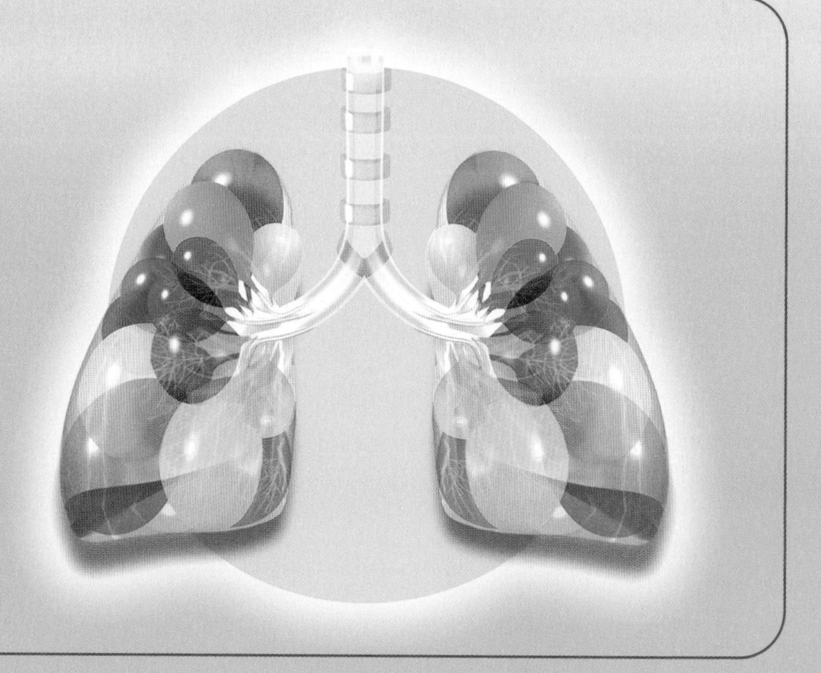

The terminal bronchioles *lead off from regular bronchioles and branch into the respiratory bronchioles.*

The respiratory bronchioles *provide air directly to the alveoli through the alveolar duct.*

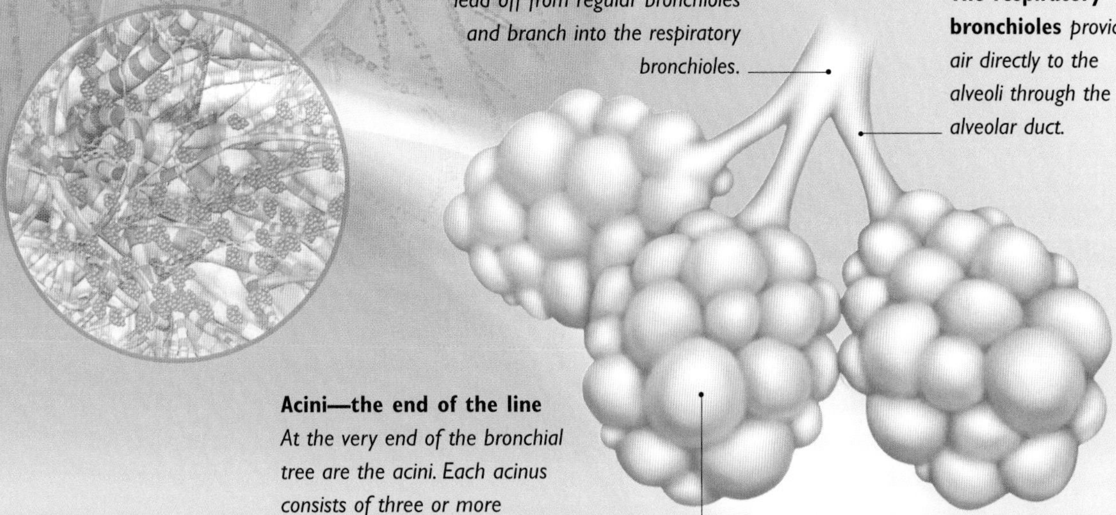

Acini—the end of the line
At the very end of the bronchial tree are the acini. Each acinus consists of three or more clusters of alveoli—the sites at which air comes into contact with your blood.

An alveolus

A capillary network *covers the external walls of the alveoli, providing the blood supply for the process of gaseous exchange.*

Life-giving connections
This close-up of a cluster of alveoli reveals the structure of the connective tissue. This tissue does more than separate the clusters from one another—it contains capillaries and elasticated fibers that are vital to the processes of breathing and gaseous exchange.

Elasticated fibers *and musclelike cells are woven through the connective tissue and combine to give lung tissue a natural elasticity. This is very important to the function of breathing; after the lungs inflate during inspiration, these elastic fibers make them spring back to their original size, causing exhalation.*

Each alveolus *is actually a hollow chamber. This arrangement allows the alveoli to hold air and provides the lungs with the vast surface area needed to keep up with the body's demand for gaseous exchange;* *see pages 28–29.*

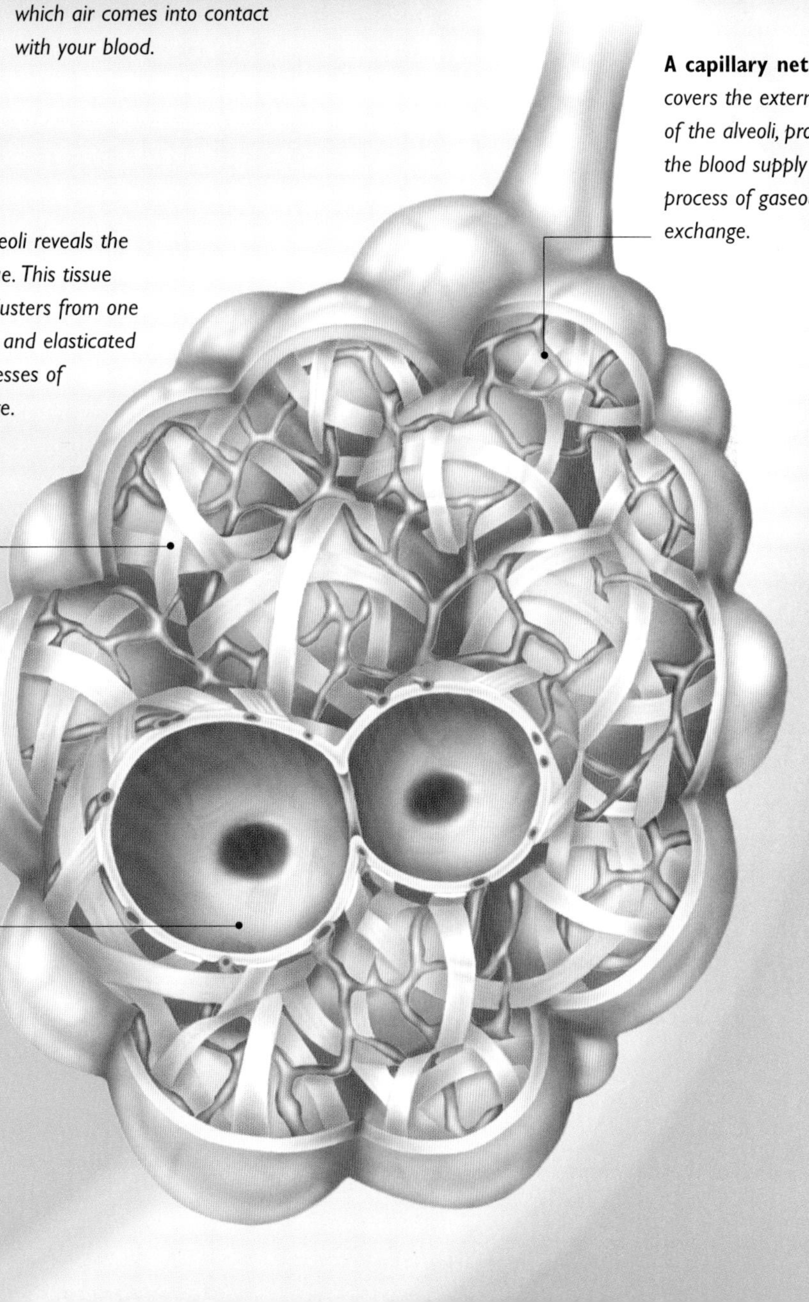

How oxygen enters the blood

The real work of the lungs goes on in the hundreds of millions of tiny air sacs called alveoli. Constructed with microscopic precision, these incredibly delicate structures allow oxygen to be taken up in the most efficient way.

GASEOUS EXCHANGE

An alveolus (plural: alveoli) is a tiny hollow ball roughly the size of this period. It is here that air comes into close contact with the blood. Together, the millions of alveoli provide a large surface area where your blood can exchange its load of carbon dioxide (a waste gas produced in the cells of the body) for oxygen from the air—a process known as gaseous exchange. Each alveolus is surrounded by a network of tiny blood vessels called capillaries, which supply the blood for the gaseous exchange process.

Keeping in shape

The function of the alveoli depends entirely on their being able to maintain their shape, which is easier said than done. The alveoli have no cartilage or bone, and because their inner surfaces are moist, they normally cling together like two wet sheets of plastic; wet surfaces attract each other because of a force called surface tension. However, type II cells in the alveoli secrete a substance called surfactant that acts as a sort of natural detergent—it weakens the bonds between water molecules that cause surface tension. With surfactant in place, the pressure of the air in the alveoli is enough to keep their walls apart, preventing them from collapsing, which causes suffocation.

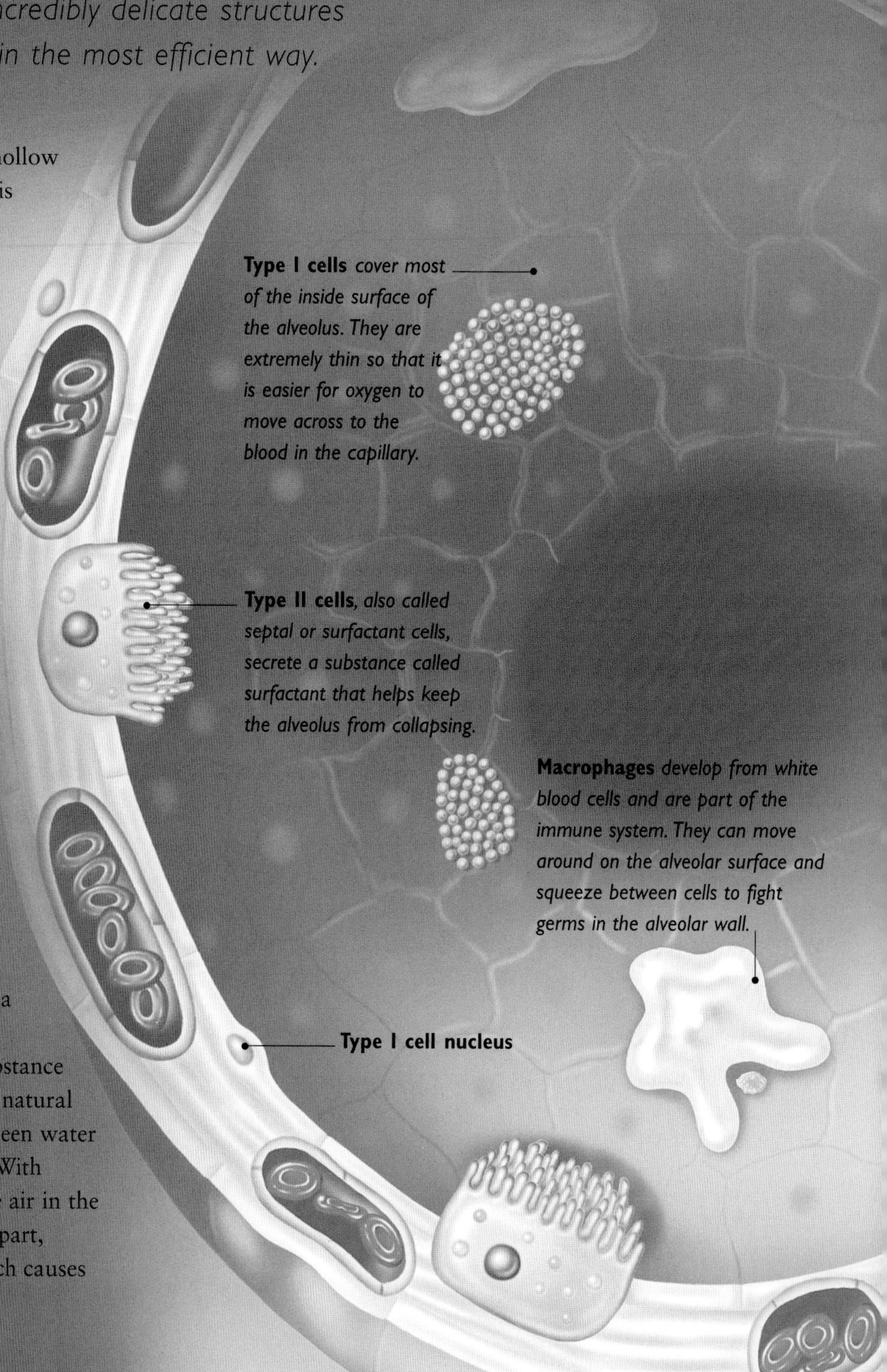

Type I cells *cover most of the inside surface of the alveolus. They are extremely thin so that it is easier for oxygen to move across to the blood in the capillary.*

Type II cells, *also called septal or surfactant cells, secrete a substance called surfactant that helps keep the alveolus from collapsing.*

Macrophages *develop from white blood cells and are part of the immune system. They can move around on the alveolar surface and squeeze between cells to fight germs in the alveolar wall.*

Type I cell nucleus

The respiratory membrane that separates your blood from the air in the alveoli is 100 times thinner than a sheet of airmail paper.

Each alveolus is approximately .01 inch in diameter.

Capillaries *spread over the outer surface of the alveolus and provide the blood for gaseous exchange. Blue indicates capillaries carrying deoxygenated blood to the alveolus; red indicates oxygenated blood being taken back to the heart.*

Air from the bronchiole *reaches each alveolus via a tiny passage called the alveolar duct.*

Alveolar pores *are tiny openings in the walls of some alveoli that allow air and macrophages to pass from one alveolus to another.*

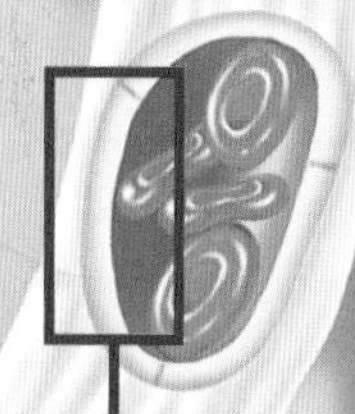

The respiratory membrane *consists of alveolus type I cells and capillary endothelial cells.*

New gas for old

Gaseous exchange, the primary function of the respiratory system, depends on the process of diffusion. This is the tendency for a dissolved substance (including gases such as oxygen) to move from an area where there is a lot of it to an area where there is not. In the lungs, oxygen moves from the oxygen-rich air inside the alveoli to the oxygen-deficient blood in the capillaries. The process works in reverse for carbon dioxide. Between the air and the blood lie the walls of the alveolus and capillary, which together make up the respiratory membrane. In places this is as thin as 0.0001 mm.

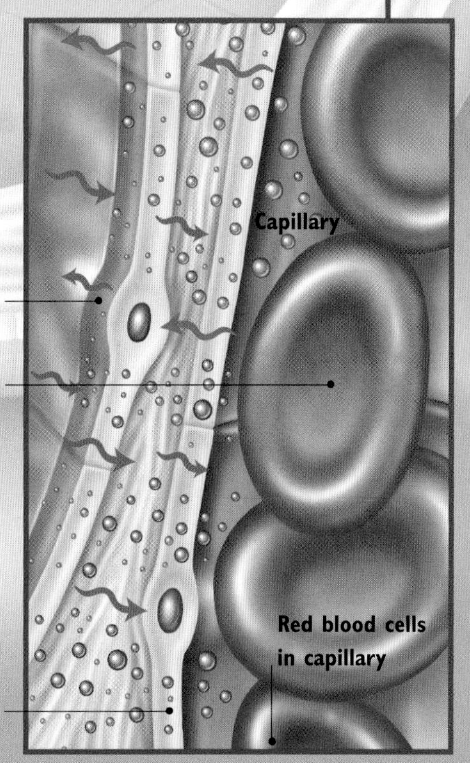

Diffusion
Oxygen (red "bubbles") dissolves in the fluid covering the alveolar surface and diffuses across the respiratory membrane in exchange for carbon dioxide (blue "bubbles") dissolving from the other side.

Uptake
The oxygen binds to hemoglobin, a protein carried by red blood cells, which picks up oxygen and carries it around the body.

Endothelial cells
make up the walls of the capillary.

Lung defenses

Your respiratory tract's surface area of fragile membranes is constantly exposed to foreign particles in the air and needs strong, efficient defense systems to stay healthy.

Pollen *and other microscopic particles are trapped in the gel of the superficial mucus layer before they reach the alveoli where they could do significant damage.*

YOUR AIR DEFENSE SYSTEM

Air is filled with things that could harm your lungs or even get into your bloodstream by crossing the respiratory membrane. To prevent this, your respiratory system is equipped with physical and immunological defences. The physical defenses clean the air before it reaches the alveoli. Immunological defenses then fight any toxins and infections (referred to as antigens) that have slipped through.

Keeping the system clean

Physical defenses start at the nose, where hairs filter out the biggest invaders, such as insects. In addition, the nasal passages are lined with sticky mucus to catch tiny particles of dirt, pollen grains, and infectious agents. Some noxious gases dissolve in the mucus before reaching and potentially damaging the lungs.

The lungs' branching airways, down to the terminal bronchioles, are lined with two layers of mucus and cilia—tiny, whiplike filaments that beat constantly. The upper gel layer is sticky for catching antigens, whereas the lower layer, called the periciliary layer, is fluid, allowing the cilia that sit in it to beat freely. Each cilium has a clawlike tip that touches the bottom of the gel layer, "clawing" it along to create a current that removes the mucus.

Other physical defense mechanisms include the coughing reflex and sneezing, which help to clear mucus from the larynx and nose; closure of the epiglottis; and the ability of the airways to constrict and block access to the alveoli. The alveoli are not equipped with cilia (which would get in the way of gaseous exchange), relying instead on cells called macrophages to engulf and digest antigens.

Immune defenses

Lymphoid tissue consists of cells specialized for immune functions and is found throughout the body. In the lungs there are some nodules of lymph cells, known as bronchus-associated lymphoid tissue (BALT). BALT includes cells that recognize antigens and produce antibodies—special molecules that lock onto antigens and either fight them directly by making them stick together in inactivated clumps or label them as targets for the killer cells in the BALT.

Respiratory cilia *are between 0.004 and 0.006 mm long and sit in the periciliary layer of mucus, which is about 0.006 mm thick. This allows their clawlike tips to make contact with the superficial gel layer of mucus (0.005–0.01 mm thick) that sits above.*

Your lungs secrete up to 3½ fl oz of mucus every day.

Goblet cells *are scattered throughout the respiratory lining, about 6,500 per mm². They manufacture mucus and secrete it onto the lining.*

Making waves

The millions of cilia lining your respiratory tract beat 12–16 strokes per second, creating waves that move mucus up and out of the lungs to the larynx at a rate of 1 centimeter per minute. Once in the larynx, the mucus can be coughed up into the back of the throat and either spit out or swallowed. This is sometimes called the mucociliary escalator. (In the nasal passages, the mucus escalator moves in the opposite direction, again toward the pharynx for swallowing.) These waves ripple up the bronchioles at nearly a thousand times per minute. In order to produce a net movement in one direction, a cilial beat has two phases. In the effective stroke, the cilium is rigid, bending only at the base to produce a stroke like an oar. In the recovery phase, the cilium bends along its entire length, starting at the base and straightening up until it is back in its starting position, ready for another effective stroke.

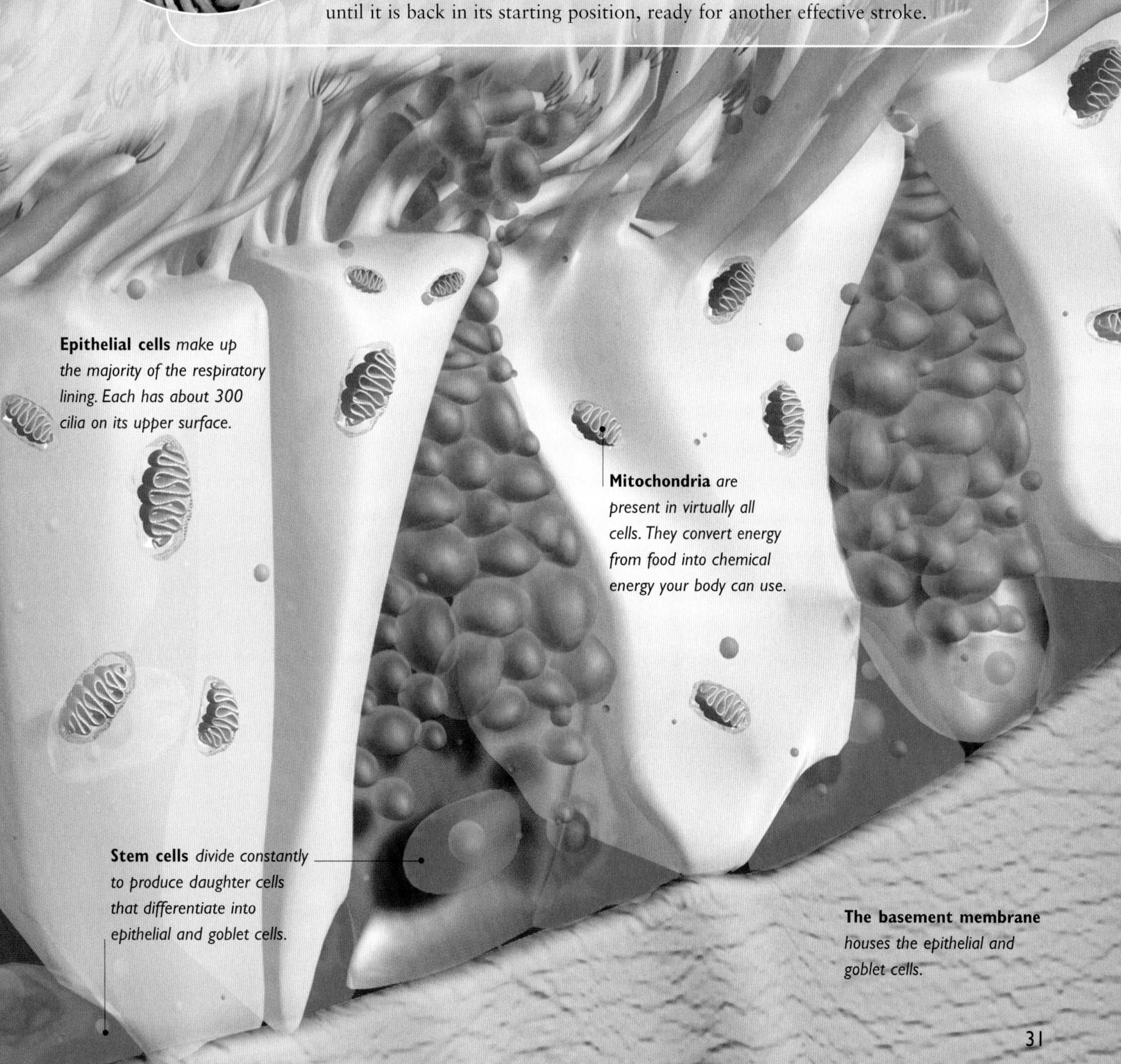

The air that we breathe

Blood is an essential component of respiration. Not only does it enable gaseous exchange in the lungs, it also delivers that oxygen to every cell in the body and returns the cells' waste product—carbon dioxide—to the lungs to be exhaled.

DOUBLE CIRCULATION

Pulmonary circulation supplies blood to the lungs for gaseous exchange. Systemic circulation supplies blood to the cells of your body. Both routes start and end at the heart, which maintains a constant flow.

The pulmonary circulation

Deoxygenated blood (returned from the body) is pumped from the heart to the lungs through the pulmonary artery, which branches repeatedly into millions of capillaries. These capillaries support the alveoli, where gaseous exchange takes place, then join up and feed into pulmonary veins, which return oxygen-rich (oxygenated) blood to the heart ready to circulate round the body.

Finely balanced

The measure of how much blood is flowing through the capillaries around the alveoli is called perfusion, and the measure of how much air reaches the alveoli is known as ventilation. The ratio of ventilation to perfusion—known as the V:Q ratio—indicates whether your lungs are working at peak efficiency. Ideally, the ratio should be balanced 1:1 so that there is the right amount of blood to pick up all the oxygen available. Factors that affect this ratio include gravity and disease.

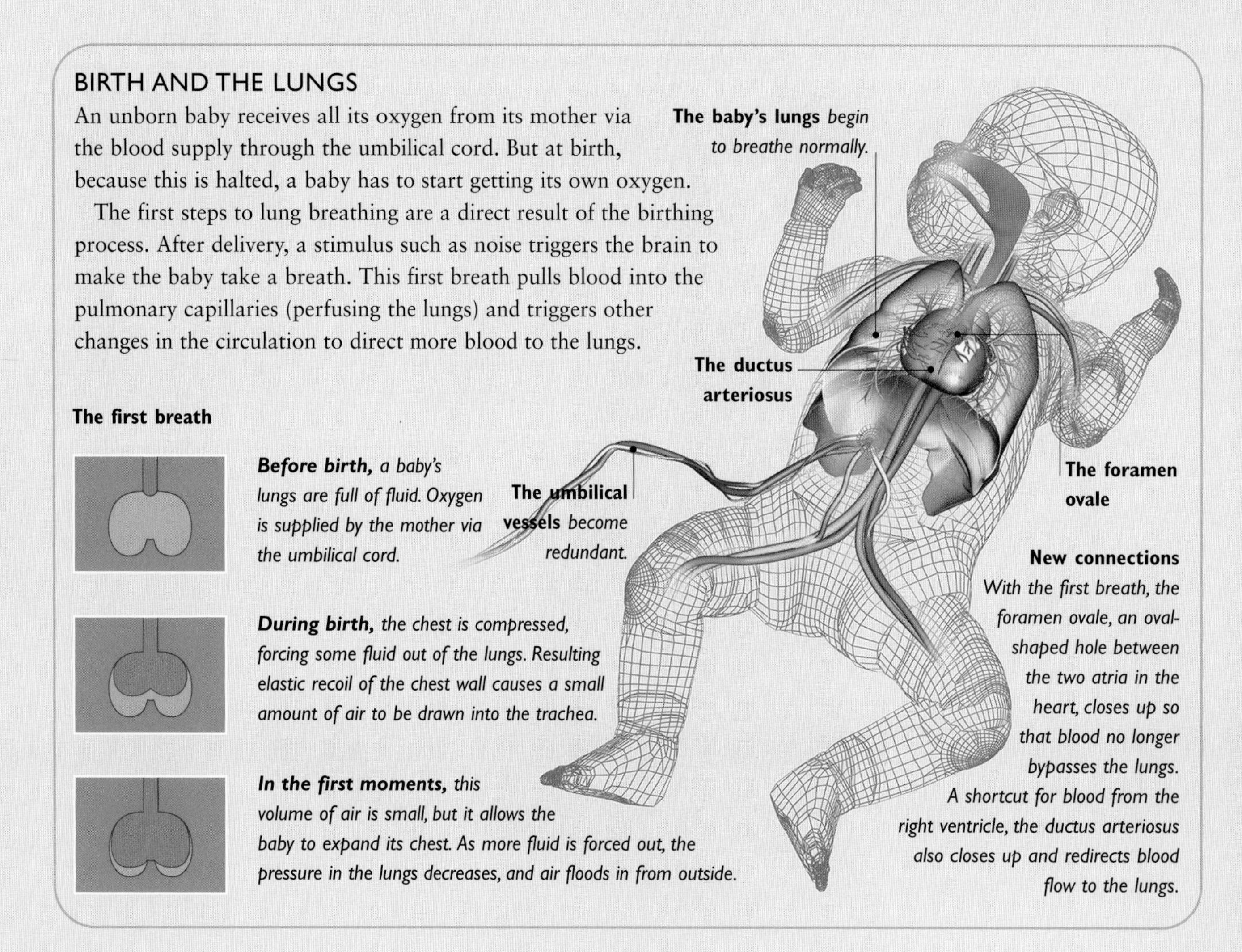

BIRTH AND THE LUNGS

An unborn baby receives all its oxygen from its mother via the blood supply through the umbilical cord. But at birth, because this is halted, a baby has to start getting its own oxygen.

The first steps to lung breathing are a direct result of the birthing process. After delivery, a stimulus such as noise triggers the brain to make the baby take a breath. This first breath pulls blood into the pulmonary capillaries (perfusing the lungs) and triggers other changes in the circulation to direct more blood to the lungs.

***Before birth,** a baby's lungs are full of fluid. Oxygen is supplied by the mother via the umbilical cord.*

***During birth,** the chest is compressed, forcing some fluid out of the lungs. Resulting elastic recoil of the chest wall causes a small amount of air to be drawn into the trachea.*

***In the first moments,** this volume of air is small, but it allows the baby to expand its chest. As more fluid is forced out, the pressure in the lungs decreases, and air floods in from outside.*

New connections

With the first breath, the foramen ovale, an oval-shaped hole between the two atria in the heart, closes up so that blood no longer bypasses the lungs.

A shortcut for blood from the right ventricle, the ductus arteriosus also closes up and redirects blood flow to the lungs.

DELIVERING OXYGEN TO THE BODY

After blood has been oxygenated through pulmonary circulation, it needs to travel through the rest of the body, delivering its load of oxygen. The passage of blood from the heart to the cells of the body and back again is called the systemic circulation. After delivering its vital load to the cells and collecting their waste products, the blood travels back to the heart, ready for another round of the pulmonary circulation.

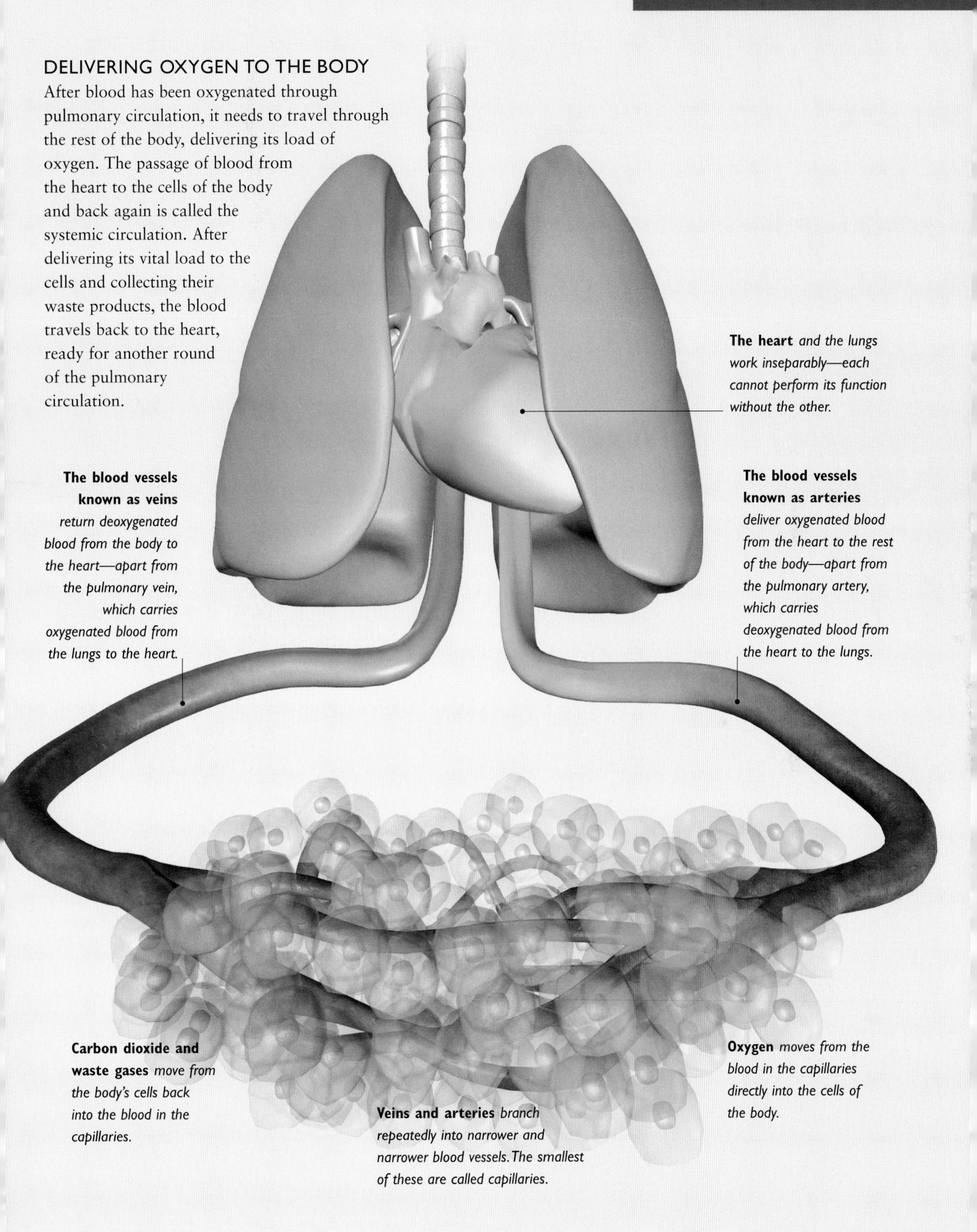

The heart *and the lungs work inseparably—each cannot perform its function without the other.*

The blood vessels known as veins *return deoxygenated blood from the body to the heart—apart from the pulmonary vein, which carries oxygenated blood from the lungs to the heart.*

The blood vessels known as arteries *deliver oxygenated blood from the heart to the rest of the body—apart from the pulmonary artery, which carries deoxygenated blood from the heart to the lungs.*

Carbon dioxide and waste gases *move from the body's cells back into the blood in the capillaries.*

Veins and arteries *branch repeatedly into narrower and narrower blood vessels. The smallest of these are called capillaries.*

Oxygen *moves from the blood in the capillaries directly into the cells of the body.*

A day in the life of the respiratory system

Your lungs adapt to different circumstances and challenges through a system of conscious and unconscious control mechanisms that oversee how much, how fast, and how often you breathe in and out.

RESPIRATORY CONTROL CENTER (RCC)

The systems of your body are adapted to work within a very precise and limited range of parameters for things like the level of oxygen and carbon dioxide in the blood. The job of your lungs is to maintain these levels whatever the condition of the environment or the activity of the body. In order to achieve this careful regulation of lung function, your body has a sophisticated system of sensors that regularly sample the blood and measure the relative concentrations of oxygen and carbon dioxide. These sensors feed information to the RCC, a mass of nerve cells located in the brain stem (the part of the brain near the base of the skull, where the spinal cord and brain meet), which processes the information and then sends commands to the muscles in and around the lungs.

7:30 A.M. A FEW MORE MINUTES

It's time to get up, but you don't want to face the world, so you are tempted to duck back under the covers. In the confined space under the covers, however, CO_2 from your expirations would build up, and the CO_2 levels in your blood would rise, too. High CO_2 levels stimulate an area of the brain that, in turn, excites the RCC, speeding up your breathing rate in an attempt to get rid of excess CO_2. It's not worth it—you have to get up anyway.

8:30 A.M. FEEL THE BURN

You're at the gym for a workout that will boost your body's oxygen demands twentyfold while increasing CO_2 production by a similar amount. But your brain doesn't wait for levels of blood gases to change. Instead, it preempts them by sending out signals to increase breathing rate at the same time as muscle activity is increased, so that your oxygen supply and demand stay perfectly matched.

5:30 P.M. OUT ON THE TOWN

Walking down a busy street, you get a blast of gasoline fumes in the face. Irritating particles trigger nerve signals from the lining of your nasal cavity to your brain stem to initiate a sneeze. You take a deep breath and then automatically shut your epiglottis and vocal cords. Your abdominal and chest muscles contract, generating tremendous pressure in the lungs. Suddenly, your epiglottis and vocal cords open, expelling the air. At the same time, your uvula is depressed, directing the air through the nasal passages and clearing out the dirt.

7:00 P.M. MUSIC LESSONS

Some activities require controlled breathing. When you sing, signals from higher brain centers bypass the RCC and affect your diaphragm, chest, and abdominal muscles directly, allowing controlled expiration. If you blow into a wind instrument, resistance increases lung pressure, driving as much as a half pint of blood from the pulmonary capillaries. The lungs store blood for emergencies, so there's plenty to go around.

4:30 A.M. STEADY BREATHING

You're in the middle of a deep sleep, and your breathing is slow and regular. This respiratory rhythm is set by part of the RCC, which emits the inspiratory signals that stimulate your diaphragm to contract, making you breathe in. The inspiratory signal builds gradually for about 2 seconds, so that you breathe in slowly, instead of gasping. It then cuts off abruptly before starting over 3 seconds later. Without stimulation your diaphragm relaxes, and the elastic recoil of your lungs and thorax expels the breath you just took.

2

Breathing free and easy

LOOKING AFTER YOUR RESPIRATORY SYSTEM

A number of factors that affect respiratory health are under your control. Being aware of common respiratory symptoms and how easily infections can spread is the first step in preventing problems. Most of us are largely unaware of our breathing until it is impaired: knowing what is normal for you is an excellent start.

Knowing what is normal

Whether you are working, relaxing, exercising, or sleeping, you don't usually have to think about your lungs: minute by minute, day after day, they are working to provide oxygen to every cell in your body so that you can live life to the fullest.

Catching your breath
Breathlessness is a common result of exercise, but its onset and duration depend on your level of fitness.

Breathing is an automatic process that we cannot control. Some people can hold their breath for a long time, even until they pass out, but at that point the human body takes over and starts to breathe again.

A relaxed adult takes a breath about every 12 seconds and with each breath takes in about 500 milliliters of air. When you exercise, however, both the rate and the depth of your breathing increase: your breathing rate may double, and the amount of air you take in may increase by up to five times. Breathing when at rest is so regular and systematic that mostly you are unaware of it. You should only feel breathless when exerting yourself.

KNOW YOUR LIMITS

When you exercise, whether intentionally or unexpectedly, it is normal to get out of breath. The point at which this happens is different for everyone: a couch potato climbing a flight of stairs will get out of breath far faster than someone used to getting regular strenuous exercise.

However, your lungs respond well to this challenge: the breathlessness you experience when you exercise requires the chest muscles to work harder, which in turn makes you breathe more quickly and deeply. This stimulates your heart to pump more blood to take the extra oxygen from the lungs to the working muscles that need it. The more you use your lungs, the healthier they will be—for most people, it is good to get out of breath through regular exercise. In fact, most people don't have to stop exercising because of breathlessness, but because the heart can't keep up or, as is common, because their muscles are tired.

Monitoring breathlessness

You can keep track of how your lungs are working by noting the point when you become breathless (after a few flights of stairs, for example). If you exercise regularly, you will increase this result. Even if you don't exercise regularly, it's worth noting your ability occasionally, because spotting a decline in function might help prevent a slight problem from becoming serious.

Is breathlessness always due to a respiratory problem?

Not necessarily: problems in many other systems can result in breathlessness. One of the most common of these is a heart condition, such as heart failure. If the heart is not pumping well, fluid may build up in the lungs, causing breathlessness. Anemia can also cause breathing problems, and nerve damage can alter your breathing patterns, which affects gaseous exchange.

ASK THE EXPERT

You may sometimes feel completely "out of breath," but in fact there is always plenty of extra oxygen in the lungs.

Healthy living
Active people will be the first to tell you that a healthy body and quality of life are undeniably linked.

THE LIFE BENEFITS OF HEALTHY LUNGS

Healthy lungs have a hugely positive impact on your quality of life, that is, on your overall health and how you feel about it, and on your ability to fulfil social, personal, financial, and family obligations. Short-lived infections of the respiratory system rarely interfere with quality of life. Chronic conditions, however, can have a profound effect on it.

Research has shown there is a direct relationship between the stage a health problem has reached—and therefore the severity of its symptoms—and the perceived quality of life of the sufferer. As a condition worsens, quality of life deteriorates.

Greater mobility

If your lungs and heart are working as they should, you will have the energy and enthusiasm to "get up and go." Your daily life—including working, getting around, shopping, and leisure activities—should not prove unnecessarily challenging. Healthy lungs also mean that you can get regular exercise, which not only improves the function of your lungs but also burns fat, thereby contributing to weight control. In addition, exercise triggers the release of endorphins. These hormonelike chemicals, sometimes referred to as "happy hormones," can lift the mood.

Improved mental well-being

Although the contribution made by your respiratory system to your physical health is more obvious than its impact on your state of mind, research has shown that physical well-being promotes mental health. People who live life to the fullest, who take work, family, and social situations in stride, are less likely to suffer from depression and other mental illnesses. They are also less likely to become socially isolated.

More life opportunities

Both work and social opportunities are affected by respiratory health. Children who are well go to school, get an education, and can join in activities, whereas those who are often ill may miss out. Adults who can breathe well have fewer illnesses

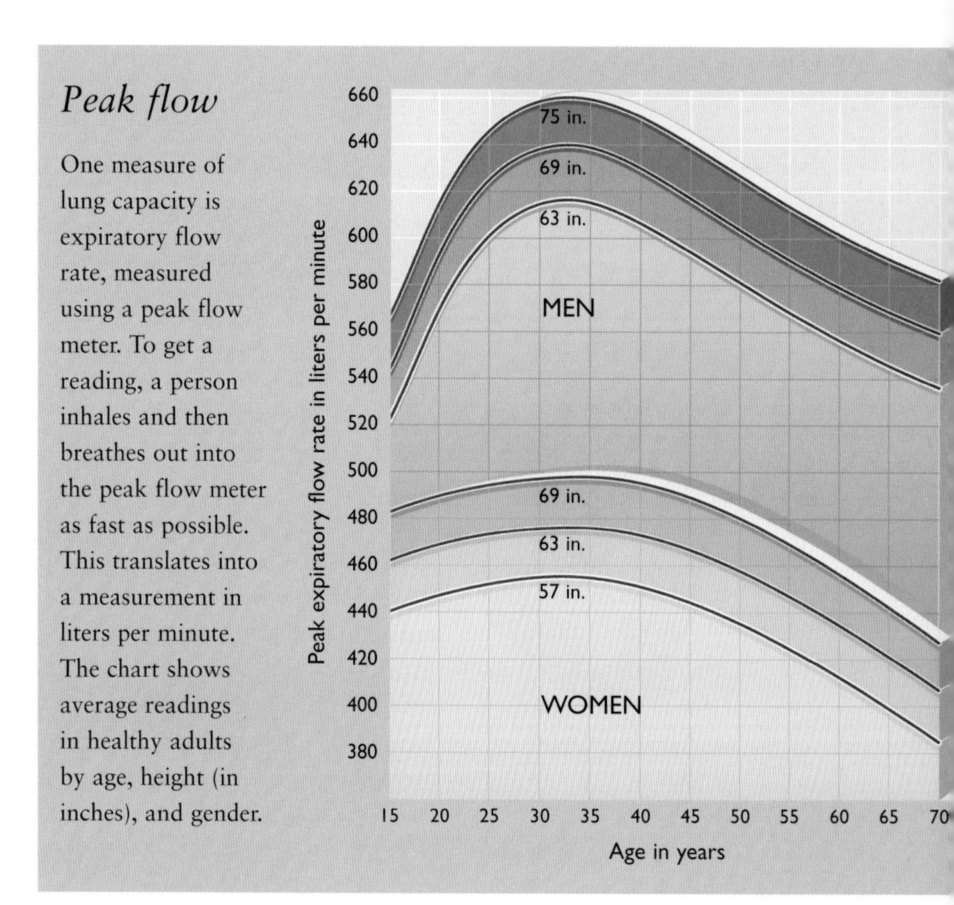

Peak flow

One measure of lung capacity is expiratory flow rate, measured using a peak flow meter. To get a reading, a person inhales and then breathes out into the peak flow meter as fast as possible. This translates into a measurement in liters per minute. The chart shows average readings in healthy adults by age, height (in inches), and gender.

and take less time off from work, which may have a positive effect on their careers.

People with healthy lungs can play sports, choosing activities to suit themselves, with the social bonus of sharing a pastime with others who are equally enthusiastic. Healthy lungs also mean opportunities for travel are boundless, because all locations and all forms of transportation are possible.

NORMAL LUNG CAPACITY

The amount of air you breathe in during a single inhalation is known as lung capacity. It depends on a number of factors, including some that you can't control, such as gender, age, height, and ethnic origin. Women have a lower capacity than men, shorter people can take in less air than taller people, white people have a greater lung capacity than African Americans, and children and the elderly have the least capacity.

Lung capacity tends to drop with age. You will lose about 20 percent of your lung capacity by the age of 60 and about 40 percent by age 75. This decline can be demonstrated by taking three deep breaths and holding a fourth. A 20-year-old should be able to hold this breath for about 2 minutes; by 40 that will have declined to less than 90 seconds; a 60-year-old will manage considerably less than a minute. Normally this has no detrimental effect on older people because it is matched to the capability of their circulation, their muscular ability, and their normal level of activity.

Limiting factors

There are also, however, factors that influence lung capacity over which you can exert some control. Damage due to genetic conditions, environmental pollutants, or disease—even a period of being confined to bed—all decrease lung capacity, putting extra strain on the heart and circulation. The good news is that lung capacity can be improved to a certain extent by deep, abdominal breathing, by posture and breathing exercises (see page 75), and by exercise (see page 68). However, if your respiratory system is not working as well as it should, exercise can be difficult.

YOUR WORKING LUNGS

A decline in lung function is a normal part of the aging process. All body tissue—including lung tissues and the muscles that surround them—becomes less taut and efficient as we age. Nevertheless, old but undamaged lungs will supply and process all the oxygen your body needs to function normally.

Smoking is the single biggest cause of reduced lung function: the more you smoke and the longer you smoke, the more likely you are to have breathing problems. Stopping smoking will improve lung capacity and quality of life and reduce the likelihood of premature death.

Improving lung capacity

The process of lung development in children is not normally complete until about the age of 8. During these early years, the cells in the lungs develop specific functions, the gaseous exchange system matures, and the protective mucosal system of the airways is laid down. As a child grows, the formation of the alveoli is completed, and lung function increases. It is the immaturity of the lungs of small children that makes them so prone to respiratory problems. Research shows that children who play a wind instrument have a greater lung capacity than those who don't. Results from at least one study illustrate this is also the case in children who suffer from asthma and play wind instruments.

Musical breathing
Not only do children who play wind instruments have improved lung capacity, they also do better emotionally and have better breath control and posture.

Take charge of your lung health

Knowing when it's "just a cold" and when your symptoms demand the attention of a doctor is the first step to keeping your lungs and respiratory system in peak condition all year.

Relief strip
Nasal dilator strips may relieve the stuffiness of a blocked nose, helping you to sleep.

Infections of the respiratory system are probably the most common health problem many of us face. In fact, it is unusual to get through a whole winter without a cold or sore throat. As September comes around and children return to school, the weather cools, indoor heating goes on, and sniffles start.

Because respiratory symptoms are so common, however, there's a chance that some people might pass off a potentially more serious problem as "nothing" or "normal." In addition, unless you visit the doctor with a health concern related to your lungs, you are unlikely to have your lung function tested. This means that you should be especially attentive to bothersome symptoms that will not go away.

COMMON RESPIRATORY SYMPTOMS

The following respiratory symptoms are usually nothing to worry about. Most are self-limiting and respond to over-the-counter medication.

Runny, blocked nose and sneezing

Rhinitis—inflammation of the membrane lining the nose, which results in it feeling blocked—may be caused by a cold or by an allergic reaction to pollen or to dust mites. If it clears up in a few days, it was probably a cold (see page 45); colds are more common in winter. If it occurs only in summer, it is probably due to an allergy to pollen; if it lasts all year, it is more likely to be an allergic reaction to dust mites. Nasal mucus changes in color and consistency as a cold runs its course; if the mucus is more consistent, it is likely to be a sign of allergic rhinitis.

Coughing

It may be annoying, embarrassing, and noisy, but coughing is also effective. Coughing is your body's way of forcibly getting rid of any irritants—large or small, wet or dry—that could potentially damage your lungs. The swelling of the airways and extra mucus production triggered by an infection will cause you to cough as your body tries to remove excess mucus.

Respiratory problems are not the only reasons why you may develop a cough, however. It can be caused by taking certain medications, particularly those for high blood pressure and heart disease, or it may be a consequence of acid reflux from the stomach. Coughing can also be a nervous habit, and people who cough for this reason can learn coping strategies to control their nervousness or anxiety.

The type and time of a cough can provide valuable information about what might be causing it. A chesty, productive cough contains the excess mucus and debris produced when the body defends itself against infection. Excess mucus draining down the throat will also make you cough.

A tickly cough is dry and caused by a short-lived irritation. It can be triggered by exercise, temperature change, smoke, aerosols, perfume, talking, or even emotion.

Night-time coughing that wakes you up should be discussed with your doctor, because it could indicate

When is chest massage used to shift a cough?

If coughing does not clear the airways of a mucus buildup, chest massage and gentle tapping, may be tried. If you can't cough up the mucus, or your body overproduces, your body provides a warm and moist environment for the growth of infectious germs. Chest massage is often used by physical therapists for hospitalized patients who cannot move effectively and is common in the treatment regimen of people who suffer from the genetic condition cystic fibrosis, in which excessive amounts of sticky mucus are produced. Tipping and tilting the body and massaging the chest encourage expectoration of the mucus.

ASK THE EXPERT

asthma. Early-morning coughing is common in smokers as they clear mucus deposits from their airways.

If a cough won't go away

Coughs usually go away spontaneously after a few days. You should seek medical advice if any of the following apply:

- The cough has lasted more than 2 weeks.
- It is severe and painful, especially if it is accompanied by chest pain.
- The mucus contains blood or dark staining.
- The cough is accompanied by shortness of breath.

Keeping coughing under control

To stop a coughing episode, breathe slowly, sip cold liquids, and suck coated candy. Cough remedies can soothe painful coughs; over-the-counter expectorant syrups and steam inhalation can help loosen phlegm. Don't try to suppress a cough: coughing is nature's way of clearing out your airways. For more on coughing, see page 49.

positive health tips

Wheeze relievers

The following home remedies may help if you suffer from a case of mild wheezing. Asthma, or severe or prolonged wheezing, needs medical attention.

- Strong tea and coffee can relieve wheezing as the body is able to convert caffeine into the chemical theophylline, which opens up the airways.
- Clear fluids, such as water, prevent mucus from becoming sticky.
- Warm fluids, such as heated apple juice or even warm water, relax the airways and loosen sticky mucus.
- A humidifier can help to clear the airways. If you don't have one, mimic the effect by closing the bathroom door and running a hot bath or shower.

Breathing problems

The most common breathing problems are breathlessness, difficulty breathing (that is, it takes more effort to breathe), and painful breathing. Attacks of breathlessness are most commonly caused by asthma and associated with known triggers (see page 50). Shortness of breath in chronic obstructive pulmonary disease (COPD) is not reversible, and a doctor will prescribe medication aimed at helping a patient lead as normal a life as possible. Breathing that takes more effort is a symptom of both asthma and COPD, but it can also be caused by chest infections, such as bronchitis and pneumonia.

Shortness of breath with tingling lips, lack of feeling in the fingers, lightheadedness, and a feeling of not being able to take in enough breath may result from tension and anxiety rather than any physical cause. Prolonged rapid breathing accompanied by such symptoms is known as hyperventilation. A person who starts to hyperventilate should be supported and encouraged to take deep, slow, calming breaths. Alternatively, the sufferer could try breathing regularly into a paper bag for a few minutes.

In the bag
Breathing into a paper bag gets more carbon dioxide into the body, helping to rebalance oxygen and carbon dioxide levels during an episode of hyperventilation.

Full steam ahead
Steam inhalation has long been used as a method for relieving wheezing or blocked sinuses. The moist vapor helps to clear the airways.

Wheezing

A common complaint, wheezing is the sound produced by air leaving a blocked airway, where the walls of the airway are so close together they vibrate. Wheezing is a symptom of chronic airway obstruction and a sign of asthma getting out of control, but it can also be a symptom of many other conditions and can be a reaction to certain medications.

Sleep apnea

The temporary interruption of breathing during sleep, sleep apnea can be frightening for those who witness the condition (those who suffer from it are not usually aware of it during the night). As the person stops breathing, oxygen levels in the blood fall, the brain triggers the waking response, and the sufferer starts to breathe regularly again.

For a diagnosis of sleep apnea, there have to be at least 5 episodes lasting 10 seconds each in an hour. Symptoms become apparent to the sufferer only during the day. They include restlessness, feeling tired despite a regular number of hours in bed, a headache when waking, irritability, and poor concentration and recall.

WHEN TO SEE THE DOCTOR

The most common respiratory problems are the symptoms of colds or the flu, and these do not require a visit to the doctor. If you are concerned, however, you can ask the nurse practitioner's advice on whether you should see a doctor. Ask your pharmacist which painkillers and fever relievers are suitable for you.

You should, however, see a doctor at the first sign of respiratory symptoms in the following cases:

- You have an underlying condition that makes it difficult for you to fight infection, such as diabetes or HIV, or you have heart disease.
- You already suffer from a respiratory problem, such as asthma or COPD.

Other indications that you should see your doctor include the following:

- A cold that lasts more than 10 days (it may be a sinus problem).
- Recurrence of fever resulting from the flu.
- Pain or discomfort in the face, ears, or throat at the same time as or following a respiratory problem.
- Coughing up sticky, colored phlegm, or if the cough's arrival coincided with starting to take new medication.
- A cough is accompanied by shortness of breath.
- A sore throat that lasts more than 2 weeks or that makes you hoarse.
- White specks on the tonsils.

Describing breathing problems

The following factors will be of the most help in diagnosing the condition behind respiratory symptoms. Before a consultation with the doctor, try to think of responses to the following questions and instructions:

- *When did the symptoms start?*
- *Were they associated with anything in particular—for example, another illness, change of environment, weather, drug use?*
- *Describe any mucus—color, consistency, amount.*
- *Describe any cough—dry, tickly, mucus-producing, spasmodic, time of day.*
- *Do you or your family suffer from any heart or lung conditions?*
- *Do you have any chest pain, do you wheeze, are you short of breath?*

Staying well in winter

The way to winter health for your respiratory system is to keep your immune system working well so that it can fight off possible infection and to understand your risk of illness at times when infections are more prolific.

INFECTION AND ILLNESS

An infection occurs when a microbe —a bacterium, virus, or fungus— invades the body and finds the body's immune system, which normally attacks and destroys any invaders, in a weakened state.

Infections spread from one person to another in several ways. Some are spread through the air, either directly on the wind, in the form of water droplets (such as the flu virus or tuberculosis), or in air-conditioning systems. Others are spread by direct contact, person to person (as in many skin infections such as impetigo), through a bite (as in malaria), by inoculation, or through the skin (as in hookworm). Some infections are spread through food or water—many of the organisms that cause food poisoning are passed in this way—whereas others need a "medium," such as a towel or bed linen, in order to be passed on.

An upper respiratory tract infection affects the nose, throat, voice box (larynx), and the windpipe (trachea). A lower respiratory infection affects the lungs, bronchi, and bronchioles. All viruses are specific to particular areas of the body and will produce symptoms only when they reach that area.

In an average lifetime of 80 years, a person can expect to have nearly 250 colds.

THE OLD AND THE YOUNG

Who gets the most colds?

Generally, the old and the young are most prone to infections. Colds are an exception, however, in that the elderly get fewer than younger people, probably because they have built up an immunity to some of the viruses. It may also be a result of greater social isolation: they come into contact with fewer people. The elderly, however, find it more difficult to recover from colds. Children can get up to 12 colds a year, but because they are generally healthy, they shrug them off quickly. Women get more colds than men, probably because they have more contact with children.

IT'S NOT TRUE!

Wet hair and cold air can give you a cold

A cold is caused by a virus passed on to you from someone else. Anything that causes you to feel cold—such as going out with wet hair, sitting in a draft, or getting very wet—won't make you catch cold. These are simply old wives' tales.

WHAT IS THE COMMON COLD?

A cold is a disease of the upper respiratory tract caused by a virus. The most common symptoms are sneezing, a runny nose, and sore, watery eyes.

How a cold takes hold

There are more than 200 known viruses that cause the common cold. All are spread by airborne droplets, through hand-to-hand transmission, or by contaminated objects. Because the viruses are parasites, they need to be transported (as in a sneeze) to their ideal host environment (a nose or throat) to thrive. Without transmission to a vulnerable host, they would be unable to reproduce and would die. The cold virus, for example, finds the mouth an inhospitable environment, and it is therefore unlikely that you would catch a cold by kissing someone who is infected.

The tiny viruses enter the body through the mucous membrane of the nasal cavity. However, they are prevented from entering the lungs by the sticky nasal mucus, which traps the virus. The mucus and virus are moved by the tiny nasal hairs, called cilia, toward the throat, away from the lungs.

The natural defense of the upper respiratory tract is to respond to any alien organism by producing extra mucus to wash it away. As the virus reproduces itself, more mucus is produced, creating the familiar symptoms of a runny nose, sneezing, sore throat, and—often—a cough. Extra blood is directed to the affected area, resulting in swelling, which you feel as a blocked nose and tight, painful throat.

The white blood cells produce antibodies to destroy the invader. These coat the viral cells, cutting them off from the food supply of the living cells. The coated virus cells eventually die along with the white cells carrying the antibody. The resultant mucus that is expelled is thick and greenish, a certain indicator that the cold is fading. Most colds last about a week. A cold that lasts longer may be from a different virus, or you may have contracted a secondary bacterial infection while your body was vulnerable.

The antibody, once stimulated, usually remains in the body's immune system forever so if it meets the same invader again, it quickly kills it, and you do not get a cold. This is the reason why some people get a cold and others do not—the latter have already developed defenses against that particular virus.

A sneeze can scatter germs up to 11 yards away in a second.

positive health tips

Use a tissue!

Disposable paper tissues are more hygienic than traditional cotton handkerchiefs when you have a cold. Infectious organisms can remain active for up to an hour after leaving the body, so they will remain in a handkerchief, especially if it is kept warm against your body, in your back pocket, for example. As a result, as well as spreading viral particles in a sneeze, an infected person will also spread them by using the same handkerchief over and over again.

Anyone who has had a cold knows how sore the nose can become after repeated blowing. Tissues with softening or decongestant agents may be more soothing to the delicate nasal area.

AVOIDING COLDS IN WINTER

BOOST YOUR DEFENSES
The key to avoiding colds is to keep your immune system working efficiently by staying fit and maintaining a healthy diet.

AVOID STRESS
Stress reduces the body's defense mechanisms. Take up yoga or meditation to combat stress, or make a plan for handling stressful situations.

SMOKE-FREE ZONE
Stop smoking and avoid passive smoking environments to keep your lungs healthy.

More than 40 million Americans contract the flu every year, at a cost of 70 million lost work days.

AVOIDING A COLD

There are lots of steps you can take to improve your chances of staying infection-free during the cold season. They include eating well, not smoking, getting regular exercise, and avoiding crowds, where possible.

- Avoid close contact with people who cough and sneeze.
- Be aware that colds are infectious for up to 4 days after symptoms first appear.
- Try to avoid traveling on public transportation that has poor or recycled air that is warm and moist—a perfect environment for viruses.
- Where possible, encourage a draft of fresh air in a room: Colds are readily spread in air that is warm and stale. Turn the heat down a couple of degrees so your house does not become too hot and stuffy, and wear an extra sweater.
- Don't share towels or washcloths with a cold sufferer: viruses live longer in just this sort of warm, moist environment.

INFLUENZA

The common cold is not caused by the flu virus, although some cold viruses can produce flulike symptoms. Like a cold, the flu is a disease of the upper respiratory tract caused by a virus. There are two influenza viruses, types A and B. Type B causes local outbreaks that are usually mild. Type A is responsible for the major outbreaks that have an international impact. This is because it has the ability to change its form and quickly create new strains. Because these strains find little resistance in the population, they spread rapidly.

Do I need a flu shot?

In the U.S., flu shots are recommended for many groups.

- People 50 years of age or older.
- People with heart or lung disease, kidney disorder, or diabetes.
- Residents of nursing homes or other healthcare facilities.
- People infected with HIV.
- Women who will be more than 3 months pregnant during flu season.
- People living in group settings, including students and soldiers.
- Health-care workers

ASK THE EXPERT

It is difficult to predict and manufacture the appropriate vaccine against each mutation. However, human flu is related to bird and pig flu; by monitoring cases in the animal and bird kingdoms, the World Health Organization (WHO) calculates the likely future forms of

AVOID CROWDS
Travel outside the rush hour if you possibly can: a crowd is likely to hold more people who are carrying a cold virus.

GET SOME OUTDOOR EXERCISE
Cold viruses can't survive in the fresh air, so take a brisk walk every day. Dress appropriately for the temperature outdoors.

WASH YOUR HANDS
Wash your hands often, and avoid rubbing your nose, because this may help the virus into your body.

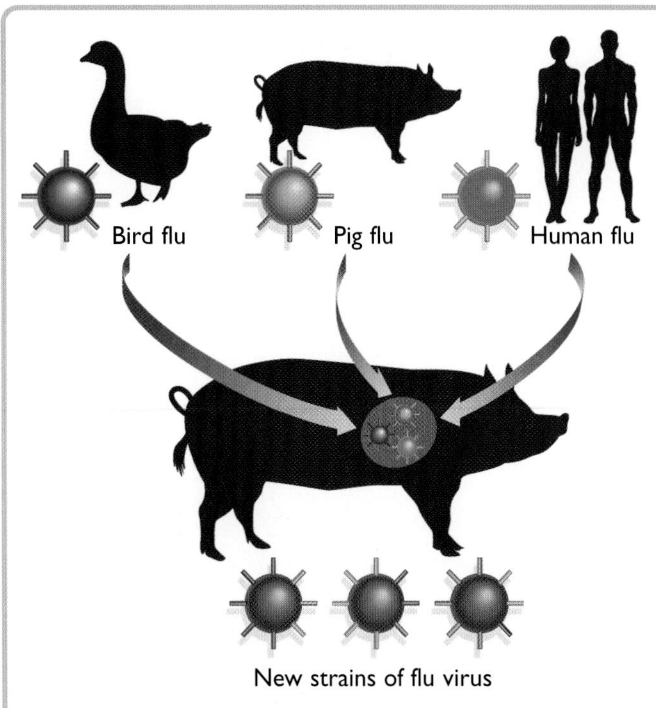

ANIMAL INFLUENCES

The 1997 Hong Kong flu virus began life as a virus of birds and may have transformed to affect people through the intermediary of pigs. Pigs are susceptible to both human and bird flu. It seems likely that in the pigs' lungs the genes of the two flu strains mutated so that the characteristics of bird flu were transferred into the human virus, creating a deadly new strain of human flu.

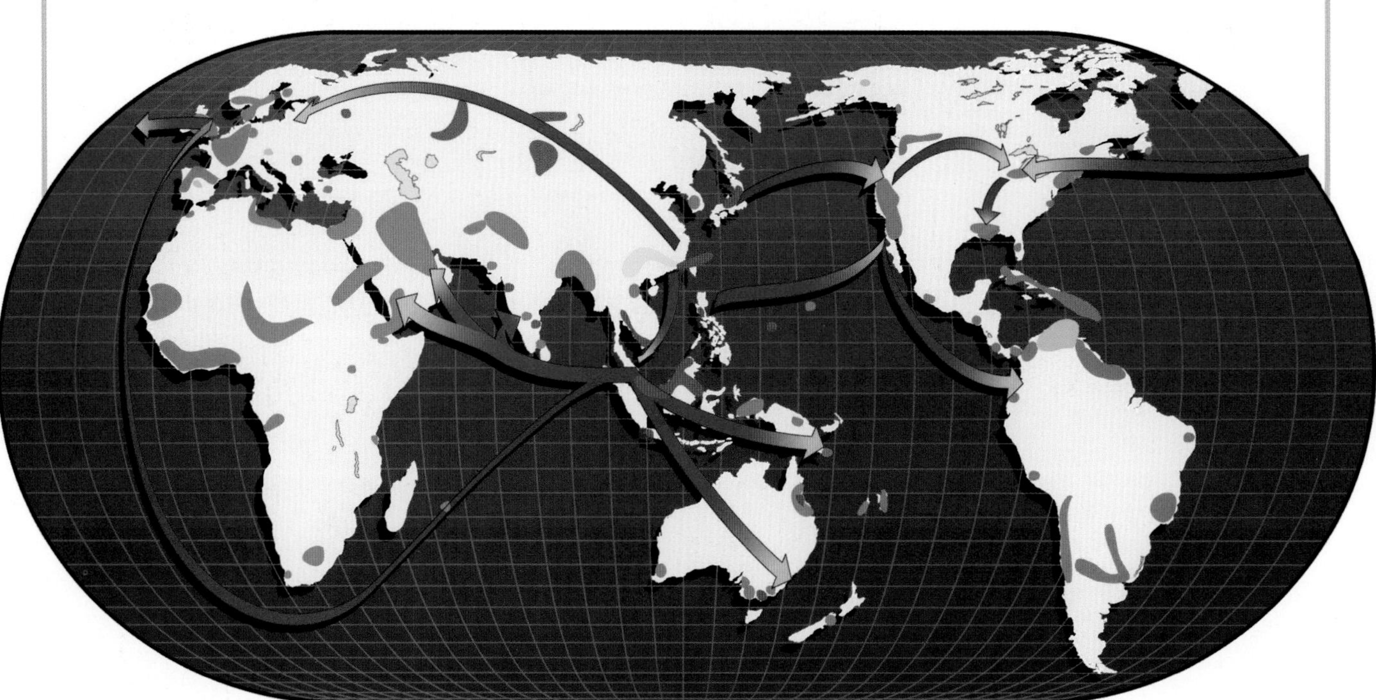

Around the world in 9 months
The global flu pandemic of 1957 began in Southeast Asia and spread eastward and westward, infecting people on every continent. The epidemics of 1957 and 1968 caused 1 million deaths.

the virus, recommending the type of vaccine to be issued each autumn. Flu shots are effective in two thirds of those who are inoculated, as long as the prediction proves accurate.

Influenza is highly infectious and tends to occur in regular annual outbreaks in most countries around the world. Occasionally, there are virulent outbreaks worldwide. This occurred in such pandemics as the 1918 Spanish flu, the 1957 mutation, and the Hong Kong flu in 1968.

The most effective ways to protect yourself from flu are the same as those that protect you from colds. In addition, you could discuss with your doctor whether vaccination would be a good idea for you.

RESPIRATORY VACCINES

There are several vaccinations available in the U.S. which reduce the risk of severe respiratory infections.

What is Zanamivir?

Zanamivir is the active ingredient in a prescription-only treatment for managing influenza, inhaled in the form of a powder. It must be given within 36 hours of the onset of symptoms and can reduce the severity and duration of flu by up to 3 days. This can be advantageous to those who belong to, or come into close contact with, vulnerable groups such as babies and the elderly. Zanamivir is not, however, recommended for people with asthma or COPD, nor is it a substitute for a flu vaccination. In addition, the safety and efficacy of repeated doses have not been fully tested.

ASK THE EXPERT

Those in a high-risk group, including those with a preexisting respiratory or heart condition, should be given priority. In fact, some vaccinations are offered routinely only to those considered to be "high-risk" by health-care professionals.

IS IT A BAD COLD OR FLU?

Because many of the symptoms of a cold are similar to those of the flu, it can be difficult to know which you are suffering from. Both colds and the flu are characterized by frequent sneezing, a runny nose with thin, clear mucus, a blocked nose, headache, sore throat, and sometimes a cough. Generally, however, flu symptoms will appear sooner after contact with an infected person and will rapidly worsen: a cold can take a couple of days to intensify, whereas flu symptoms can be acute within hours.

Cold symptoms are often mild, but flu symptoms are always severe. The flu always produces a high fever, whereas you may not have an elevated temperature at all with a cold. The flu is accompanied by chills, sweating and shivering, aching muscles, exhaustion, and sometimes persistent depression. If you suffer from any of these symptoms, you have the flu, not simply a bad cold.

Finally, if you have a cold, you can still be fairly active, depending on how you feel; if you have the flu you must rest—you may be unable to do anything else. A cold may last from a few days up to 2 weeks, but the flu usually lasts at least a week, and you can be left feeling very washed out for a while after symptoms have gone.

WHEN TO SEE THE DOCTOR

A cold should not require a visit to your doctor, and over-the-counter remedies to relieve symptoms and rest should be all the treatment you need for the flu. However, it is worth calling or visiting the doctor if:

- There is no improvement in your condition after a week.
- You have a fever that lasts more than 48 hours.
- You experience breathlessness or breathing difficulties.

If you suspect you have the flu, inform the doctor early if you have close contact with anyone who has a higher-than-average risk of infection, such as babies, the elderly, those with heart or lung disease, or those whose immune systems are already compromised (such as those with HIV or diabetes). Your doctor may prescribe Relenza for you.

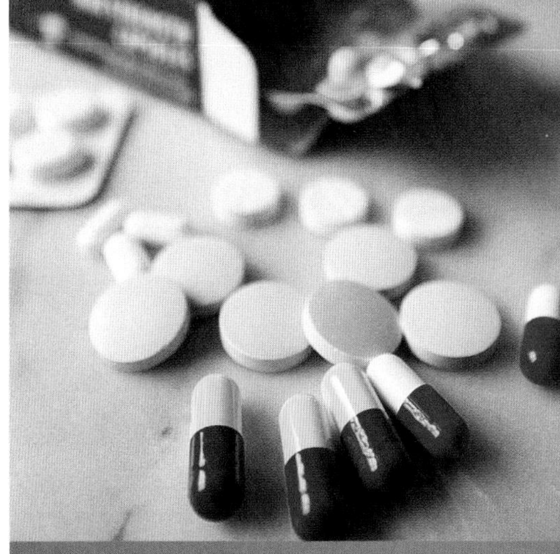

Over-the-counter medication

Cough remedies *These may be soothing but have little medicinal value; do not use them to suppress a cough unless it keeps you awake at night.*

Combined remedies *Formulations vary, but most contain an analgesic, a throat soother, and sometimes caffeine.*

Analgesics *Acetaminophen, aspirin, and ibuprofen relieve pain and lower a fever. Do not give aspirin to children younger than 12.*

Home remedies

Traditional soother *Lemon, honey, and hot water can soothe a sore throat.*

Teas *Ginger tea can soothe a sore throat, and mint may help a blocked nose. Both help to augment your fluid intake.*

Throat remedies *Hard candy may relieve throat symptoms.*

Chest rubs *Eucalyptus or menthol oil rubbed on the chest may ease a blocked nose; olbas oil on a handkerchief has the same effect.*

Managing asthma

Asthma is the only treatable condition whose incidence has increased in the Western world in the past 20 years. It is the most common chronic childhood illness in the U.S. and the most common chronic-disease-related reason that children miss school.

BREATHE RIGHT
Therapies such as yoga, in which you concentrate on your breathing, can aid relaxation and may improve asthma.

HOME SENSE
Curtains and carpets trap millions of dust mites; hardwood floors and blinds are more user-friendly for asthma sufferers.

PLAYGROUND RULES
If grass triggers your child's asthma, try play areas without grass. Some playgrounds are "floored" with rubberized mats or bark chips, which may not cause problems.

Asthma is a chronic condition of the lung airways, characterized by wheezing, a productive cough, tightness in the chest, and shortness of breath. It can't be cured, but it can be controlled by avoiding trigger factors, using appropriate medication, or both.

TRIGGER FACTORS

Identifying what causes asthma is the first step to controlling it. Many factors can precipitate an attack—some unique to an individual. Among the most common are:

- **Infection** The allergic response is triggered as a reaction to a virus in the upper respiratory tract.
- **Allergens** Many people find that asthma is triggered by an allergic reaction to a particular substance in their surroundings. These include pollens from trees, grasses, and flowers; the spores from molds; dust mites; feathers; and animal dander and saliva.
- **Exercise** The rapid intake of air can bring on breathing difficulties and a tight chest in some people. Sufferers of exercise-induced asthma should take particular care to warm up properly and stimulate their own body epinephrine prior to exercising more vigorously. It may be advisable to take a dose of relief medication 15 minutes before exercising.
- **Weather** The inability to warm cold air quickly can cause asthma symptoms. A scarf wrapped around the nose and mouth helps.
- **Emotions** Laughing and strong emotion may trigger an asthma attack, most likely through an associated rapid intake of air.
- **Drugs** Some drugs, including aspirin, can precipitate an asthma attack.
- **The environment** Environmental irritants can include cigarette smoke, other types of smoke, fumes, chemicals, and aerosols.

Occupational asthma is a response to irritant substances in the workplace.

TAKE CONTROL OF ASTHMA

An important part of managing asthma is monitoring peak flow, that is, the force at which a full breath is exhaled. Asthma patients ascertain their normal peak flow (see page 99), then can monitor their condition by taking twice-daily readings when they have symptoms. This allows an individual to adjust treatment and dosage according to a personal management plan formulated by the doctor. A patient-held plan enables people to take control of asthma themselves.

Children younger than 5 years cannot use a peak flow meter, but they can follow a symptom plan to identify deteriorating asthma. If your children have asthma, you should involve them in taking control of their condition as soon as possible.

About 17 million Americans, 6.4 percent of the population, have asthma.

IT'S NOT TRUE!

Steroids for asthma stunt growth and build excess muscle and fat

The steroids used to treat asthma are corticosteroids, not the anabolic steroids that body-builders use to bulk up their muscles. When taken orally, corticosteroids can cause side effects, including growth restriction, but when they are inhaled—as they are by asthma sufferers—these side effects are reduced. Studies have shown that high doses of inhaled steroids can slow children's growth but that final height is unaffected.

TREATING ASTHMA

Avoiding known triggers whenever possible is the best way to keep asthma under control. In addition, there are two categories of drug treatment for asthma, one or both of which suit most asthma sufferers.

- **Rescue drugs** These drugs bring relief within 15 minutes by relaxing the muscle constriction of the airways. They are known as bronchodilators and are inhaled. They should not be needed regularly; if you are using them daily, it signals your asthma is not well controlled.
- **Preventive medication** Usually in an inhaler, these drugs reduce swelling and excess mucus production by acting on the inflammation that is blocking the airway. They are steroids (corticosteroids) and take 48 hours to become active, so preventive medicine does not help during an attack. Treatment must be maintained for some months to prevent recurring inflammation. The dose is reduced gradually, often by the user.

A regular maintenance dose of preventive medication can stop airway sensitivity and allow an asthma patient to live a normal life. A child who needs preventive medication should keep an inhaler at school. Not needing to use rescue inhalers indicates that preventive medication is controlling the asthma effectively.

Depending on the individual's circumstances, medication may occasionally include other inhaled drugs or tablets (see pages 114–116).

Symptom relief
Rescue inhalers are a common sight in sports and exercise venues, and a child with asthma should always carry one.

COMPLEMENTARY THERAPIES

There is no conclusive evidence that sole reliance on any complementary therapy, such as acupuncture, homeopathy, or aromatherapy, can effectively treat asthma. Combined with medication, however, some therapies may bring about an improvement in symptoms or in an individual's attitude to the asthma.

Stay healthy on the move

Whether you are driving to the store, taking a train to work, or enjoying a well-earned vacation, you will find travel easier and more enjoyable if your lungs and respiratory system are in peak condition and stay that way.

THE AIR WE BREATHE

Some experts suggest that the increase in the number of cases of respiratory disease results from atmospheric pollution (certainly proved in the case of asthma); others believe that we are simply documenting problems better.

Pollutants in the atmosphere are increasing, largely because of emissions from automobiles, airplanes, and factories. Although cars have become "cleaner," the fact that there are more of them on the road has an effect on overall pollution levels. This is exacerbated by heat and by cloudy conditions that trap the polluting air molecules. Some cities, including Athens and Paris, have introduced measures restricting car use in the city center on days when climatic conditions and toxic atmospheric molecules pose a risk to health.

Commonly known as particulates, or particulate matter, some of these polluting particles are extremely small: PM10s, for example, are less than 10 microns in diameter (a micron is a millionth of a meter). These can float for some time in the atmosphere and can penetrate deep into lung tissue. This can have severe consequences for people who are susceptible to irritants in their lungs and for those who already have reduced lung function because of disease or age.

HOW TO TRAVEL

Almost all forms of transportation—including walking—pose some problems to travellers. Your aim should be to minimize the risks to yourself. Good nutrition and regular exercise are important in the fight against infections.

Be aware that cars can concentrate atmospheric particulates within the vehicle, and studies have shown that levels of pollutants can be higher in a car than in the environment outside.

Walking and cycling have health benefits greater than those of other modes of transportation, but here too you need to be vigilant about atmospheric pollutants.

Cycling for good health
If you cycle in heavily polluted air, your lungs may be getting more than you bargained for.

Should I wear a face mask while cycling?

Wearing a face mask will reduce the risk of absorbing atmospheric pollutants while you cycle or jog along busy roads. Although not particularly attractive, they filter noxious particles, trapping them in the mesh. However, some experts argue that masks are unnecessary. Cyclists have been shown to have lower concentrations of carbon monoxide in the bloodstream, but this may be because their breathing is more effective and regularly gets fresh oxygen into their lungs.

ASK THE EXPERT

HEALTHY TRAVELING

Many of us don't have a choice about how we travel. Traffic congestion may mean that city dwellers rely more on public transportation than on cars, whereas those who live in rural areas may have no choice about using the car every day. Whichever form of transportation you use, however, there are ways to reduce the risks to your health.

WALKING AND CYCLING

- *If you are allergic to pollen, check expected levels before starting out: call the weather bureau and listen for the Air Quality Index, or read or listen to the weather forecast.*
- *Try to avoid going out on very sunny or foggy days, especially in the late afternoon when the tiny airborne particles are settling at ground level.*
- *Wear wraparound sunglasses to avoid absorbing pollen or pollutants through the eye membrane.*
- *Consider wearing a face mask (see opposite).*

TRAVELING BY CAR

- *Start by making an objective assessment of whether your journey is necessary. Could you walk or use public transportation or combine two trips in one?*
- *Keep your car properly maintained and serviced to be sure it works to maximum efficiency. This prolongs the car life, increases fuel economy, and leads to fewer harmful emissions.*
- *Drive effectively: try to avoid stop-and-go by planning to drive outside the rush hour whenever possible.*
- *Keep a distance between your vehicle and the one in front to reduce its exhaust emissions entering your car.*
- *Use air-conditioning wisely. Air-conditioning filters out stale, dry air and trapped particulates, which is good for you and your passengers, but it uses more fuel so that you put more pollution into the atmosphere.*

USING BUSES AND TRAINS

- *Travel outside the rush hour wherever possible.*
- *Ask yourself if you really need to travel in the confined space offered—could you walk part of the way?*
- *Steer clear of children with runny noses and anyone who is sneezing.*
- *Choose the non-smoking section whenever possible.*
- *Avoid crowded public transportation where the air is poor or recycled—warm, moist air is a perfect environment for viruses.*
- *If possible, try to sit by an open window.*
- *On a bus, try to sit near the door, where frequent stops will provide an exchange of air, or open a window.*
- *Wear gloves and a scarf around your mouth and nose if you are concerned.*

Keep on moving

If you are confined to an airplane seat for extended periods—through bad weather and turbulence, for example—you should make sure that you move your feet and legs regularly to encourage normal blood circulation. This will reduce the risk of respiratory problems caused by a deep vein thrombosis.

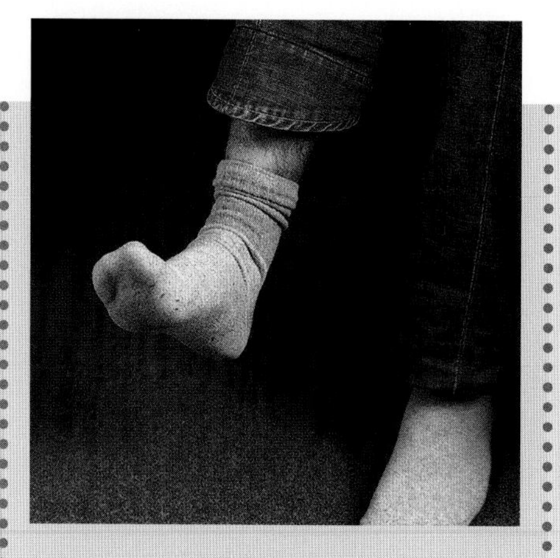

Rotate your ankles
At least every hour that you are on a plane, lift and rotate each foot approximately 10 times clockwise, then counterclockwise.

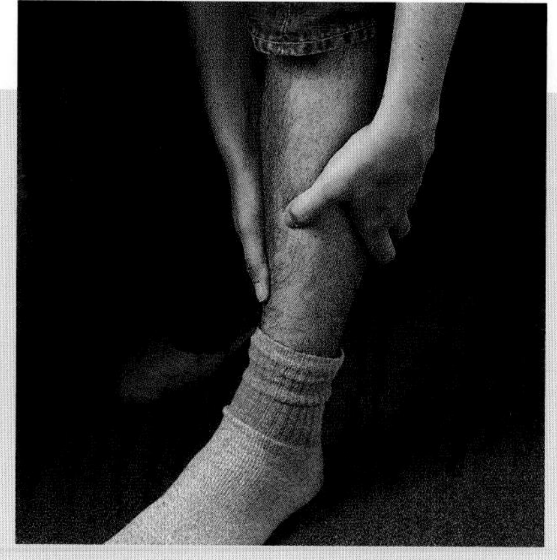

Massage your calves
Hold your calf in both hands near the ankle and gently massage your leg, working up to the knee. Do this to both legs at least once an hour.

positive health tips

Stay healthy in the air

You can reduce your risk of developing a deep vein thrombosis by taking the following measures:

- Don't remain seated the whole flight: walk around every hour.
- Keep your legs uncrossed and raised where possible.
- Increase your fluid intake, but avoid alcohol and caffeine.
- Do not wear tight clothes, including socks and shoes.
- When taking long trips, try to arrange flights that include layovers.
- Contact your doctor if you have a family history of thrombosis, a heart condition, are taking diuretics, or are significantly overweight. You may be advised to take medication to reduce the clotting capacity of your blood.

FLYING

If you already suffer from shortness of breath, you may find your difficulties exacerbated by flying. Planes are pressurized for the comfort and survival of passengers. Cabin pressure is equivalent to being 6,000–8,000 feet above sea level. If you are unable to walk 100 yards at sea level without getting out of breath, you should consult your doctor about the advisability of flying. A small reduction in cabin pressure will pass unnoticed by a healthy person, but someone with a respiratory disease will be affected by the reduced volume of oxygen in the bloodstream and may need to be given additional oxygen.

Because of the pressure, the volume of gas in your body expands by approximately 30 percent during a flight, which explains why your clothes and shoes often start to feel uncomfortably tight. If you have a heavy cold or blocked sinuses, you will almost certainly feel the effect of this increased pressure as pain behind your nose and eye sockets.

Evidence of the risk of developing a deep vein thrombosis in the leg and of a blood clot travelling to the lung is under review at present. A blood clot in the lung is extremely painful and can prove fatal because it blocks oxygen exchange in the lung tissue. The effect of a clot forming is mostly felt 24 hours after flying, and those with poor lung health generally are more susceptible.

If possible, discuss any doubts or difficulties with the airline medical staff before traveling. They can be extremely helpful, and it is in their interest that you and other passengers have a stress-free journey.

TUBERCULOSIS: A GLOBAL PROBLEM

In the United States, the virtual eradication of tuberculosis (TB) was one of the 20th century's medical success stories. From more than 84,000 cases in 1953, the rate fell to

2 billion people worldwide are infected with tuberculosis.

Contagious agent
Mycobacterium tuberculosis, *a rod-shaped bacteria, is highly infectious and responsible for causing tuberculosis.*

22,000 cases in 1984. After that, the disease started to return, however, and in 1993 the World Health Organization (WHO) declared TB a global emergency. U.S. rates have fallen again since 2000.

How TB spreads

TB is highly infectious. When a person who is infected coughs, sneezes, talks, or spits, TB bacilli (or germs) are propelled into the air, where they can survive for up to an hour. It is necessary to inhale only a few of these bacilli to become infected, although an otherwise healthy person may not immediately develop the disease. The bacilli, however, remain in the body, and when the immune system is challenged by another infection, TB may develop.

Why is TB likely to develop?

Since 1953, the TB case rate has dropped dramatically. However, foreign-born people living in the U.S. have a higher rate of developing the disease. The Centers for Disease Control is working with public health partners to implement TB control initiatives among recent international arrivals and residents along the U.S.-Mexico border.

Having a weakened immune system, whether through social deprivation, a dependence on drugs or alcohol, or through infection with HIV, also plays a part in the rise in TB infection rates. TB generally strikes those who are least able to fight it—the young, elderly, sick, deprived, and undernourished—and it also affects those living in poor or crowded conditions, such as those in homeless shelters and refugee centers.

One case of tuberculosis can take up to 6 to 8 months to treat.

Some strains of the bacterium have become resistant to antibiotics. This may be because some people do not complete the lengthy course, which can lead to the development of resistant strains of the disease. Strains resistant to the single drugs commonly used to treat TB have been documented worldwide, and these are the strains that are being passed on.

Staying TB-free

If you belong to a high-risk group, are in contact with high-risk people (if you are a health-care worker, for example, or work in a shelter for the homeless), or plan to travel to a high-risk area, you should get vaccinated. When you travel overseas, eat a healthy diet, get plenty of sunlight, and avoid people visibly coughing or sneezing.

Remember that being infected with TB bacilli does not mean you will develop active TB. One of your best defenses is keeping your immune system healthy by eating well, exercising, and getting enough sleep.

People in close contact with an infected person will be tested and treated if necessary; if not infected, they will be offered vaccination.

Restricting spread
TB bacteria cannot survive in sunlight, so in a high-risk holiday destination, get plenty of sun, but be sure to use adequate sunscreen.

Medicines and breathing

For most people, most of the time, modern medication has a positive effect on health and well-being. However, in some cases of respiratory illness, medicines that are usually considered safe can prove harmful.

Modern medicines have improved quality of life for most people. Drugs relieve pain, alleviate symptoms, and slow down or reverse the process of a disease. There can be a downside to medication, however, and it is important for overall health to understand what this may be. This is especially true for people who suffer from respiratory problems. Certain medications can suppress breathing or respiratory rate and others may interact with prescribed treatments, such as those for asthma.

When you start taking a new medicine or change the dose of an existing one, be on the lookout for side effects. These might include a rash, nausea, dry mouth, headache, or feeling bloated. If you develop a side effect, seek advice from your doctor or pharmacist, especially if you think your asthma medication is less effective than usual.

When medication should be taken with care

Several common medicines can cause problems for people who have especially sensitive airways, such as asthma sufferers and young babies. Always let your doctor and pharmacist know if you take regular medication for a condition when something new is prescribed: there may well be a better alternative that is not potentially harmful.

Common name	Examples	Used for	Side effects
NSAID PAINKILLERS	Aspirin, ibuprofen	Rheumatic problems; aches, pain, flu, fever; aspirin often taken to thin the blood	Can worsen asthma or cause an attack up to 2 hours after taking. Use acetaminophen instead.
OPIATE PAINKILLERS	Morphine, pethidine, dihydrocodeine, high-dose codeine, fentanyl	Relief from severe pain	Impairs central nervous system and depresses breathing, usually only in excess of recommended dose. Those especially sensitive may have problems at normal dose.
SEDATIVES	Sleeping pills Tranquilizers Antihistamine	Inducing sleep Reducing anxiety Relief of hay fever	Taken in excess, all these drugs—as well as alcohol—can slow the rate of breathing.
BETA BLOCKERS	Eye drops Regular tablets	Glaucoma Heart disease and high blood pressure	Constricts the muscles, so works against asthma relievers. If beta blockers are vital, your doctor may also prescribe a bronchodilator aerosol.*
VOLATILE OILS	Menthol or eucalyptus rub	Clearing nasal congestion	Do not rub directly onto the skin of babies.
ACE INHIBITORS	Captopril, enalapril. lisinopril	High blood pressure	Causes a cough as a side effect, which may hide asthma symptoms or make asthma worse.
AMIODARONE	Cordarone	Heart rhythm abnormalities	May cause inflammation of the lung: risk is greatest during the first 12 months in those older than 40, but rare with doses of less than 400 mg/day.

* Bronchodilators affect the heart rate, so these need to be prescribed with caution for those with heart problems, high blood pressure, or an overactive thyroid.

YOUR HEALTHY LIVING CHOICES

Many aspects of our lives, including many that relate to health, are under our own control. We can all make informed choices about our habits—we can choose not to smoke because of the dangers to health; we can exercise, which we know is the key to general and respiratory fitness. Other options may have a less immediate effect on health but over time can have far-reaching benefits. Relearning the breathing skills you had as a child, for example, can greatly improve your respiratory health and well-being.

58

Smoking is addictive and can destroy your lungs. Many people successfully quit each year—and if you are a smoker, you can, too.

65

Eating well is the cornerstone of health, helping you fight off infection. If you get sick, the right foods can make you well again.

68

Exercise increases your rate of breathing, helping you get more oxygen into your bloodstream and to expel used carbon dioxide.

75

If you breathe using your diaphragm and all the breathing muscles, you will stand taller and sit better, alleviating possible problems.

Smoking: the deadly habit

Of all the steps you can take to safeguard your lungs and respiratory system, not smoking—or stopping smoking if you already do—will have the greatest impact on your health and well-being.

Tobacco was introduced to Europe almost immediately after Columbus's voyages. The methods of indulging used in North and South America included smoking, sniffing, and drinking various tobacco preparations. Native Americans associated its use with medical and religious rituals, and its early growth in popularity was a consequence of its supposed healing properties.

By the 17th and 18th centuries however, an increasing number of physicians were warning of the dangers of tobacco consumption, including cancers of the nose (in those who took it as snuff) and of the lip (in pipe smokers).

Patterns of consumption in the U.S. and Europe changed, as first the pipe, then snuff, then cigar smoking became the favorite way to get tobacco into the body. It was only in the 20th century that cigarette smoking became the most common form of tobacco consumption, 50 years after the invention of the cigarette. The proliferation of manufactured (as opposed to hand-prepared) cigarettes resulted in tobacco smoking becoming a habit adopted by the majority of the population, to the extent that cigarettes formed part of the daily rations issued to soldiers in World War I. The prevalence of tobacco smoking in the United States reached 55 percent in men and 50 percent in women between the 1950s and 1960s but started to decline at the beginning of the 1970s for men and in the late 1970s for women, as evidence identified the health consequences of tobacco use.

THE SMOKE HAZARD

The two main components of cigarette smoke that cause damage to the smoker's body are carbon monoxide and tar. Carbon monoxide is a poisonous gas also found in car exhaust fumes. It is toxic because it binds to red blood cells, thereby reducing the oxygen-carrying capacity of the blood. As a result, up to 15 percent of a smoker's blood can be carrying carbon monoxide rather than oxygen. (This is one of the reasons why cigarette smoking is so dangerous during pregnancy, because the fetus receives all of its oxygen from the mother's blood.)

Tar is a compound substance made up of several of the chemicals in cigarette smoke that form a thick, sticky residue. The nicotine in a cigarette gets into the lungs by binding to tar droplets. Cigarette smoke causes the airways to narrow

IT'S NOT TRUE!

Cigar and pipe smoking are not as bad as cigarette smoking

The pH (acidity) of cigar and pipe smoke is different from that of cigarette smoke. This means it can be absorbed through the lining of the mouth and does not need to be inhaled into the lungs to have its effect. Because the nicotine in cigar and pipe smoke dissolves in saliva, the risk of oral and esophageal cancer is higher than in cigarette smokers. The risk of lung cancer is not as great, but a recent study showed that cigar smokers are still nine times more likely to develop lung cancer than nonsmokers.

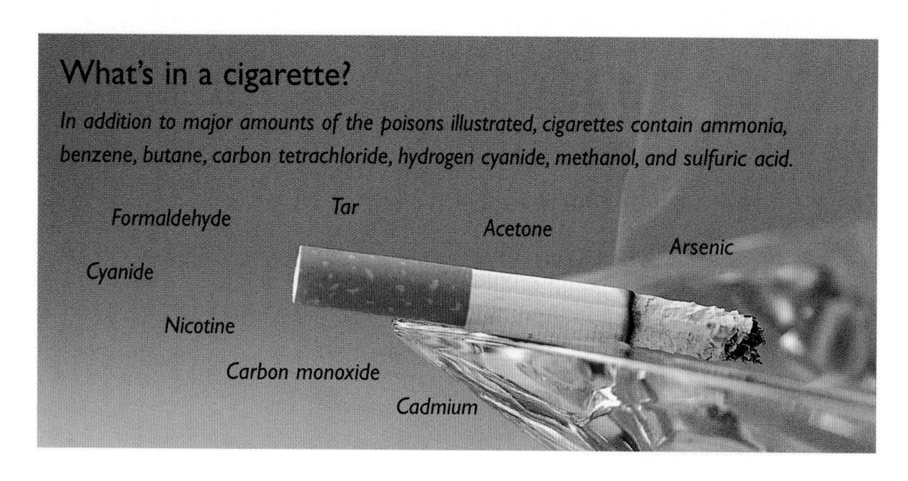

A well-known mineral water was withdrawn from sale when a batch was found to contain 4.7 micrograms per liter of benzene; one cigarette contains 190 micrograms.

Carbon monoxide and smoking

The blood of smokers contains more carbon monoxide than that of nonsmokers. Doctors and pharmacists may have a meter that measures the carbon monoxide in your body; the good news is that if you quit smoking, levels return to normal.

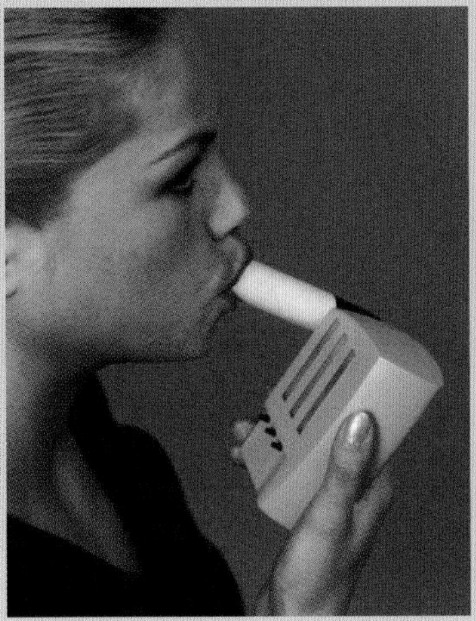

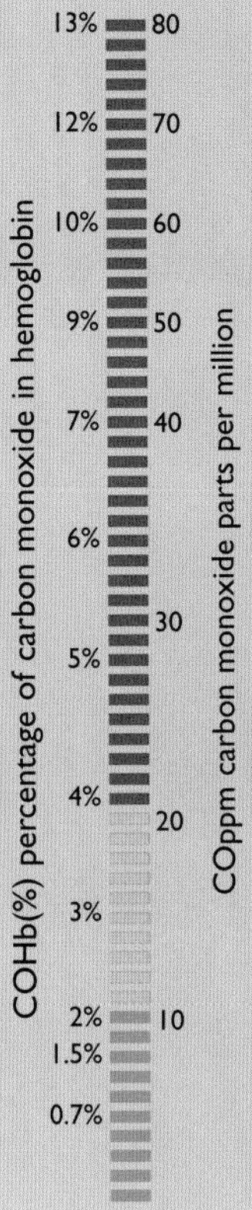

COHb(%) percentage of carbon monoxide in hemoglobin

COppm carbon monoxide parts per million

COHb(%)	COppm
13%	80
12%	70
10%	60
9%	50
7%	40
6%	
	30
5%	
4%	
	20
3%	
2%	10
1.5%	
0.7%	

Over 78 CO ppm
Uncommon: seen only in chain-smokers.

40–78 CO ppm
Frequent smokers of cigars, pipes, and cigarettes.

21–40 CO ppm
Smokers: the red blood cells are carrying less oxygen than they need; the heart is having to work harder.

11–20 CO ppm
Light smokers: every cigarette raises CO level.

5–6 CO ppm
Non-smoking city residents.

1–4 CO ppm
Nonsmoker, living in an unpolluted environment.

in response to the irritant effects of the tar. This makes the smoker cough and causes the airways to produce excess mucus in an attempt to protect themselves from the irritants. Smoking also damages the small hairs, called cilia, that protect the airways and lungs from dirt and infection, making them less able to clear the airways.

As a result of constant exposure to carbon monoxide, tar, and other chemicals, smokers are at a greater risk of illness and early death than nonsmokers. They are also more likely to suffer more frequent and more severe respiratory complaints such as coughing, sneezing, and breathlessness. Cigarette chemicals suppress the immune system, too, putting smokers more at risk from infectious diseases like influenza.

Other effects of smoking include a yellowing of teeth and fingers, a poorer complexion, and an increase in wrinkling of the skin, especially around the eyes. Smokers also have to pay higher life insurance premiums.

KNOW YOUR TAR

Many people try switching to low-tar cigarettes in the belief that low-tar brands are less harmful. In theory, less tar means fewer irritants in the airways and less nicotine reaching the lungs. However, research has shown that there is little difference in the amount of nicotine consumed by smokers of low-tar and high-tar brands. Definitions of low and high tar are based on readings from a machine that "smokes" cigarettes and measures the extracted chemicals. A machine, however, does not smoke the way people do. Real smokers can vary the amount of nicotine they extract from a cigarette in the following ways:

- By varying the length and number of puffs they take so that more smoke is inhaled for each cigarette smoked.
- By varying the amount of time they hold smoke in their lungs.
- By holding the cigarette so their fingers cover up many of the gaps in the filter tip so that less air is drawn in with the smoke.

This means that cutting down on cigarettes might not mean that the smoker is consuming less nicotine or tar, because more of either might be extracted from each cigarette. Often a smoker isn't aware of this change: it occurs unconsciously as the body demands its accustomed level of nicotine.

Why is smoking so addictive?

The speed with which nicotine reaches the brain is one reason cigarettes are so addictive, but the habitual behaviors associated with smoking also play a part. Some people smoke at specific times and in specific situations and find it hard to overcome this behavior. On average, each cigarette is puffed between 10 and 12 times. As well as being addicted to nicotine, smokers find it difficult to stop habitual movements that they may have performed for several years.

ASK THE EXPERT

HOOKED ON NICOTINE

The Surgeon General's office has long reported on the addictive qualities of cigarettes, particularly of nicotine. Regular cigarette smokers need to maintain a certain level of nicotine in their bloodstream and feel the craving for another cigarette as soon as this level begins to drop. Nicotine reaches the brain in 8 seconds, immediately putting the body into a "fight or flight" mode, raising the blood pressure and heart rate. It also increases levels of dopamine in the brain, initially resulting in improved attention and better psychological performance. Once these levels start to fall, however, the craving for a cigarette to raise them results.

The fact that nicotine is so addictive is reflected in the difficulty most smokers have in quitting. Seven out of every 10 smokers say they want to quit, but the success rate is low. Half of all smokers light up within half an hour of waking. Overnight, levels of nicotine fall so that the smoker wakes up feeling deprived of nicotine and needing a cigarette to manage the resulting craving, beginning the cycle again.

Withdrawal effects that result from stopping smoking include irritability, restlessness and sleep disturbance, poor concentration, increased appetite, and weight gain. Mouth ulcers are common because the bacterial content of the mouth changes once you stop; why this happens is still debated.

HOW SMOKING AFFECTS THE BODY

Smoking is widely known to have detrimental effects on the lungs and respiratory system and on the heart, but there are few parts of the body that are not affected by it. Although these problems may not prove fatal, they can result in years of ill health.

HEAD

Smoking causes eye damage including cataracts, macular degeneration, loss of vision, infection, and abnormal eye movements. It is responsible for gum disease, and tooth loss, and hearing loss.

DIGESTIVE SYSTEM

Duodenal and stomach ulcers, Crohn's disease, colon polyps, and diabetes can all be attributed to smoking.

SKIN

Smoking may cause psoriasis and wrinkling of the skin.

CANCERS

In addition to lung cancer, smoking is associated with cancers of the kidneys, stomach, pancreas, bladder, esophagus, breasts, cervix, mouth, and tongue.

SKELETAL SYSTEM

Smokers suffer more back and neck pain than nonsmokers; smoking causes osteoporosis and osteoarthritis and makes muscle and tendon injuries more likely.

THE RISKS TO HEALTH

Smoking is the most preventable cause of premature death in the United States. More than 400,000 Americans die from cigarette smoking every year. One in five deaths in the U.S. is smoking related. Much of the loss associated with cigarette smoking is a result of smokers dying far earlier than nonsmokers: 5 million years of life are lost in those younger than 65. A 35-year-old who has never smoked can expect to live about 7 years longer than a similar person who smokes regularly.

SMOKING AND THE LUNGS

In addition to nicotine, cigarette smoke contains several thousand other chemicals, many of which are poisons or are known to increase the risk of cancer. The carcinogens in cigarettes damage the cells in the lungs. In time, these cells may become cancerous. Some of these carcinogens are additives that are not present in tobacco; for example, ammonia is added to cigarettes to improve the absorption of nicotine. Other chemicals are added to reduce the bitterness of the smoke or to numb the airways so that the irritant effect of the smoke is not felt.

Lung cancer was rare before the invention of cigarettes. As smoking became more common, so too did lung cancer, although there is about a 30-year delay between a person starting to smoke and developing cancer. As a result, there was an explosion in the number of cases in men in the 1950s and 1960s. Women only started to smoke in large numbers in the 1930s. By the mid-1960s rates of cancer in women had risen, and by the late 1990s lung cancer had overtaken breast cancer as the leading cause of death from cancer among women. Some experts believe that this rate has peaked.

CHRONIC OBSTRUCTIVE PULMONARY DISEASE (COPD)

COPD, which includes emphysema and chronic bronchitis, is rare in people who do not smoke: 80 percent of deaths from COPD can be attributed to smoking. COPD is progressive and irreversible. The airways in the lungs gradually become narrowed, and the air sacs are slowly destroyed. As a result, less oxygen reaches the lungs, and there is less surface area for the exchange of gases to take place. By the time a sufferer notices breathing problems, as much as half of the lung has probably been destroyed.

Pneumonia

An infection of the lungs, pneumonia causes a cough, raised temperature, and breathlessness. Not only is pneumonia more common among smokers, but it is also more likely to be fatal in those who smoke.

Asthma exacerbation

Cigarette smoke is a common precipitating factor in asthma. Smoking and smoky atmospheres make the symptoms of asthma worse, adding extra strain to already compromised airways. People with asthma should not smoke.

Cigarette smoke contains about 4,000 chemicals, including 200 known poisons and almost 60 known carcinogens.

Males and females
The number of regular smokers is increasing among those younger than 25, including teenagers and especially women.

SMOKING HABITS

More than 80 percent of smokers take up the habit as teenagers, and there is evidence that smoking is on the increase among this age group, especially in those younger than 16. Half of all teenagers who are currently smoking will die from a smoking-related disease if they continue to smoke. The younger a person starts smoking, the greater the risk of lung cancer. A recent study revealed permanent genetic changes in the lungs of teenage smokers; these changes predispose people to lung cancer, even if they stop smoking.

Trends in smoking

About a third of teenage girls smoke at least one cigarette per week. The number decreases in the 25–34 age group and among those older than 60. The number of smokers is unchanged in those between ages 35 and 59.

10-POINT PLAN TO STOP SMOKING

Quitting for good

Quitting smoking is not easy, even when you are absolutely determined to do so. All the evidence suggests that it is easier to stop completely than to try cutting down first. If you aren't ready and don't genuinely want to stop, it is almost certain that your attempt will fail. This creates a vicious circle by promoting a sense of failure, which will make you less likely to want to try to stop again. As a starting point, ask yourself what, if anything, you enjoy about smoking. Then ask yourself why you want to stop. Make a list of the reasons for and against quitting, and read through the two lists. If you genuinely think you're ready to stop, this plan may work for you.

1 Decide on the date

Plan a "quit-smoking" day ahead of time so that you can quit on a day that will be free of stress. Write this down, along with the reasons why you want to stop and the people you will ask to help you to stop.

2 When do you smoke?

People often smoke in particular situations, without even craving a cigarette. Identify these cues and write them down so you can avoid them—perhaps by not going to a party in the first few weeks—or think of strategies to deal with them. Leave the table right after a meal if lingering will tempt you to light up.

3 Remove temptation

The night before your "quit-smoking" day, throw away all your cigarettes, lighters, and ashtrays: You will not need them anymore.

4 Get support

It can be helpful to ask a friend to call you every day to check on your progress, and ask people you socialize with to respect the fact that you are trying to stop. It can also help to stop with someone else so that you can support each other. Try calling a state-sponsored helpline, visiting the American Lung Association (ALA) Web site, or joining an Internet support group.

5 Snack attack

Have lots of healthy snacks on hand, for those times when you crave a cigarette. Suitable choices include raw vegetables, dried and fresh fruit, or sugar-free gum. But be pragmatic: If a bar of chocolate will help to keep you away from cigarettes, it's worth it!

10 Spend spend spend

Smoking is an expensive habit that costs more each year. Even smoking five cigarettes a day costs more than $300 a year: that's time in the sun or two new pairs of shoes. Writing down what you plan to do with the money you save—then going out and buying what you promised yourself—can be a great incentive to stay away from smoking.

9 Take regular exercise

Gyms and swimming pools are non-smoking environments, and exercise will prevent you from gaining weight, a common problem in ex-smokers. Getting exercise will demonstrate the effects of not smoking on your breathing: within days you will breathe more easily. Finally, exercise triggers the release of endorphins in the brain, chemicals that can block the craving for nicotine.

TALKING POINT

Zyban: a wonder drug?

Buproprion, marketed under the tradename Zyban, is an aid to quitting smoking, available only with a prescription. It contains no nicotine and works by reducing withdrawal symptoms through changing the levels of the chemicals dopamine and norepinephrine in the brain. Zyban comes in tablet form and is taken over two months with smokers setting a date to stop smoking during the second week. Some people experience side effects, such as difficulty sleeping, dry mouth, and headache, although these normally last only for a short time. Zyban should not be used by people who have had eating disorders or who suffer from epilepsy. There are risks associated with Zyban, however. It should not be taken along with certain other medications, such as MAO inhibitors for depression. It has been reported as causing seizures, and may exacerbate mental problems in some users.

8 Keep your hands busy

Many smokers miss having something to do with their hands. Taking up an activity that keeps your hands busy can be a good way to get over this problem: You can try anything from writing to all your friends to taking up knitting to learning to play a musical instrument.

7 Relieve stress

If stress is a factor in your smoking, find other ways of dealing with it before you quit. Good stress-busters include therapies like yoga and meditation or energetic sports such as tennis and squash.

6 Nicotine substitutes

Discuss with your doctor or pharmacist whether nicotine replacement therapy (NRT) might be suitable. NRT products include patches, gum, nasal sprays, inhalers, and tablets to place under the tongue. Products can be tailored to individual needs: patches, for example, offer continuous nicotine and thus are suitable for regular smokers, whereas gum may be better suited to irregular smokers.

NRT and a quit-smoking plan can help reduce withdrawal symptoms and boost morale—but they can't stop for you or make it easy to quit.

FOR CHILDREN

Children and passive smoking

Smoking particularly affects babies and children. Exposure to secondhand smoke means exposure to the same tars and chemicals that are damaging the smoker, but because babies' lungs are still developing, they are at a greater risk of respiratory diseases such as asthma, bronchitis, and pneumonia. Every year thousands of children younger than 5 are admitted to the hospital because of their parents' smoking, and more than a quarter of crib deaths may be related to parental smoking in pregnancy and after. Child passive smokers have a higher risk of developing cancer in later life, and the more smokers there are in the house, the greater the risk. There is also evidence that children who grow up with smokers are also likely to smoke.

THE FUTURE OF SMOKING

There has been a trend toward increasing cigarette taxes and banning smoking in certain places, combined with increased health education and more stringent advertising laws. This in part is responsible for the decline in the percentage of regular smokers over the last 30 years. This has also resulted in a decrease in the number of deaths related to cigarette smoking. This encouraging evidence has led to efforts in the U.S. to reduce cigarette smoking by 50 percent by 2010.

Antismoking policies are not new, although the example of California is often cited to support them as a means of changing public opinion. In the late 1980s, California introduced strict clean-air laws, began an aggressive campaign of public awareness, and provided support for local stop-smoking groups. The initiative was funded in part by a 25 percent increase in tax on tobacco. Studies of the results of the program after 10 years showed that cigarette consumption had fallen by 50 percent, and there had been a 14 percent decrease in lung cancer in the state (compared with a 2 percent average national decrease).

The California experience may be copied elsewhere. Public opinion regarding smoking, however, appears to be cyclical, and it may be that we are at the bottom of such a cycle, with cigarette smoking generally regarded negatively. There are still groups, however, for whom smoking has a positive image.

Clean-air California
The California experience demonstrates the positive effects on rates of lung cancer deaths of strict no-smoking laws, a steep rise in taxes, and comprehensive antismoking education.

Eat better, breathe better

By maintaining a balanced diet, you help keep your immune system functioning as it should. This reduces your risk of picking up a respiratory infection from any harmful bacteria, viruses, and fungi that enter your lungs as you breathe.

Severe deficiencies or excesses of vitamins are rare in developed countries such as the United States. Even so, different vitamins and minerals do influence the normal working of our immune system.

- Vitamin A This vitamin is essential to the development and functioning of mucous membranes, including the lining of the lungs and bronchi. It is found in milk, margarine, butter, cheese, egg yolk, liver, and oily fish. Carrots, tomatoes, and dark green vegetables are rich in beta carotene, which can be converted to vitamin A in the body. Deficiency in vitamin A is associated with lowered resistance to respiratory tract infections.
- Vitamin E Helping to protect the lungs from disease caused by pollution and smoke, vitamin E is found in dark green leafy vegetables, such as cabbage and spinach. A deficiency makes the immune system less efficient.
- Vitamin C By enhancing the ability of the body's white blood cells to destroy bacteria, vitamin C helps defend the body against foreign agents. It is found in fresh fruits, especially citrus fruits, green vegetables, and potatoes.
- Iron A deficiency in iron leads to a range of defects in the immune system. Meat is the richest source of iron, and bread, cereals, fortified breakfast cereals, and green leafy vegetables contain some iron.
- Zinc Lack of zinc in early infancy delays the normal development of the immune system. Zinc is found in milk, cheese, meat, eggs, fish, whole-grain cereals, and legumes.
- Minerals and trace elements A shortage of some minerals and trace elements such as calcium, magnesium, manganese, and copper depresses the body's ability to defend itself against bacteria and viruses. Calcium is found in milk, cheese, fish with edible bones, tofu, and dark green leafy vegetables. Milk, bread, potatoes, and vegetables contain magnesium. Manganese is present in nuts, spices, and whole-grain cereals. Copper is found in shellfish, liver, meat, bread, potatoes, dried beans, and dark green leafy vegetables.

FIGHTING COLDS AND THE FLU

Most people have a favourite cure for colds and the flu. Among the most popular are high-dose vitamin C tablets, zinc lozenges, the Echinacea plant, and chicken soup. There are conflicting opinions on whether these effectively prevent or alleviate the symptoms of colds and flu, and scientific evidence does not always support the anecdotal evidence.

Vitamin C

Linus Pauling, a double Nobel prize winner, was the first person to extol the virtues of vitamin C when he published his book

FOODS RICH IN VITAMIN C

PRODUCT	VITAMIN C CONTENT (mg)	RDA %
FRUIT AND FRUIT JUICES		
7.5 oz orange juice	87.8	146
Small orange	64.8	108
2.6 oz strawberries	57.8	96
Large peach	46.5	78
1 slice papaya	43.4	72
Kiwi fruit	34.5	59
20 raisins	32	53
Half grapefruit	28.8	48
6 oz apple juice	24.5	41
15 raspberries	19.2	32
7.5 oz tomato juice	18	30
20 blackberries	15	25
1 banana	11	18
4 apricots	9.6	16
VEGETABLES		
2.6 oz red/green pepper**	105	175
5.2 oz broccoli*	66	110
2.6 oz red cabbage**	41.3	69
5.2 oz white cabbage*	30	50
Medium baked potato	25.2	42
2.6 oz spinach*	19.5	33
2.6 oz endive	9.6	16
2.6 oz asparagus*	3.8	6

* raw
** cooked

Diet and your immune system
A healthy, varied diet protects your immune system which, in turn, helps to keep you healthy. These dietary guidelines, in addition to helping you eat well, may go a long way towards year-round health.

Vitamin C and the Common Cold in 1970. In it he claimed that large daily doses of vitamin C reduce the chances of catching a cold. However, in 1997 a review of 30 trials found that long-term supplementation with vitamin C in large daily doses (up to a gram) does not appear to prevent colds. Some of the trials had found a modest benefit in reducing the duration of cold symptoms.

Grandmother's chicken soup

Chicken soup has long been reputed to relieve the symptoms of upper respiratory tract infections. Some studies have tried to identify specific compounds within chicken soup that have medicinal properties, and more than one concluded that chicken soup may contain compounds that have anti-inflammatory effects. A study at the University of Nebraska, for example, found that both the chicken soup and its individual ingredients, boiled and eaten separately, prevented the action of the immune cells that results in inflammation of the lining of the nasal passages.

Zinc

Zinc lozenges are marketed for their ability to shorten the duration and reduce the severity of symptoms of the common cold, although how they do this has not been explained. Two recent clinical trials, however, demonstrated that zinc lozenges did not have any effect on the duration of a cold or provide any relief from its symptoms.

Comfort food
All fluids are good for you when you have a cold, and the warmth of chicken soup is very soothing. Traditional chicken soup with chicken, sweet potatoes, onions, turnips, carrots, celery, and parsley prevents mucus buildup and swelling of the nasal passages.

Echinacea

Extracts of the Echinacea plant are reputed to boost the immune system and have been used widely in the United States for the prevention and treatment of the common cold. A review of 16 studies comparing using Echinacea against no treatment, placebos, and other treatments for colds did suggest some preparations of Echinacea were better than placebos. At present, however, there is not enough evidence to recommend specific Echinacea products for the prevention or treatment of the common cold.

FOOD ALLERGIES

A food allergy is a specific type of food intolerance that involves an abnormal reaction of a person's immune system to a food constituent that, for most people, is harmless. The immune system protects the body from harmful foreign compounds, known as antigens, by generating a response to eliminate them. In food allergies the response can be immediate—as soon as a food is eaten, or in some cases just from inhaling the smell—or it can take several hours to develop.

The immediate response releases a number of substances, including histamine, which causes symptoms in the respiratory system: a runny nose, asthma, flushing, swelling, and difficulty breathing. The allergic response usually occurs in just one or two organs in the body, but if it is widespread it can lead to an anaphylactic reaction.

Anaphylactic reactions affect the whole body and vary in severity, but at their most acute can be life-threatening, leading to a fall in blood pressure and coma. Allergies to nuts (especially peanuts), eggs, shellfish, milk, and seeds have all been known to cause anaphylaxis.

MIRACLE MICRONUTRIENTS

Some of the vitamins and minerals that are important for fighting infection are also antioxidants, which can help to protect the body against developing certain cancers.

What are antioxidants?

Antioxidants are compounds present in some foods that can help to neutralize harmful molecules called free radicals. Free radicals cause changes in the structure of proteins, fat (or lipids), and DNA—our genetic makeup. Damage to the DNA may be one of a sequence of events in the development of cancer.

How do antioxidants work?

Antioxidants work in several ways, all of which inhibit the change in structure (or oxidation) of our DNA. For example, some trap free radicals to get them out of harm's way, and others protect against the oxidation of lipids, thereby keeping the microscopic structure of all our cell walls intact and functioning properly.

Foods rich in antioxidants

Fruits and vegetables are the major sources of antioxidants in the average diet. Antioxidant nutrients include vitamins C and E and carotenoids such as beta carotene, leutein, and lycopene.

In addition, the body's defense system against free radical damage includes several enzymes functioning as antioxidants. These enzymes rely on the diet to provide a regular supply of essential minerals such as selenium, zinc, and magnesium.

Other antioxidants include compounds called flavonoids, which are found in fruits and vegetables, soy beans, and tea. These may prevent or counteract free radical damage.

8 Great ways to boost your intake of antioxidants

If you find it difficult to eat the five-servings-a-day of fruit and vegetables recommended for good health, try these simple suggestions.

1. Have a glass of fruit or vegetable juice with your meals.
2. Add a handful of chopped fresh or dried fruit to a bowl of whole-grain cereal or a cup of reduced fat yogurt.
3. Serve a side salad with your meals—the greater the variety of vegetables the better.
4. Add extra chopped vegetables such as onions, leeks, carrots, and tomatoes to stews and casseroles. Vegetables can be canned, frozen, or raw.
5. Eat fruit or raw vegetables as snacks.
6. Include legumes and beans in your diet, for example, bean salads or a tofu stir-fry, or add them to stews.
7. Always have two servings of vegetables with your evening meal. If you don't have fresh, use frozen.
8. Finish off each meal with a piece of fruit or a bowl of fresh fruit salad.

Exercise and your lungs

Giving your lungs a workout through exercising improves the way they function, helping you breathe more freely and easily. Choosing suitable activities is not difficult, but it's important to take sensible precautions and not overdo it.

Aerobic exercise—walking, jogging, cycling, swimming, or any activity that allows you to work at a moderate intensity for an extended time—is the best exercise for your lungs. You should aim to exercise for at least 20 minutes three times a week, but if you are new to exercise, start gradually and work up to this level. Lungs love aerobic exercise because it allows them to carry out their primary function of supplying oxygen to the working muscles in the most efficient manner. As you increase the rate and depth of your breathing during exercise, you use more of your lung capacity, and this encourages your diaphragm and intercostals, the respiratory muscles, to work harder.

During aerobic exercise, lung volume can increase from 6 liters per minute to 150 liters per minute.

Steady, deep rhythmical breathing increases airflow to the alveoli, the tiny blood vessels deep within the lungs where the transfer of oxygen to the blood and the elimination of the waste product of respiration—carbon dioxide—takes place.

At rest, about 250 milliliters of oxygen leaves the alveoli and enter the blood every minute. During a vigorous exercise session, however, up to 25 times this quantity of oxygen can be transferred across the alveolar membrane each minute.

HEART AND LUNGS—AN INTIMATE PARTNERSHIP

The primary function of your lungs, during rest and also during exercise, is to maintain a fairly constant concentration of oxygen and carbon dioxide within the alveoli. The heart and lungs work together in a tightly controlled relationship so that you regulate the rate and depth of your breathing to continue to supply enough oxygen to the muscles, no matter how hard they are working.

Physical activity affects oxygen consumption and carbon dioxide production more than any other form of stress on the body. Alveolar tissue has the largest blood supply of any part of the body, and when you exercise, the alveoli need everything the heart is pumping out.

When you start to exercise, carbon dioxide levels within your blood begin to rise. This triggers the brain to increase the rate of your breathing. As you breathe faster, you breathe out more carbon dioxide. At the same time your muscles are demanding more oxygen and so your heart begins to beat faster in order to transport more oxygen-rich blood to the muscles and more blood back into the lungs to be oxygenated.

There are two ways in which our bodies work to keep the right balance of oxygen and carbon dioxide—nervous control and chemical control. Both means of control begin in a group of nerve cells in the brain called the respiratory center.

YOGA PROGRAM FOR HEALTHY LUNGS

Practically all regular exercise is good for a healthy body, but yoga can be particularly beneficial for the heart and lungs. This series of postures can help you to improve breathing by enhancing awareness of the senses, muscles, and joints. It may look difficult but it gets easier with practice.

Warming up

This exercise stretches the respiratory muscles while increasing the size of the lungs, allowing you to breathe deeply. It can also be used to improve respiratory health if you find the exercises on the right too difficult to begin with.

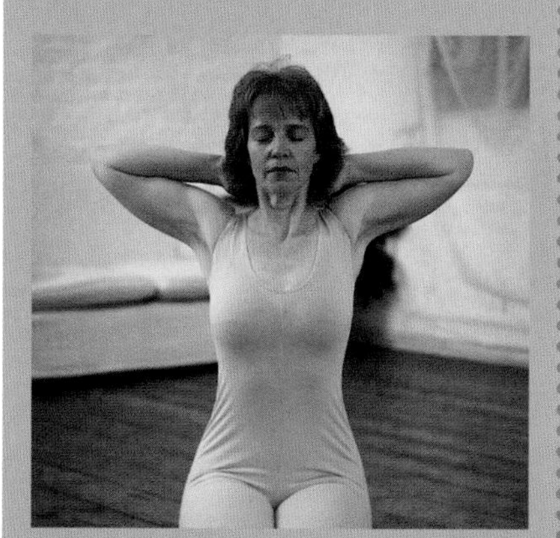

1 *Kneel, then, with a straight back, place both hands behind your head and breathe deeply.*

2 *Drop one elbow toward the floor, hold this position for a few seconds, then return to upright. Repeat, dropping the other elbow toward the floor.*

Chest opener

This posture stretches the chest and the front section of the lungs as well as the airways themselves.

1 Kneel on the floor, clasp your hands behind your back, and link fingers. Push out your chest and drop your head back, stretching the muscles of the front of your chest.

2 Exhale as you lean forward to rest your head on the floor, while slowly bringing your arms, still clasped behind your back, toward your head.

3 As you inhale, lift your buttocks off your heels so that your torso becomes almost vertical. In this position, take a few deep breaths. Lower your buttocks back to your heels as you lift your head.

The Cat

The Cat stretches the muscles in your sides, from the edge of the armpits all the way down your ribs and including the area from your lowest rib to your hip bone, thereby opening up your breathing. The movements are also designed for relieving tension.

1 Kneel with your hands on the floor, shoulderwidth apart. Your knees should be hipwidth apart. Inhale and hollow your back. Breathe normally, keeping your back hollow.

2 Begin to exhale while slowly rolling yourself back to a horizontal position. Hold this position and breathe in again.

3 While continuing to breathe out, slowly curve your back. When your back is as rounded as possible, breathe in. When exhaling, roll yourself back to a horizontal position.

4 From the horizontal, breathe out and bend your elbows outward. Exhale and hollow your back. As you breathe in, let your back be pulled back toward your heels.

5 Exhale while you slowly stretch out your back and lower your elbows to the floor. Repeat steps 4 and 5, which should give you a wavelike movement down your spine. Finish in the step 4 position so that you can kneel upright from this position, then stand up.

AEROBIC EXERCISE

The word *aerobic* is derived from Greek and means "with air." In the context of exercise, it refers to the mechanism by which our muscles receive the energy they need. Energy is created in the muscle cells by combining oxygen with fat and carbohydrate to produce ATP, or adenosine triphosphate, which is the body's energy fund.

The purpose of aerobic exercise is to improve the amount of oxygen the body can obtain and use in time. You should be able to sustain aerobic exercise for long periods: your body has plenty of carbohydrate and fat stores, and your bloodstream is supplying plenty of oxygen.

Aerobic exercise is different from anaerobic exercise, that is, exercise in which oxygen is not used in producing energy. When you sprint, for example, your heart and lungs cannot keep up with the amount of oxygen your body needs to convert carbohydrate and fat into energy. The extra energy, therefore, comes from stored glucose, which can be turned into energy without needing oxygen. This produces a waste product, lactic acid, which makes your muscles ache.

The benefits of aerobic exercise

The secret of successful aerobic exercise is long duration. The longer you exercise, the more you will improve the way your heart and lungs function. It's not unusual for physically fit people to exercise for an hour a day, 5 days a week. By asking your heart and lungs to work for an extended period, you will reap many health benefits.

Good forms of aerobic exercise

There are lots of ways you can get enough aerobic exercise to stay healthy, and many of them don't require any special equipment or a visit to the gym. Brisk walking, for example, can be carried out by anyone anywhere. You need to buy good running shoes if you are planning to take up jogging, but otherwise that too can be done anywhere and at any time.

Swimming is excellent aerobic exercise and one of the best sports for developing the health of the lungs

Oxygen-dependent
Theoretically, when your body is receiving sufficient oxygen from the blood, you should be able to exercise for an extended period.

LONG-TERM REWARDS OF EXERCISE

Although beginning regular exercise can seem like a painful prospect if you are unfit, remember that positive effects will be felt by the body almost instantly. The longer-term benefits could be life-saving and include:

CHOLESTEROL CONTROL
With regular exercise, your total body cholesterol falls and the level of HDL ("good") cholesterol rises.

BENEFITS FOR THE HEART
Your resting heart rate falls as your heart becomes more efficient, raising the amount of blood pumped out with each beat.

BLOOD PRESSURE
Regular exercise lowers blood pressure; this effect can be seen in as few as 3 months.

MAJOR HEALTH RISKS CUT IN HALF
Your risk of heart disease and stroke is half that of someone who does not exercise.

and the circulatory system. The rhythmic movements of swimming use all the major muscle groups and raise the heart rate. The respiratory muscles are strengthened as they work against the additional resistance of the weight of the water compressing the upper body. Swimmers also tend to pick up fewer injuries than other athletes because the buoyancy of the water relieves pressure on the bones and joints. This makes it a good choice for anyone with painful joints

There are many other excellent forms of aerobic exercise to do on or your own or in a group. If group activities appeal to you, you could try step classes or line dancing. Rowing, cross-country skiing, and cycling—either outdoors or on a stationary bike—are good if you prefer to work alone. Around the home, heavy gardening and digging are also excellent aerobic exercise. Stop–start sports such as football, squash, and tennis are not good aerobic exercise.

TALKING POINT

Should athletes have oxygen after intense periods of activity?

The idea behind using oxygen after an intense training session was to help the athlete recover as fast as possible. However, there is little scientific evidence that inhaling oxygen will improve recovery time. The practice was based on laboratory studies that showed breathing extra oxygen while exercising on a treadmill or stationary bicycle could increase the time that a person can exercise before becoming completely fatigued. This, however, does not take into account the fact that the body uses oxygen differently during exercise and recovery. While we exercise, the body needs oxygen to help the muscles cope with the extra demands being made of them. After exercise, oxygen aids the conversion of the by-products of muscle activity, such as lactic acid, into energy for recovery. Taking extra oxygen is not harmful, although research in the late 1980s and early 1990s showed that walking around was as effective.

Easy does it

When you first start aerobic exercise, the keys to improved health and fitness are to start slowly and to choose activities that you enjoy. If you don't like swimming, for example, you are unlikely to stick to it; if you love walking, on the other hand, walking farther, faster, and more regularly than you normally do will probably be easy.

Because the goal is to perform aerobic exercise for a lengthy period, the exercise cannot be so intense that

BREATHING MORE DEEPLY
The amount of air you inhale and exhale when you breathe deeply increases.

IMPROVED BLOOD FLOW
The flow of blood to the muscles increases. At the same time, the network of capillaries—the smallest blood vessels in the body—gets denser so that oxygen and nutrients are delivered to the muscles more efficiently.

KEEPING BLOOD SUGAR UNDER CONTROL
Less insulin is secreted, which helps to prevent or to control diabetes.

GREATER LUNG CAPACITY
The lungs' ability to absorb oxygen increases.

What is a stitch?

A stitch is a sharp pain on one side just below your rib cage, although it is sometimes felt further up the torso. A stitch is thought to be caused by a cramp in the diaphragm, intestinal gas, or food in the stomach—this is why it is important not to exercise just after eating. If you experience a stitch while exercising, try the following remedies:

- Stop or slow down, and breathe deeply from your abdomen until the pain disappears.
- Lift your hands above your head, with your elbows back, and breathe deeply.
- Apply pressure to the painful area as you exhale, and massage.
- Bend over a few times and tighten your stomach muscles.

If none of these techniques work, stop exercising and walk slowly, breathing deeply into your abdomen until the pain subsides.

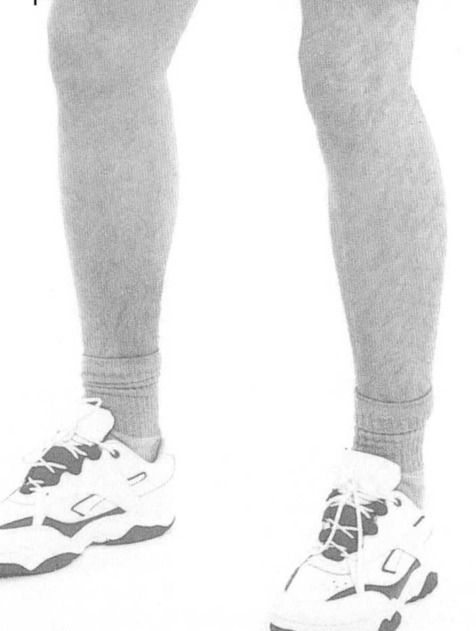

you can't maintain the pace. Aerobic exercise does not need to be strenuous to be effective—in fact, the most effective aerobic exercise is moderate in intensity. However, moderate intensity is a subjective measure. What's moderate for you may be too light or too hard for someone else. Probably the easiest measure of moderate intensity is the talk test. This simply means that you should still be able to talk or hold a conversation while exercising. If talking is difficult or impossible, the exercise is too intense for your current state of health and fitness, and you should slow down. If, on the other hand, you can manage to sing while exercising you are not working hard enough and need to increase your pace.

Start by exercising for 20 minutes three times a week on non-consecutive days. Try the talk test, or take your pulse as you exercise, initially aiming to raise it to around 60 percent of 220 minus your age. If you are 40, for example, your pulse rate as you exercise should be about 60 percent of 180, which is 110 beats per minute. As you become fitter, your pulse should be closer to 75 percent of 220 minus your age, so a 40-year-old should be aiming for a rate of 135 beats per minute. When you can sustain this level of activity fairly easily, increase your sessions to 30 minutes three times a week.

PROTECTING YOUR LUNGS

When we exercise, we need to move air in and out of our lungs rapidly and thus tend to use mouth breathing, which bypasses the nasal passages, the body's natural air filter. Air pollutants such as carbon monoxide, ozone, carbon dioxide, and sulfur dioxide can damage your lungs. When you exercise, you breathe more deeply and more frequently so that you breathe in more pollutants. This sounds like bad news, but research has shown that you don't retain them. Cyclists in rush hour traffic breathe in more carbon monoxide than most car drivers do, but they have lower blood levels of carbon monoxide because they are exhaling actively.

You can minimize your exposure to air pollution during exercise by following some simple guidelines, which are particularly important if you live in an area that is susceptible to air pollution.

- Choose your time Sunlight and time are necessary for pollution formation, so the highest levels of ozone typically occur during the afternoon. Because carbon monoxide is produced primarily by motor vehicles, the highest carbon monoxide levels usually occur during rush hour or at other times

Why should I breathe in through the nose rather than through the mouth?

Air breathed in through the nose undergoes several changes that help to preserve lung health. It is warmed by the heat from the blood in the capillaries of the nostrils, then dampened by passing over moist mucus. It is also cleaned by the cilia, which sweep dirt and dust on to the mucus, and filtered by the fine hairs in the nostrils.

ASK THE EXPERT

when traffic is congested. Good times to exercise are first thing in the morning or in the evening, after the main rush hour traffic has eased.

- **Choose your place** Avoid congested streets, because pollution levels can be high up to 50 feet from the road. Unless you have problems with pollen, choose a park rather than the road for your walk or jog.
- **Watch the weather** Pollution levels are often given with weather reports and printed in newspapers. You could also consider wearing a face mask (see page 52).

Vulnerable groups

Children, the elderly, and those with existing respiratory problems are more at risk of lung damage caused by exercising in areas and at times susceptible to pollution. Children are especially vulnerable because not only are their lungs still developing, but they also have a faster breathing rate than adults (see page 83). Some children don't cough or wheeze, even when pollution levels are high, which means that they may not realize the harm being done to their lungs. As a result, they continue to play outdoors, putting their lungs at risk.

The elderly, too, are more at risk because part of the natural process of aging is a reduction in overall lung function. Combined with breathing poor-quality air, this can lead to irritation of the lungs, wheezing, and coughing.

Timing and location

It is sensible for everyone to be aware of the problems pollutants may cause to their lungs, but different groups have different requirements.

CHILDREN
Ensure that children who have asthma are not regularly exercising in a polluted atmosphere. Encourage indoor activities such as swimming, gymnastics, or martial arts at times when the air quality is particularly poor.

TEENAGERS
An exercise bike can give you the same workout as a road bike—without the pollution. Or you could invest in a face mask if your preference is to ride outdoors.

THE ELDERLY
Indoor activities like dancing are good aerobic exercise—and don't irritate the lungs. But best of all, dancing is fun, whether done with a partner, such as waltzing, or in a group, such as line dancing.

ADULTS
Be wise about time and place: walk or jog away from roads, especially during peak traffic times. Try to find a park or a route where traffic is minimal, or exercise in the early morning before pollutants have time to build up.

Air temperature and your lungs

If cold air hits the lungs, they respond by releasing histamine. In people with sensitive airways or asthma, this causes wheezing. The nose is designed to condition inhaled air in order to protect the delicate lung tissues.

When you breathe in cold air, the tissues lining your nose swell as the capillaries dilate, bringing warm blood to heat the cool air. The mucus normally present in the nose increases and becomes thicker. Thus, cold air by itself can produce congestion and stuffiness, which can make it more difficult for your body to get rid of inhaled germs.

Of course, cold is not the only environmental change that may affect your breathing. Hot and humid air, and the pollens and dust that are prevalent in spring, can also cause problems.

If you have a lung problem

Research has shown that people who have asthma or COPD benefit from exercise, which increases their ability to exercise further and reduces shortness of breath.

These sessions normally consist of exercises to strengthen the muscles used for breathing and conventional aerobic exercises to tone the rest of the body. If you have asthma or COPD, always pay attention to your body, and rest when you are tired. Avoid exercising when it is too cold, too hot, or too humid, or when the air quality is poor.

GETTING USED TO ALTITUDE

Athletes must acclimatize if they are to compete at high altitudes. The length of this acclimatization period depends on the altitude. As a general guideline, 2 weeks are required to adapt to altitudes of up to 7,700 feet, with an additional week for every 2,000 feet climbed, up to an altitude of 15,000 feet.

Intense training can begin as soon as is comfortable during the acclimatization period, but strenuous activity before that is dangerous, because the body is still learning to cope with the reduced levels of oxygen in the air. The benefits of acclimatization are probably lost within 2–3 weeks of returning to sea level.

Less strenuous activity at high altitudes does not need a long period of acclimatization, but it is wise to take care. If you are walking or skiing at a high altitude:

- Try not to fly straight in to a high-altitude destination. It's better for your body if you can climb gradually, perhaps by landing lower and driving up.
- Be aware of the symptoms of mild altitude sickness: tiredness, nausea, and headaches. Do not climb any higher for a couple of days if you experience these symptoms. Rest, and take painkillers if required.
- Vomiting, chest pain, and breathlessness indicate severe altitude sickness. Move to a lower altitude for a couple of days; if you don't feel better, you may need hospital treatment.

BREATHING HIGH

When you arrive at an altitude of more than 7,700 feet, your body will need to make rapid adjustments to compensate for the reduced concentration of oxygen in the air. There are two immediate changes: the first is an increase in breathing rate; the second is that your heart starts to work up to 50 percent harder.

BREATHING LOW

Scuba diving puts your lungs in a high-pressure environment. As a dive deepens, the pressure increases, and nitrogen in breathed air dissolves into the blood and body tissue. If a diver surfaces too rapidly, the falling pressure causes the nitrogen to be released suddenly as bubbles—a painful condition known as decompression sickness or "the bends."

People born and raised at high altitude have larger lungs and bigger areas of respiratory tissue than those living at sea level.

Breathing and posture

How you breathe, stand, and sit are intricately linked. People with good posture are likely to breathe efficiently, getting maximum oxygen into their bodies. This in turn stimulates the muscles to keep the body looking good.

How we breathe can be crucial to health. Babies and young children usually breathe well, that is, they take deep breaths, so that on an in-breath the abdomen, lower ribs, and lower back draw the diaphragm deep into the abdomen, allowing the lungs to draw in air and become fully inflated. On the out-breath, the diaphragm moves up, helping to push stale air out of the lungs.

Abdominal breathing increases the oxygen supply to the brain and muscles, raises energy levels, helps relaxation, and improves concentration. As we get older, however, many (some experts suggest, most) of us neglect this ability to breathe deeply and well, tending instead to breathe only with the upper chest, shoulders, and neck. So-called thoracic breathing makes little use of the diaphragm. In time, we become accustomed to this shallow way of breathing, and the volume of air breathed in and out, and the speed of breathing change.

There are several reasons why this happens. One is cosmetic: we hold in our stomachs so that they look flat, which means that the diaphragm does not have room to move down and let the maximum amount of air into the lungs. A sedentary lifestyle contributes on more than one level: It leads to weight gain and sitting poorly in front of the TV or computer makes it more and more difficult to breathe well. Finally, stress is a major influence on how we breathe.

Why does holding the breath cure hiccups?

Hiccups result from an irritation in the diaphragm, which pushes it upwards in a jerky way. When the resulting breath hits the voicebox, it causes a hiccup. Taking a deep breath stretches the diaphragm, relieving the irritation; remaining still and holding the breath allows the diaphragm to recover its equilibrium.

ASK THE EXPERT

STRESS AND BREATHING

Many of us adopt incorrect breathing positions without even realizing it, especially when we are stressed. In response to stress—physical or mental—your body mobilizes its

Using the diaphragm

Rapid diaphragmatic breathing gets more oxygen into the lungs and is a technique well worth learning. As well as improving the efficiency of the lungs and making you more aware of your breathing, it is also relaxing—and so is ideal if you feel stressed—and good exercise for the abdominal muscles. Keep your chest and shoulders still during this exercise; the movement should be felt only in your abdomen.

Emptying the lungs

Take in a complete breath, but breathe out only about three quarters of the breath. Quickly contract your abdominal muscles so that the remaining air is breathed out of your nose in a fast, noisy exhalation.

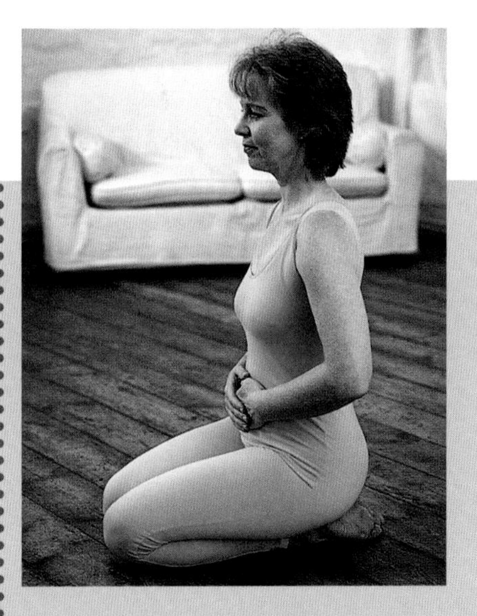

Encouraging deeper breathing

Relax your abdominal muscles as you inhale a quarter of a breath, then contract them again to exhale quickly and loudly. Repeat this 20 times to begin; as you become more proficient, increase the number gradually to 50.

POSTURE PERFECT

Everyday actions—such as lifting, holding the telephone, and making repetitive motions—play a major role in the development of poor posture. Sitting for long periods, for example, can encourage you to slump, thereby restricting your breathing. To open up your chest and breathe more easily, remember these guidelines as often as you can.

SITTING

- *Make sure your feet are flat on the floor or supported by a footrest.*
- *Check that there is a space of at least three quarters of an inch between the back of your knees and the edge of the chair seat, so that you do not cut off the circulation behind your knees.*
- *Make sure your knees and hips are angled at approximately 90° so that your back is not slouched in the seat.*
- *Hold your head up straight, with your chin in. Do not tilt your head forward, backward, or sideways.*
- *Ensure that your lower back is comfortably supported by the chair backrest.*

STANDING

- *Keep your earlobes in line with the middle of your shoulders.*
- *Keep your shoulder blades back.*
- *Stretch the top of your head toward the ceiling.*
- *Tuck your chin in a little.*
- *Push your sternum out slightly.*
- *Tuck your stomach in. Keep your pelvis neutral, tilted neither forward nor backward.*
- *Lean forward slightly from your hips.*
- *Keep your knees facing forward.*
- *Make sure that your knees are not locked.*
- *Stand with your feet side by side, about shoulderwidth apart.*
- *Rise up on the balls of your feet, then gradually lower your heels until they just touch the floor, and make sure your weight is balanced evenly on your feet.*

AT WORK

- *Try alternating your tasks between sitting and standing.*
- *Take frequent, brief rest periods, particularly from working at a computer screen.*
- *Do some gentle stretches once every hour.*
- *Ensure that there is adequate lighting in your work space so that you don't have to lean over to see what you are doing.*
- *Hold the telephone receiver in your hand: never prop a telephone on your shoulder while you talk and type or write at the same time.*
- *Open a window to get some fresh air if you possibly can.*
- *Go for a brisk walk, a run, or a swim during your lunch break to improve your breathing and circulation.*

positive health tips

Breathe—and relax!

Voluntary breath control is probably the oldest and best-known stress reduction technique. When we feel stressed or anxious, our involuntary bodily response is to gather tension into our necks and shoulders and to begin to take quick, shallow breaths from the top of our chests. Breath training helps to control your respiration rate and improves the position and function of the respiratory muscles. If you feel anxious or stressed, inhale through your nose and exhale with your lips pursed together in a whistling position. Make each out-breath longer than an in-breath—a good rule is 4 seconds for an in-breath and 6 seconds for an out-breath.

resources to get ready to fight or flee. Your muscles—particularly those in your shoulders and chest—tense, ready for action; your heart beats faster; and your breathing becomes quicker and shallower. Known as hyperventilation, this form of breathing has many negative effects on physical and emotional health.

When you breathe too fast, you reduce the level of carbon dioxide in the blood disproportionately to the level of oxygen. Paradoxically, this increased level of oxygen leads to lack of oxygen in your body, because the oxygen–carbon dioxide imbalance constricts the blood flow throughout the body. This heightens the fight or flight response, so you find yourself in a vicious circle.

The best ways to break the circle are to breathe through pursed lips (see above) or to breathe regularly into a paper bag (see page 43).

ABDOMINAL BREATHING.

Take note of how you are breathing now. Place one hand on your chest and one hand on your stomach, and breath normally. Notice which hand has the most movement. With abdominal or diaphragmatic breathing, the hand on your stomach should clearly move while the hand on your chest barely moves.

Practicing abdominal breathing

Place both hands on the lower part of your stomach, and breathe in so that the incoming air expands that area and gently pushes against your hands. Then, gently push with your hands as you exhale slowly. Relax for a moment, then inhale again. Inhale through your nose and exhale through your mouth. If using an image helps, picture a balloon in your stomach, which inflates when you inhale and deflates when you exhale. Practice this several times. Now, imagine the tension and stress leaving your body as you exhale while saying to yourself, "I am becoming more and more relaxed."

GENTLE THERAPIES FOR BETTER BREATHING

The Eastern therapies of yoga and qigong both combine fluid body movements with breath training. Both are best learned in a class at first but can then be practiced at home and incorporated into your everyday life. Becoming aware of how you breathe is central to both yoga and qigong.

Deep abdominal breathing is an important element of qigong. An in-breath brings positive energy into the body and is associated with "opening" movements. An exhalation, by contrast, forces negative energy out of the body and may be associated with "closing" movements.

"Receiving energy from the sky"
Qigong consists of sequences of movements, each subtly different, so that they flow into one another. Many sequences begin with "opening" movements to bring qi into the body by breathing in positive energy.

In yoga, you are encouraged to fill your lungs with air by focusing on three separate areas of your torso:

- Diaphragm The diaphragm contracts and lowers as you breathe in, and the abdominal region swells to fill the lower part of the lungs with air.
- Intercostals Raising the ribs—and therefore the chest wall—like a pair of bellows fills the middle section of the lungs.
- Clavicles Air is introduced by raising the collar bone and shoulders so that the upper part of the lungs receive air. (This is the type of shallow, or thoracic, breathing many of us tend to do most of the time.)

Equally important as inhalation is exhalation, which rids your body of stale air so that you can inhale more fresh air. In some yoga exercises, it is not unusual for the out-breath to take up to four times as long as an in-breath.

Other types of yoga breathing teach an awareness of breathing and may improve your breath control.

STAND TALL, BREATHE EASY

Most of us are aware that posture greatly influences breathing. However, many of us have developed ways of using our bodies that limit our ability to breathe efficiently. Rounded or slumped shoulders restrict the rib cage and therefore the volume of our breathing. People who sit up straight tend to look alert because breathing correctly allows the maximum amount of oxygen to reach the brain.

Sing your heart out

Breathing properly makes a huge difference to a singer's voice. To sing properly, you must take deep, balanced breaths to allow the vocalization process to become more natural. This continuous airflow means that you don't strain your vocal cords, you can hold notes longer, and you may achieve a vibrato.

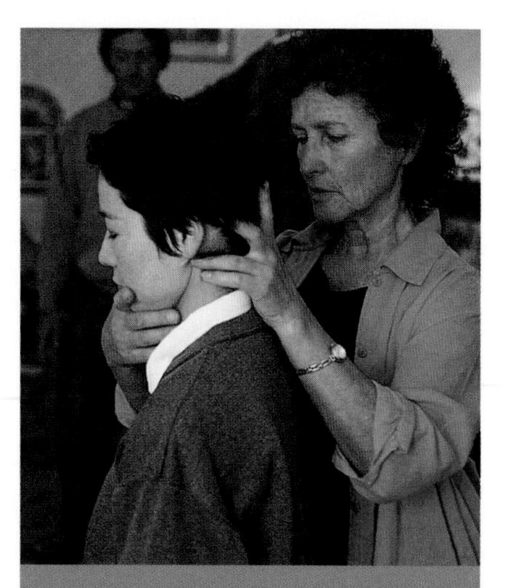

Alexander technique

Developed by F. M. Alexander (1869–1955), an Australian actor, the Alexander technique teaches you awareness of poor postural habits. Alexander suffered from a vocal problem that threatened his career, and he spent many years developing ways to improve his posture, allow him to breathe correctly, and help with his voice control. Today there are teachers of the technique all over the world who use it to solve the common movement problems that cause chronic pain, back injury, and stress.

The Alexander technique releases stress in the muscles and improves breathing. It offers a way to streamline actions and movements and to move more easily. Posture, movement, and breathing capacity improve, making you look and feel better. The Alexander technique is best taught by a registered teacher at first, but the lessons you learn can then be translated into your everyday life.

YOUR HEALTHY ENVIRONMENT

The world around us probably has more impact on respiratory health than on any other body system: after all, every minute of our waking and sleeping hours we take in lungfuls of air. If that air has poor quality—even if there is nothing really wrong with it but it contains a substance to which an individual suffers a poor reaction, such as pollen—our health and well-being, even life itself, may be compromised. Knowing which substances may be harmful and why, at home, work, and in the air around you, is an important part of staying well.

What is air pollution?

You have no choice but to breathe the air around you, but there are times when that air can be harmful. If you know the risks to respiratory health posed by the environment, you are in a better position to minimize their impact.

Airborne substances that make an environment unpleasant or harmful to the health of living things are called air pollution. The Air Quality Index (AQI) uses a scale of 0–500, divided into six levels, each with a representative color, to describe air pollution. Green means "good," or 0–50. Yellow is "moderate," or 51–100. Orange means air quality is unhealthy for sensitive groups,with 101–150. Red is "unhealthy," or 151–200. Purple means "very unhealthy," or 201–300. Finally, maroon is "hazardous," or 301–500.

Healthy people do not usually notice any effects from air pollution, except at times when it is very high. Even then, they should be aware only of the pollution rather than suffer any ill effects from it.

People who are sensitive to air pollution—those with heart or lung problems, including COPD and asthma, especially if they are elderly—should not notice any effects on days when pollution is mild. On days when the level is moderate, they may notice the pollution but should not need to take special action.

When the pollution level is high, sensitive people will notice adverse effects and may need to take action.

CONSTITUENTS OF AIR POLLUTION

There are six major constituents of air pollution: sulfur dioxide, nitrogen dioxide, ozone, carbon monoxide, lead, and particulate matter (dust and pollen, for example). Information is gathered on these substances from centers nationwide to produce a pollution index and issue pollution warnings. A raised level of any one of these pollutants automatically raises the index, so that if levels of sulfur dioxide, for example, are found to be high, the pollution index is classed as high, even if levels of all other pollutants are within acceptable limits.

Road vehicles are responsible for half of the nitrogen dioxide and three quarters of the carbon monoxide in the atmosphere.

If I can't even tell that I'm inhaling pollutants can they really be that bad for me?

The simple answer is yes. Just because some airborne pollutants do not irritate your nose and throat does not mean that they are not being absorbed into your body. Take smog for example: sensitivity to ozone levels in smog varies from person to person so many of us do not notice its presence, and are unaware it is doing us harm. In addition, not all pollutants are detectable to the eye or nose. Carbon monoxide, for example, is an odorless and colorless gas, yet it is potentially fatal in high doses.

ASK THE EXPERT

WHAT YOU CAN DO

Anyone with respiratory problems should check the pollution index for the next 24 hours. This information is available from weather forecasts or via the Internet.

When pollution levels are high or very high, people with respiratory problems may have to use their relief medication or spend more time indoors.

Industrial hazards

Smoke and toxic chemicals are regularly pumped into the air above our cities where, with the action of sunlight, they may become hazardous to lung health.

Knowing the pollutants

Two facts are important when thinking about potential risks from air pollution; first, there is a lot you can do to avoid exposure to irritants; second, governments and independent advisors monitor safe levels, indoors and out.

The major air pollutants, which are all potentially damaging to your respiratory system, fall into two broad categories: particulate matter and chemical pollution. Some chemicals are classed as particulate matter, but more often than not this is made up of nonchemical particles that irritate the airways and, if small enough, invade lung tissue. Chemical pollution includes gases, such as carbon monoxide, and hazardous air pollutants, which are chemicals released as part of several industrial processes.

PARTICULATE MATTER

Particulate matter can come from a number of sources, from road construction to agriculture. Because your nose and throat filter out larger particles, it is the smaller ones that are potentially harmful to your lungs. Particles that manage to get past your nose and upper respiratory tract can reduce mucous clearance, impair lung function, and cause respiratory disease. Inhaling particulate matter can provoke wheezing and other symptoms in people with sensitive airways. If you already suffer from asthma, you may find that pollen and dust make it worse.

It can be difficult to protect yourself against particulate matter; you can't always avoid pollution, but you can give your body's natural defenses a helping hand by wearing a face mask near busy roads and when the air quality is generally poor.

GASES

Gases can occur naturally, or they may be produced in a chemical reaction. Most are harmful only in high doses or in combination. Almost every type of gas is present in the environment but in concentrations so low that they provide no risk to health. In many cases, it is only when these gases build up that they are harmful. Often, people contribute to this buildup; in order to safeguard your health, prevention is as important as protection.

More than 500 people die of unintentional carbon monoxide poisoning every year; 2,000 use it to commit suicide.

Carbon monoxide

Traffic is a major pollutant, with emissions of many harmful gases, including carbon monoxide.

Carbon monoxide is odorless, colorless, and tasteless and affects your health by entering the bloodstream and preventing the normal delivery of oxygen, via the blood, around the body. In high doses, carbon monoxide can cause or worsen heart and respiratory disorders and reduce oxygen supply to the heart. There are, however, steps you can take to reduce the risk of carbon monoxide poisoning.

- Be on the lookout for symptoms These include headaches, fatigue, dizziness, and chest pains.

Good gas

Many gases make life on Earth easier and more pleasant.
Ozone (O_3) is a gas of the upper atmosphere that shields us from the sun's ultraviolet radiation.
Carbon dioxide (CO_2) is used by plants for photosynthesis, the process by which they grow and process nutrients. It is considered one of nature's fundamental building blocks.

Bad gas

Problems occur when gases are present in large quantities in the wrong place.
Ozone (O_3) causes problems at lower atmospheric levels and in heavy concentrations; this is common on smoggy days.
Carbon dioxide (CO_2) is dangerous to humans in high concentrations, whereas carbon monoxide (CO, which has only one oxygen molecule, rather than two) impairs the blood's ability to transport oxygen around the body.

- **Understand the risks** Carbon monoxide is produced by the incomplete combustion of carbon-based fuels, such as oil, gas, and wood. Dangerous levels are often caused by leaking or poorly installed gas appliances, including water heaters, boilers, and fires.
- **Get appliances serviced** Regular servicing of gas appliances by qualified engineers reduces the risk of carbon monoxide poisoning.
- **Get a detector** Carbon monoxide detectors are a good idea in both the home and garage; they should have an audible alarm and a long-term warranty and comply with government safety standards. Most of the cases of carbon monoxide poisoning have occurred in multi-tenanted rental accommodations. If you or someone you know lives in this type of housing, a detector is especially recommended.

positive health tips

Avoid radon pollution

- Test your home. Testing is the only way to determine radon levels in a building. Reliable radon testing is not difficult to find. Home tests are often available at hardware stores.
- Open windows. Opening the windows can reduce radon levels dramatically.
- Ventilate. Power fans can be used to extract radon through pipes to be sure that the building is well ventilated.
- Preventive measures. It is important to prevent radon from entering the building: ventilating the surrounding soil so that radon can be released into the atmosphere before it leaks into the building is a good start.
- Seal the building. This can be done by undersealing the ground floor with impermeable sheeting. Plastic piping run from beneath the sheeting can vent radon safely through the roof. A louvered airbrick can help to dilute radon beneath suspended concrete or wooden floors.

Ozone

Traffic fumes include other gases that aggravate respiratory conditions. Low-lying ozone is produced when hydrocarbons (from vehicle exhausts, for example) and nitrogen dioxide in the air combine in the presence of sunlight. Hydrocarbons are also released from refineries and chemical plants and from solvents and paints.

Low-lying ozone damages crops and the environment as well as health. Ozone irritates the eyes, nose, throat, and respiratory tract, and in sensitive people it causes coughing, headaches, chest pain, and impaired breathing. It can aggravate existing lung problems and increase susceptibility to infection.

Because ozone is mostly an outdoor pollutant, it is difficult to avoid it altogether. A sensible approach is to do your best to avoid contributing to low-lying ozone levels by reducing the use of your motor vehicle. Don't use the car on days when the air is already heavily polluted or for any journey when you could reasonably walk.

Monitor air pollution and smog reports in the local press or on local radio. Summer is the worst season for smog because sunlight is needed for its production, so wear a face mask during peak smog periods if you expect to be outdoors.

Radon exposure is the most common cause of lung cancer in non-smokers, and is responsible for up to 15,000–20,000 deaths in the U.S. each year.

Radon

Radon is a colorless, odorless, radioactive gas released as uranium breaks down. If a house is built on rock or soil containing uranium—common in areas of granite or limestone—radon gas can seep up through cracks and drains and is trapped indoors. Exposure can cause lung cancer because inhaled particles can become lodged in the lungs where they radiate and penetrate mucous membranes, bronchi, and other tissue, initiating the cancer process. Smoking increases this risk because radon attaches to fine dust and smoke particles. There are no short-term symptoms of radon exposure.

Other harmful gases

In large quantities, carbon dioxide can make you breathe faster. In a confined space, too much carbon dioxide excludes oxygen, which can be fatal. Carbon dioxide is produced by burning coal, gas, and oil.

Nitrogen dioxide (and related oxides) is produced when fuels such as coal are burned, especially in power plants. Nitrogen oxide is part of the chemical process that produces smog, which can cause respiratory problems and has an effect on the body similar to that of ozone.

Sulfur dioxide is produced when fuels containing sulfur are burned; these include coal and oil. Some industrial processes, such as smelting metals and producing paper, release sulfur dioxide. Even very low levels of sulfur dioxide can impair breathing. It constricts the air passages, which is dangerous for asthma patients and for children.

Hazardous air pollutants (HAPs)

The chemicals in our environment that cause cancer or other serious damage are known as HAPs. Unfortunately, such substances may be harmful at very low levels of exposure. These chemicals include volatile organic compounds (VOCs).

Special hazards for children

Children may be more at risk from exposure to air pollution than adults. They are likely to play outdoors and be more active close to the level of vehicle exhausts. Children running around tend to breathe through the mouth, so pollutants bypass the nose's natural filters and go straight to the lungs.

Volatile chemicals are those that produce vapors easily, and organic compounds may occur naturally or be synthesized by chemists. VOCs include gasoline and industrial chemicals such as benzene and solvents. They are present in motor vehicle emissions and are released from burning fuels including coal, gas, and wood.

The good news is that environmental protection agencies the world over are monitoring processes that produce HAPs, and there are strict emission guidelines for all industries.

THE EFFECT OF THE WEATHER

Although pollution emissions are often fairly constant, their concentration in the air varies greatly with the weather. Pollutants are usually dispersed through the air, becoming diluted naturally.

- Still or stagnant air usually increases the concentration of pollutants in the area where they are emitted.
- Shifting winds can move pollutants to other locations.
- Different air temperatures at different heights can produce weather features, such as eddies and temperature inversion, that have an impact on the rate of pollutant dispersal.
- Sunshine influences air pollution. When sunshine heats the ground, it leads to lower pollution concentrations. However, sunshine is also an important ingredient in the production of smog.

In the battle against air pollution, the key is not to fight the weather but rather to be informed about it. Simply knowing when poor conditions are predicted means you can take preventive steps to avoid being outdoors for extended periods. Daily air pollution forecasts and measures such as the AQI let you know when extra caution may be necessary.

Pollution in the workplace

Air pollution is not simply an outdoor phenomenon; it can also affect indoor spaces such as homes, factories, and offices. Because workplaces are environments where we tend to spend a lot of time, this can pose risks to health.

At work, people are not only potentially exposed to a wide variety of pollutants, but they are also exposed on an ongoing basis. Many workers are at risk for respiratory problems, and still more go on to develop workplace-related, or occupational, asthma.

It is important to remember, however, that respiratory problems can often be avoided by being aware of potential risks, keeping yourself fit and healthy so you are better able to fight off infection, and following safety guidelines.

Occupational lung diseases are a prominent cause of work-related illness.

It is important for everybody not to smoke, but even more so for people in "risky" occupations who need every encouragement to quit the habit. Not only does smoking increase the risk of lung disease in the first place, but it also exacerbates the severity of any symptoms.

SERVICE INDUSTRIES

Workers in stores, banks, and hotels face a combination of hazards, many of them common to workers in other areas, particularly offices. These include formaldehyde from store fixtures, bedroom furniture, and carpets; bacteria from air-conditioning systems; and ozone-forming agents in cleaning products.

FARM WORKERS

Hay and straw release dust when forked, and if they are stored in a damp atmosphere they may become moldy and release spores. In a confined atmosphere, this can cause problems for farm workers, provoking immediate symptoms such as a blocked or runny nose, in addition to leading to delayed symptoms, including breathing difficulties and coughing. A study in Ontario, Canada, found that up to 90 percent of pig farmers suffered from acute bronchitis at some time.

What you can do

Good farming practices can reduce the risk of symptoms and enable workers to stay well.

- Wear a face mask when handling hay, silage, and grain, particularly if hay is moldy. The mask needs to be capable of filtering particles as small as one micrometer (see page 52).
- Keep storage areas clean, dry, and well ventilated. This will cut down on mold formation and reduce the dust in the air.

OFFICE WORKERS

Office workers are at risk from several types of pollutants. Often, these substances are present in very small amounts, and it is simply the fact that there are so many of them that may combine that causes respiratory problems for workers. Office pollutants can include:

- **Ozone** This is emitted from some printers and photocopiers.
- **Formaldehyde** Used for bookshelves and furniture, many board products contain formaldehyde (see page 89). It may also be present in fabrics and glues.
- **Bacteria** Air-conditioning systems and humidifiers can be sources of infectious organisms.

What you can do

The banning of smoking in many offices or its restriction to clearly defined areas has improved the air quality for workers, but there are still many precautions you can take.

- Ensure that photocopiers and laser printers are located in well-ventilated areas.
- Check that air-conditioning and ventilation systems are serviced regularly and that filters are changed.
- Improve ventilation: if windows can be opened, do so; otherwise, ask for fans to be installed.
- Get outside into the fresh air at lunchtime.

MINING AND INDUSTRIAL WORKERS

A major group of occupational respiratory problems involves industrial chemical inhalation. The chemical industry, however, is highly regulated, so excessive exposure to toxins is likely to be accidental.

Chemicals in the air of the workplace can take the form of gases, vapors, dusts, or fumes. In all of these forms, they are easily inhaled, often passing all the way to the lungs where they can do significant damage. They can also pass into the bloodstream, where they are carried to and can damage other parts of the body.

Miners, who inhale coal dust, risk coal worker's pneumoconiosis. Some miners are also at risk for silicosis, caused by inhaling crystalline silica. Workers in foundries and stone and glass manufacture are also at risk for silicosis. Radon (see page 82), present in uranium mines, is associated with an increased risk of lung cancer. Results of a 30-year study published in 1995 showed the lung cancer risk for uranium mine workers was seven times the normal risk and that the risk of tuberculosis or pneumoconiosis was also increased.

Dust from processing flax, cotton, and hemp can irritate the lungs of textile workers, causing chest tightness and shortness of breath.

THE AUTO INDUSTRY

Mechanics are at risk of respiratory problems caused by carbon monoxide from car exhaust. Constant running of engines to check repairs can lead to a dangerous buildup of this gas. Diesel fuel, too, is associated with lung problems, and body shop workers are exposed to isocyanates and polyurethanes used in paints and varnishes. These have been shown to cause a variety of problems from irritation of the mucous membranes to cancer.

What you can do

There are several commonsense precautions you can take to reduce your risks of respiratory problems.

- Run car engines only in well-ventilated areas or out of doors.
- Don't rev an engine unnecessarily.
- Wear a protective face mask when spray painting.

Train and car spray painting carries almost 40 times the average risk of causing occupational asthma.

The problem with asbestos

Asbestos was once hailed as a wonder material because it is virtually indestructible by fire. It was widely used in buildings—industrial, commercial, and domestic—as a fire retardant and insulating material. It is, however, dangerous to health when its fibers are released into the air; this generally only happens as it decays and becomes crumbly. The resulting fine dust can be inhaled and reach the lungs where it has been shown to cause several different diseases, including cancer.

Although building workers are at particular risk of exposure, electricians, carpenters, and plumbers all face exposure. People who work with building materials, such as cable installers and window-blind fitters, may also be exposed. Shipbuilders are also at risk.

Because the symptoms of asbestos exposure are usually not evident for a number of years (at least 10 and commonly as many as 30), people are still dying despite stringent regulations introduced in the 1970s. The number of asbestos-related deaths is falling, but associated diseases still have not been eliminated.

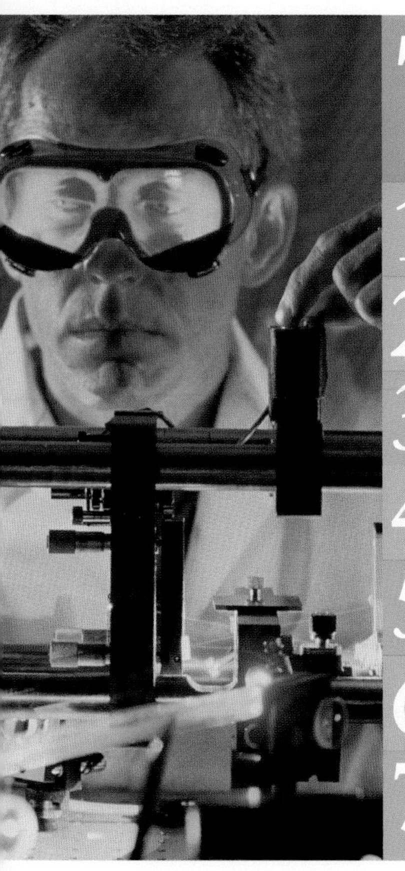

7 Ways to protect your lungs

These safety measures will protect your lungs as well as safeguard your overall health.

1. Be tidy. By keeping your workspace clean of spills and free of clutter and dust, you help to ensure that it is pollution-free.
2. Be informed. Adhere to safety advice displayed on doors, the labels of chemicals, and safety information provided by your employer, including company policies.
3. Be thoughtful. Only handle toxins in workspaces that have been designated for this purpose and are well-ventilated or have extractor fans.
4. Be prepared. Use protective clothing and a face mask. Employers must provide protective equipment and train you to know how and when to use it.
5. Be clean. When you have been exposed to toxins, clean your protective clothing and equipment and any part of you that has been exposed to the air.
6. Be smoke-free. Smoke only outside your work area, because the heat from a cigarette can chemically alter in the workplace into far more toxic substances.
7. Be alert. Strange smells, chemical spills, or leaking fumes should be reported to your employer as soon as possible, as should any signs of human distress.

PROTECTING YOURSELF

Employers are required by law to test workplaces for pollution and comply with government-set levels. They are also required to inform employees of any risks to health and the proper use of control methods and to provide any training that might be required by employees to perform their jobs safely.

Plant detective

Ozone-sensitive plants can be used to monitor ozone levels in an office. The nicotiana, for example, develops spots on its leaves in the presence of ozone—the more spots, the higher the concentration of ozone.

Your safety is also your own responsibility, however, and there are a number of precautions that you can take.

OCCUPATIONAL ASTHMA

Asthma sufferers may find that they suffer symptoms in the workplace, from inhaling dust or fumes, for example. There are, however, many people who were not previously diagnosed as asthmatic who start to suffer wheeziness, chest constriction, and cough in response to substances encountered in the workplace. Estimates suggest that up to 15 percent of cases of adult asthma, or 1.8 million cases, are related to the working environment. Some jobs carry a higher overall risk than others, but asthma has been triggered in workers in many different industries.

Allergies

If you already have an allergy such as hayfever (even if you have never had any asthma symptoms), it would be wise to avoid those jobs that are at high risk of triggering asthma. Working with animals, whether with a groomer or as a veterinarian, for example, may not be a good idea because cats, dogs, and other animals produce powerful allergens, and heavy exposure is likely to sensitize your lungs if you are already allergic.

Allergens causing occupational asthma are often derived from plants and animals. "Biologicals" include detergent enzymes, laboratory animals and insects, flour and grain (which can include mites), natural rubber latex (exuded from trees), wood dusts, resins, and glues.

Other respiratory irritants

Less obvious irritants may trigger asthma in some professionals. Chemical processing, for example, including plastics manufacture, welding, and soldering, carries 17 times the average incidence of occupational asthma. Irritants are also encountered in office and hotel cleaning and in "outdoor jobs," such as bus and cab driving, which involve sitting in traffic fumes. Traffic police may get more exercise, but they also spend much of their day among exhaust fumes and other outdoor pollutants. Flight attendants are exposed to recycled air that may contain germs breathed out by infected passengers, but this is unlikely if the air is well filtered.

How to reduce risk

The best way to reduce risk is to remove the irritant altogether. Unfortunately, it is not always possible to either stop using the irritant or to replace it with a safer substance in the workplace, and therefore steps to reduce exposure need to be undertaken carefully.

Efficient air filters and extractor fans at work can help to reduce allergens and irritants, eliminating some of the specific causes of occupational asthma. If at all possible, closing off the workspace that contains the risk is desirable.

Professional baking carries 25 times the average risk of developing occupational asthma.

Partially enclosing the process that produces the risk may prevent some people from developing symptoms.

In cases of extreme pollution, protective clothing and a face mask—designed to withstand the smallest particles—are vital.

Several agencies in the United States keep statistics on work-related injuries and illnesses; these include the National Institute for Occupational Safety & Health (NIOSH) and The Occupational Safety and Health Administration (OSHA). According to OSHA, part of the U.S. Department of Labor, dust diseases of the lungs and respiratory conditions caused by toxic agents are down since 1995.

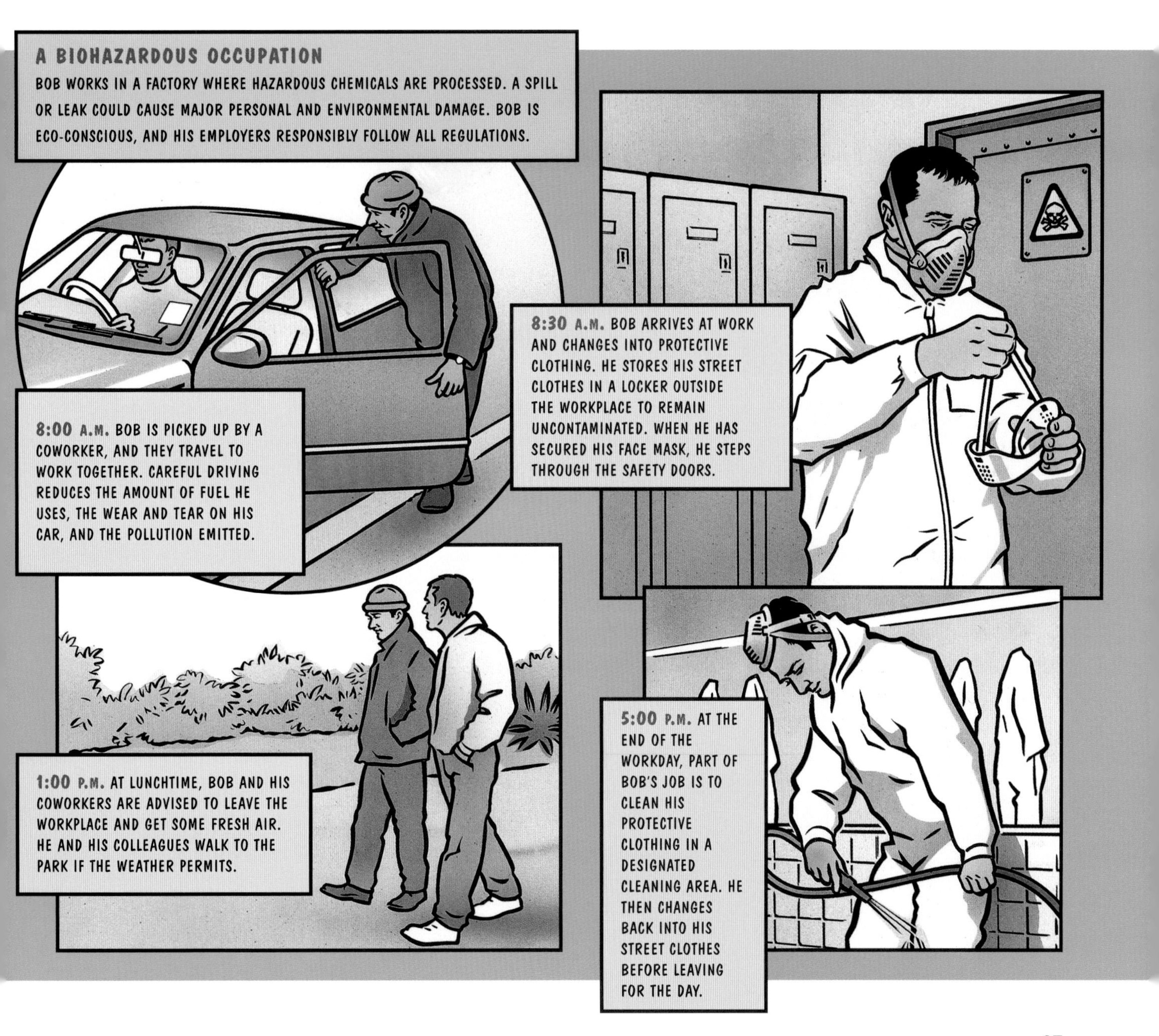

A healthy home for your lungs

Some experts consider that we are most at risk from harmful pollutants in our own homes, where there are fewer guidelines on acceptable levels and checks on how we live and which products we are storing and using.

Mighty mite
The dust mite is one of the major triggers for asthma and other respiratory problems.

Although the health risks from older houses, principally relating to lead paint and asbestos, are widely recognized, some homes still contain these substances. If you are unsure if your home is hazardous, have it assessed by professionals and have any lead paint removed. Asbestos can be removed or sealed, but in either case this is a job for a professional.

CLEAN AIR

Paradoxically, increased environmental awareness and energy-conscious building practices are partly to blame for domestic air pollution today. It makes sense to minimize heating costs by building well-insulated houses. Inadequate ventilation, however, when combined with warm, humid indoor conditions, helps dust mites thrive.

Adequate ventilation

Good ventilation is the key to air quality, but opening windows depends on the weather and may bring outdoor pollution into the house. If you suffer from asthma and live near a busy road or if pollens trigger your symptoms, keep windows and doors closed at times.

Dust control

Dust control is essential throughout the house. Apart from mite allergens, dust particles small enough to enter the lungs (up to 5 microns) may trigger asthma symptoms by irritating the bronchial tube linings.

When dusting, use a damp or electrostatically charged cloth or mop to collect, not scatter, the dust. Vacuum frequently, especially where floors are carpeted, and close the door and open the windows of the room being cleaned to allow floating dust to escape. Change the filters regularly. This ensures that dust is not blown back out through the air exhaust. Consider buying a vacuum fitted with a high-efficiency particulate air filter, which is designed to trap fine dust more effectively. Empty canister vacuums (those without bags) directly into the trash to avoid releasing dust in the house.

Smoke-free zones

Tobacco smoke is detrimental to indoor air quality, especially where there are children. If you smoke, do so in one or two well-ventilated areas only: efficient ventilators and air cleaners may help to reduce smoke particles, but some air cleaners do generate irritant ozone.

Pets

If you develop asthma after getting a pet, assume that it is to blame. Stop handling your pet directly, and keep it out of your bedroom. You may need to find a new home for it if it continues to cause symptoms. Pet allergens are too small to trap, and it is difficult to restrict a pet to certain parts of the house.

SAFE HEATING

Make sure all heating appliances are fully vented and serviced, especially gas heaters (see pages 82–83). Watch out for the following signs:

- Yellow or brown staining on appliances
- A yellow or orange pilot light
- A pilot light that goes out often
- Condensation

All indicate that an appliance is functioning poorly and may be

ON THE CUTTING EDGE

Allergen-free cats

A company has announced plans to produce an allergen-free cat. The protein that causes the allergic reaction is carried on only one of the cat's genes: the company believes that it can modify this gene to stop it producing the protein. Modified skin cells will be fused with egg cells from which the genetic material has been removed. Once these cells reach the embryo stage, they will be implanted into a surrogate mother. Initially, cats with the modified gene will be neutered or spayed to protect the "normal" cat population, but once there are enough modified cats, in theory they will be able to breed nonallergenic kittens.

leaking carbon monoxide. A different form of heating may be preferable. However, allergens and dust can be circulated by fan heaters and convectors, and central heating and electric space heaters may dry the air, causing breathing difficulties.

HOME IMPROVEMENTS

Doing it yourself has short-term effects on indoor air quality. A few sensible precautions will protect you:

- Decorate one room at a time. Keep the room well-ventilated and doors closed to prevent fumes and dust from spreading around the house.
- Washing down wallpaper before starting to strip it will help to keep the dust down.
- Increase the ventilation when stripping paint, sanding wood and plaster, drilling, and welding. Take a break outside while dust settles.
- Wet paint gives off chemicals that can trigger asthma. Low-odor water-based gloss paints may be a better option than oil-based gloss or water-based emulsion.
- Store unused chemicals in a ventilated cupboard or a shed. General household cleaning fluids and solvent-based products should also be stored safely, because many of them release chemicals that can cause breathing difficulties.
- Use a face mask when spraying paint or sawing wood and board products.

The problem with fiberboard

Some widely used compressed wood products, such as fiberboard, release formaldehyde. This colorless pungent gas can severely irritate the lungs and also trigger asthma symptoms.

- Before use, store board products upright, and leave space for air to circulate to eliminate odors.
- Coat pressed wood shelving with polyurethane or laminates.
- Keep the room at a moderate temperature (maximum 80°F) and humidity (about 45 percent).
- Make sure any room containing a new carpet, curtains, furnishings, or wallpaper is well aired for a few days—all can emit formaldehyde.

A SAFE HOME

Many of the products we use to clean our homes—especially the kitchen—are potentially harmful. Formaldehyde, phenols, ammonia (used in window cleaning products), and chlorine (in bleach) are particularly toxic and dangerous to the lungs.

An oven hood should be vented through an external wall. Use as much external ventilation as possible.

Outdoor-vented extractor fans remove indoor air intermittently and replace it with air from outside. Extractor fans are effective at reducing moisture levels (which can cause the formation of molds).

Flat-fronted cupboards and fittings are easy to wipe clean, and dust cannot collect in moldings.

Chemical cleaners, disinfectants, pesticides, and air fresheners should be stored in cupboards—all are potentially damaging to the lungs.

Never mix bleach with any other cleaning product: This gives off chlorine gas, which damages lung tissue.

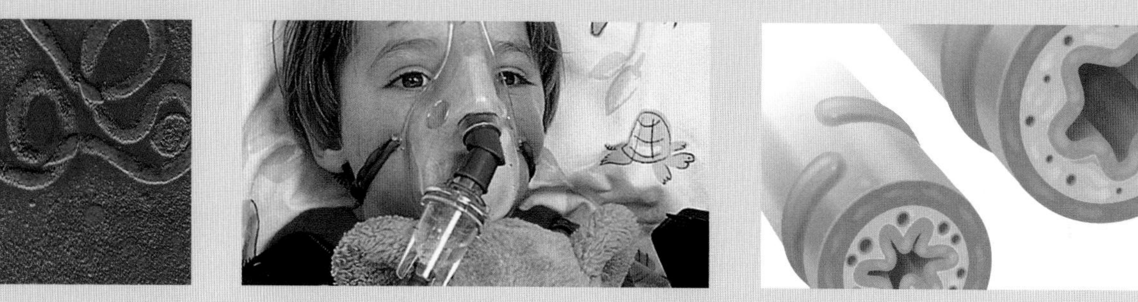

3 What happens when things go wrong

Knowing what can go wrong

Breathing is one of the body's most essential functions. When something disrupts the intake and outflow of air, it has a far-reaching effect and can, in extreme cases, be deadly. Being aware of what can go wrong, and why, may help you to reduce your risk of problems.

Problems with the lungs and respiratory system fall into two broad categories: those you can do something about, and those that are more difficult to influence.

SMOKING-RELATED DISORDERS

Almost all disorders of the respiratory system are made worse by smoking, and smoking is the major cause of chronic obstructive pulmonary disease (COPD) and lung cancer. All forms of smoking affect the bronchi and the lungs directly. They increase the production of mucus and, at the same time, they reduce the clearance of this mucus by impairing the function of the cilia, which sweep potentially harmful organisms away. Left to stagnate, the mucus is more liable to infection—a risk magnified by the fact that a smoker has a less efficient immune system. On its passage into the lungs, smoke irritates the bronchial muscle, triggering an inflammatory response and causing the muscle and airways to constrict and restrict breathing.

The chemicals in smoke damage the alveolar walls by introducing free radicals. These overwhelm the body's repair mechanisms and set up a chain reaction of tissue destruction, which can lead to COPD or to a permanent enlargement of the air spaces and walls in the lungs.

The association of smoking with lung cancer was identified as long ago as the 1950s by Dr. Richard Doll and Sir Austin Bradford Hill. Smoking is also linked with cancers of the nose, mouth, and esophagus. The risk of developing cancer depends on the number of years of smoking and the number of packs smoked. It is never too late to benefit from quitting. Someone who quits in middle age can avoid much of the risk; someone who gives up in his or her twenties avoids almost all of the risk.

Lung cancer kills 155,000 people a year in the U.S.—that's approximately one in four cancer deaths.

POLLUTION-LINKED PROBLEMS

There is overwhelming evidence that air pollution levels correlate with both the incidence of asthma and allergic rhinitis and the severity of symptoms. Outbreaks of asthma and worsening COPD symptoms have been shown to be directly related to the level of atmospheric pollutants, which varies from day to day.

Experiments have demonstrated that exposure to atmospheric pollutants increases the sensitivity of the airways, damages the cilia, and causes the inflammatory response seen in asthma. The main substances responsible are ozone, nitrogen dioxide, and particles generated from car exhausts, especially diesel fuel. It is now widely believed that tackling the issue of pollution levels in cities would lead to improvements in respiratory health.

Exposure to a wide range of industrial chemicals and biological agents at home and in the workplace may provoke an allergic reaction and, in extreme cases, lead to permanent ill health and forced early retirement. Even relatively low levels of domestic exposure to irritants like bleach have been shown to trigger asthma symptoms.

MORE COMMON

COLDS
Adults have 2–4 colds each year. Children have 6–8.

HAY FEVER
About 9% of adults were diagnosed with hay fever in the past year.

INFLUENZA
About 10%–20% of U.S. residents get the flu each year. On average, 20,000 will die from it and 114,000 will be hospitalized.

ASTHMA
Approximately 17.5 million adults and 4.8 million children have asthma. About 4,000–5,000 die each year.

COPD
There are about 16.4 million people with COPD in the U.S. and 120,000 die from it annually.

PNEUMONIA
There are over 60,000 pneumonia deaths and 1.3 million cases treated in the hospital every year.

LUNG CANCER
There are 164,000 cases diagnosed annually and about 155,000 deaths.

SARCOIDOSIS
Sarcoidosis affects 5–11 in 100,000 whites and about 40 in 100,000 blacks.

INFECTIONS

Infections are the most common form of illness affecting the respiratory system, from acute conditions, such as colds and influenza, to chronic, debilitating disorders, such as the recurrent infections experienced by COPD sufferers. Infections can strike anyone and be fatal, especially among elderly people. Antibiotics treat bacterial infections, and vaccination against influenza is available.

TUMORS

Growths of abnormal cells, or tumors, in the lungs may be benign or malignant. Benign tumors are uncommon and include hamartomas, lumps composed of several types of tissues. Adenomas, or glandular tumors, may also occur in the bronchi. Benign tumours rarely cause problematic symptoms but are often removed if there is any suspicion that they may be malignant or if they are growing rapidly.

Malignant lung tumors are the leading cause of death from cancer in both men and women in the U.S., having overtaken breast cancer in women. This rise results from smoking: Tobacco smoke is responsible for 85 percent of lung cancer cases, but asbestos and radon exposure contribute to a small number of cancer cases.

Milestones IN MEDICINE

The link between smoking and lung cancer was proved only a few years after Sir Austin Bradford Hill and Dr. Richard Doll started a study of British doctors in 1951. Curious that many of their patients who had lung cancer were also smokers, Doll and Hill sent a questionnaire on smoking behavior to everyone in the British Medical Association register; 40,000 doctors replied and were subsequently studied at intervals. Patients who smoked were shown to be 25 times more likely to die from lung cancer than those who did not.

ALLERGIES

An allergy causes the body to produce an exaggerated and inappropriate immune response to an everyday substance, such as pollen, dust, some foods, and the skin and hair of domestic animals. Large amounts of the antibody IgE are produced, which under normal circumstances would be called upon to protect the body against certain parasitic organisms that are now rarely encountered.

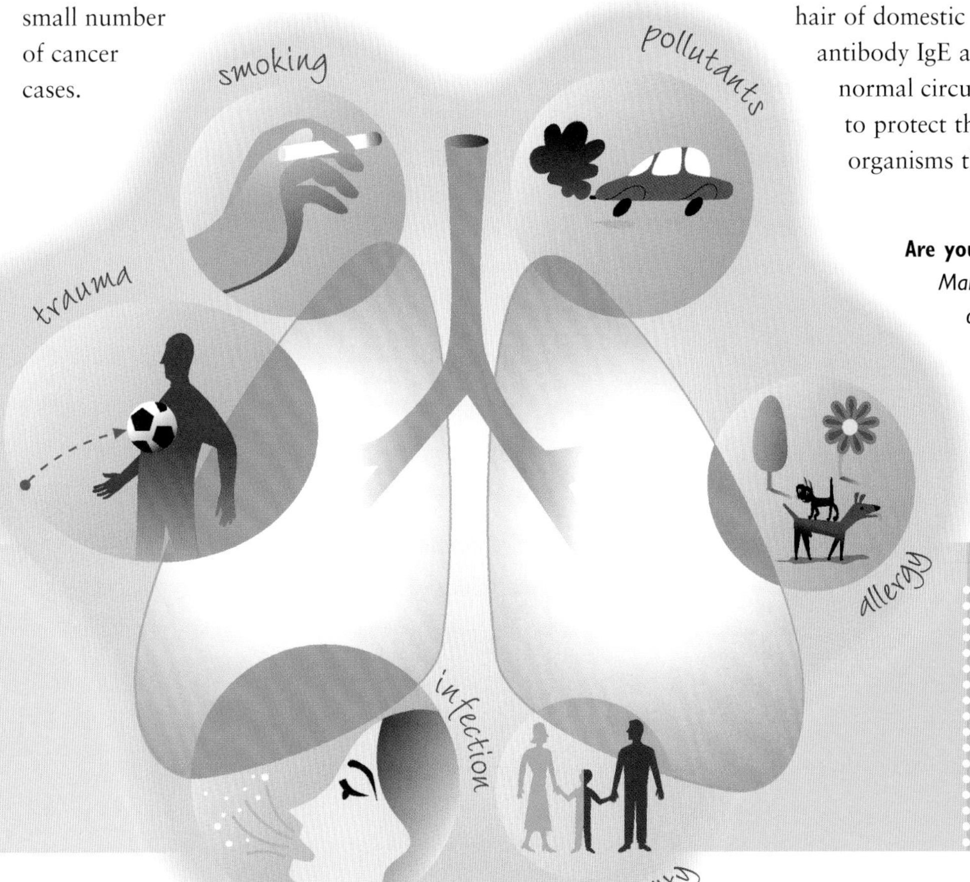

Are you at risk?

Many factors influence individual risk of respiratory problems. Some common and not-so-common conditions are highlighted below with an indication of how many people suffer from them each year in the U.S.

LESS COMMON

CYSTIC FIBROSIS

About 30,000 Americans have cystic fibrosis, but 12 million are carriers. Every year 2,500 babies are born with it.

TUBERCULOSIS

More than 16,000 cases were reported in 2000.

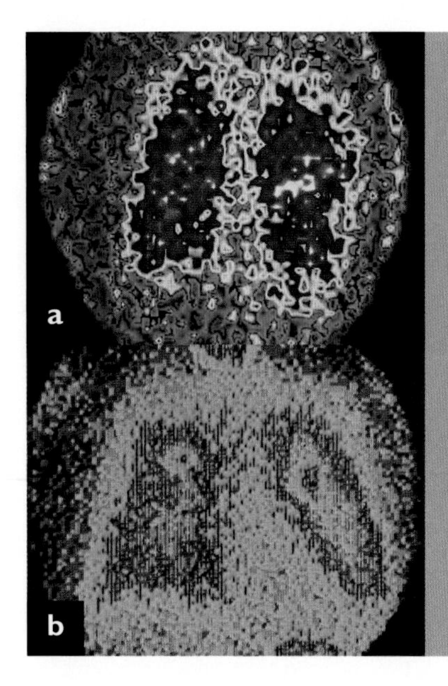

Working lungs

a Asthma and cigarette-smoking reduce the area where gaseous exchange takes place (shown here as red and white). This often causes severe breathing problems. **b** In healthy lungs the area is large: the lungs are said to be well ventilated.

Allergies are most common in childhood (up to 20 percent of children have one or more), and about half of those affected "grow out" of the condition. Allergies can, however, appear for the first time in adulthood.

Allergic conditions have increased dramatically over the last 40 years, and many people believe pollution may be to blame. Other scientists think that raised standards of living have resulted in a lack of exposure to microorganisms in early childhood and that this leads to faulty programming of the immune system and the development of allergies. This theory is called the hygiene hypothesis.

GENETICS AND HEREDITARY FACTORS

There is a genetic component to many respiratory diseases. Some, such as cystic fibrosis, are predictable. When two carrier genes are inherited, the disease develops. Other diseases are more complex. The chances of a child developing asthma are higher if members of the immediate family suffer from the condition. The situation is not straightforward, however. First, there is no certainty that the disorder will develop in a child with a strong family history of asthma, and second, the mother's influence appears to be greater than the father's.

FOREIGN BODIES AND PHYSICAL INJURY

Damage to the respiratory system can come from external sources. Inhaled foreign matter, for example, can cause lung problems. Physical injury may also affect the lungs in a variety of ways, from being "winded" by a soccerball to a broken rib piercing a lung. Sudden deceleration or blunt trauma, such as is often sustained in a car crash, can cause internal bleeding, and the pain of bruising to the ribs can restrict breathing and coughing.

CONGENITAL ABNORMALITIES

Nonhereditary conditions present at birth or developing in childhood include kyphoscoliosis, or curved spine, which can restrict breathing. Other abnormalities include hypoplasia, in which part or all of a lung does not grow; an extra segment of lung, which may require removal; and bronchogenic cysts, the interruption of lung tissue by empty spaces surrounded by cartilage and muscle.

AGING PROCESS

Lung tissue deteriorates with age, with loss of elasticity and a decline in function. There is a reduction in muscle strength, and the ribs and spine become stiffer, resulting in decreased lung expansion. There may also be scarring of the pulmonary arteries and veins, leading to a reduced blood supply. The result is a loss of performance.

Family history and the risk of asthma and allergies

British research into the genetic component of asthma and allergies has found many links but has still not revealed the whole story. It seems likely that a group of genes predisposes a child to atopy, a sensitivity to common allergens. Different genes may then control whether the atopy affects the skin (as eczema), the lungs (asthma), or the nose (hay fever), and how severe the condition is.

FAMILY HISTORY	RISK OF ASTHMA AND ALLERGIES
All children (UK)	1 in 7
Neither parent affected, older sibling has atopy	1 in 7
One parent has an atopic condition	1 in 3.5
Both parents have an atopic condition	1 in 2.5

Who's who—meet the respiratory specialists

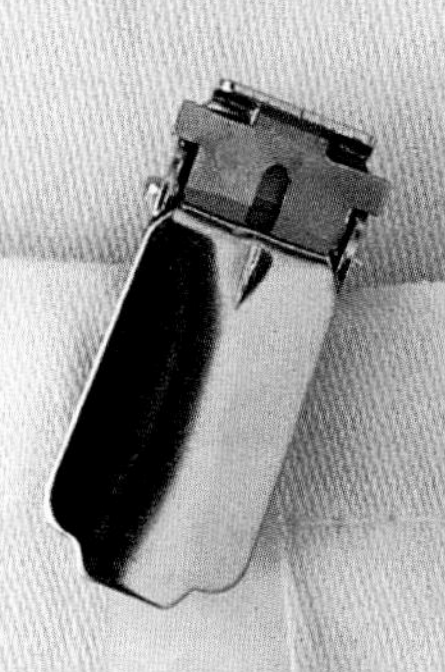

Minor respiratory problems are extremely common and often clear up without medical intervention; after all, who has not suffered from the common cold? However, some conditions, once identified, will need to be treated by the experts.

CARDIOTHORACIC SURGEON

Surgery is sometimes required to remove lung tumors that have not spread. Cardiothoracic surgeons specialize in such operations. They also perform biopsies of lung masses suspected of being cancerous and of areas of fibrosis (scarring) to help determine the cause.

RESPIRATORY NURSE

These nurses educate respiratory patients about their illnesses. They are particularly important in asthma care, where they provide links between the patient and the hospital and community care. By following the progress of patients after discharge from hospital, they may help prevent further admissions. They give advice on the correct choice and use of inhalers and supervise patients' use of devices such as noninvasive ventilators, which help to tackle sleep problems caused by a lack of oxygen.

RESPIRATORY TECHNICIAN

The respiratory technician conducts tests of respiratory function (see pages 99–101), using various machines that patients breathe in and out of in a special laboratory. These tests are not easy to perform correctly and require exceptional patience from both technician and patient.

PHYSICAL THERAPIST

The physical therapist assesses and makes the most of the patient's ability to move. This involves advice on the most efficient use of the body and the introduction of exercises for specific muscle groups. Specialists in respiratory conditions advise on general and specific breathing techniques and use manual and positional techniques to bring up sputum in conditions such as bronchiectasis.

CLINICAL ALLERGIST

There are relatively few clinical allergists in the U.S. They specialize in diagnosing and treating conditions that have an allergic component, such as asthma, eczema, rhinitis (nasal allergies such as hay fever), and food allergies. They administer tests, such as skin pricks (see page 105), monitor blood antibody levels to help confirm whether there is an allergy, and advise on allergen avoidance.

CONSULTANT PULMONOLOGIST

The consultant pulmonologist is in charge of a patient's clinical care in the hospital, making the major decisions regarding a patient's treatment, although day-to-day care is the responsibility of junior doctors. Children may be cared for by pediatricians experienced in dealing with asthma and cystic fibrosis in childhood. The consultant is also in charge of outpatient clinics and should be available to discuss the treatment.

CLINICAL ONCOLOGIST

Specializing in cancer care, the clinical oncologist works with respiratory consultants and palliative care specialists, communicating about illness and its care and administering treatments such as radiation and chemotherapy, together with dealing with the side effects of such therapies.

PALLIATIVE CARE SPECIALIST

Doctors and nurses who specialise in palliative care (treatments intended to alleviate pain and anxiety) are involved with cancer patients soon after diagnosis, when they are usually still in relatively good health; they also specialize in other conditions, such as COPD. They prescribe medication for pain relief and give patients much-needed support, advice, and reassurance.

FINDING OUT WHAT IS WRONG

The complexity of the respiratory system and the enormous range of respiratory symptoms mean that reaching a diagnosis may not be easy. Today's doctors have access to a number of techniques when trying to pinpoint the cause of a problem. These range from simple methods, such as asking a patient to describe symptoms and their duration, to highly sophisticated imaging techniques that can give a clear view of a possible problem area. No doctor works in isolation, however, but relies on the skills of laboratory technicians in interpreting the results of blood and microbiological tests to help build a complete picture.

Medical history and examination

The first step toward diagnosing a disease of the respiratory system is to discuss a patient's symptoms and history and to do a physical examination for signs of pain or breathing difficulties.

The introductory consultation between patient and doctor, during which the symptoms and background of the patient are discussed, is often referred to as the medical history.

PRELIMINARY INFORMATION

A medical history should cover the nature of the disorder and include a history of the patient's health and treatment as well as information on lifestyle and background. This helps to form a diagnosis and points to future treatments.

Explaining the symptoms

The first thing a doctor will want to have is a full account of the symptoms—what they are, when they started, whether they came on suddenly or gradually, what eases them ("relieving factors"), and what makes them worse ("exacerbating factors"), and whether any symptoms seem to come and go together.

The most common respiratory symptoms include coughing, wheezing, breathlessness, sputum production, and chest pain. How these and other symptoms are described has a direct bearing on further investigations and the form and success of treatment, so it is important to be clear and as detailed as possible. For example, symptoms that have developed quickly can point to infection or acute inflammation, whereas slower-onset symptoms that are prolonged may indicate scarring or tumors, especially if they are associated with weight loss.

Medical history

The illnesses an individual is currently suffering from or has suffered from in the past are extremely important in diagnosis. This is because respiratory symptoms may be linked to other diseases affecting many body systems. These so-called "multisystem" disorders include tuberculosis and sarcoidosis. A medical history is also useful in deciding issues such as the safe prescription of medication and fitness for possible surgery.

The medical history also includes a drug history and any sensitivities to past treatments. The doctor will list all the medications currently being taken, including over-the-counter drugs, herbal remedies, and supplements. Whether the patient suffers from allergies will also be discussed, because some people are sensitive to antibiotics, aspirin, anesthetics, or even adhesive bandages. These questions ensure the safe prescription of new medications.

Family and social history

The doctor will also want to hear about the patient's family history. Many diseases, including pulmonary emboli and certain cancers, may have an inherited component, which can be established through examining the history of illness in close relatives.

At the same time, lifestyle and habits can be telling. Smoking is associated with many respiratory diseases, including lung cancer and COPD. It also worsens other respiratory problems. An honest smoking history is therefore vital, detailing the total number of years as a smoker, the method of smoking, and the average number per day.

Other important factors that may be asked about include alcohol consumption, domestic environment (exposure to pets or dampness can create respiratory problems, for example), and past and present occupation (knowing that a patient works with asbestos or coal or with allergens in organic dusts may help the doctor start forming a diagnosis).

PHYSICAL EXAMINATION

Further investigation into respiratory complaints requires the doctor to undertake a physical examination of the patient. For a suspected lung or respiratory problem, this largely centers around the chest, although there are many other indicators in the body for which the the doctor will look, feel, or listen.

Inspection

A doctor can tell a great deal about a patient's general health simply by looking. For example, skin color is a useful indicator: pale skin may point to anemia, whereas dusky skin may suggest low blood oxygen. A closer inspection reveals more.

The doctor will inspect the patient's neck for bulging of the neck veins. The height of the column of blood in the visible neck veins provides an estimate of the pressure in the jugular vein. This, in turn, is a guide to the pressure in the right atrium (where blood from the veins first collects in the heart). The jugular vein may bulge further if the right heart is failing as a result of COPD, for example.

All the relevant details

a The doctor will want to know as much as possible about your lifestyle and habits. The presence of a fluffy pet in the household, for example, may be contributing to breathing difficulties.

b Hobbies may be relevant in respiratory problems. Regulations to control dust in the workplace do not apply at home. Anyone sawing wood or board products should wear a mask and work in a well-ventilated area.

Feeling and hearing

a The neck and shoulders are felt to check for enlarged lymph nodes, which may be present in inflammatory diseases and cancer. The doctor will also manipulate the chest to check for tenderness and then feel the patient's upper back while the patient takes a deep breath to check that chest movement is symmetrical and adequate. Reduced lung expansion on one side may indicate disease on that side.

b The stethoscope allows a doctor to listen to breathing. Normal breathing is usually regular and smooth, with the in-breath sounding louder and longer than the out-breath. If fluid is present in an area of lung, as in pneumonia, the sounds from the large airways such as the bronchi are conducted straight to the surface through the fluid rather than being heard filtered through the bronchioles, producing harsh, hollow sounds known as bronchial breathing.

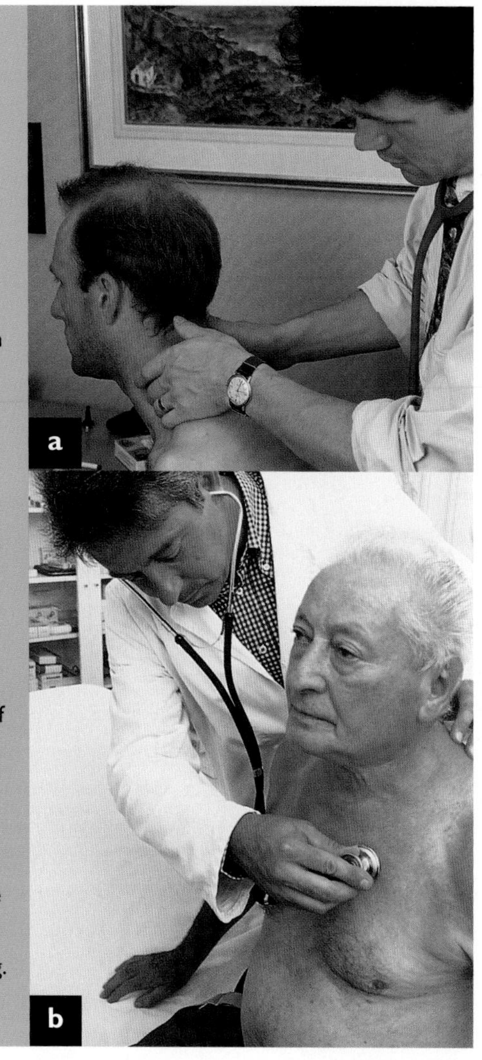

The doctor will examine the chest for scars and deformities. This includes looking for curving of the spine, or scoliosis, which could interfere with breathing. Chest movements are observed, with the doctor looking for asymmetry, which could indicate a restriction on one side. Breathing rate will be measured; this normally varies between 12 and 16 breaths per minute at rest. The fingers are inspected for signs of clubbing, a drumstick-like appearance of the finger pads, which may be associated with scarring diseases and lung cancer. The lower eyelid is examined—paleness can indicate anemia—and the mouth is inspected for cyanosis, blueness of the lips and tongue, which can be a sign of low blood oxygen.

Feeling for problems

Palpation is the hands-on exploration conducted by the doctor and usually begins by feeling for the position of the windpipe at the base of the neck. This pipe may be pulled to one side by scarring or by the collapse of one lung or be pushed aside by a pleural effusion—fluid between the lung and the chest wall. The doctor will feel the left side of the chest for the so-called apex beat, the lowest, outermost point at which a heartbeat can be discerned. It is normally felt under the left nipple, but in certain conditions, the point at which the doctor can feel the beat shifts. These include:

- when the heart is enlarged, which can happen when the left ventricle fails;
- a collapse in the left lung; and
- fluid in the cavity surrounding the right lung.

The position of the trachea can give the doctor a clue to what is causing the shift in the apex beat. In heart problems, the trachea remains in the center of the chest; in lung problems, it will be pushed or pulled to one side or the other.

By listening to the noise created when a partially hollow body cavity, such as the chest, is tapped, a doctor can gain valuable clues as to what is wrong with a patient. In percussion, one finger is held against the chest while the index or middle finger of the other hand taps against it. Normally, the lung resonates because of the air inside it, but fluid or solid masses obstructing the sound can make it dull and unclear. Alternatively, if there is air between the lung and the chest wall, as in pneumothorax, the echo is particularly resonant. By holding a hand against the chest to feel the vibrations when the patient talks, the doctor may elicit the same information.

The doctor will listen through a stethoscope for "crackles"—noises that occur when breathing in. These noises are caused by fluid in the alveoli, causing them to "snap" open suddenly, rather than gently, when filled. Breath sounds may be difficult to distinguish where there is a pleural effusion. Wheezing, on the other hand, may indicate asthma or, occasionally, a heart problem. You can mimic these sounds by forcibly breathing out with your throat open.

Investigating lung function

There are various nonintrusive methods for exploring the lungs, most of which involve measuring an individual's breathing and lung capacity. They can yield a surprising amount of information about possible causes of the patient's distress.

The doctor has a battery of simple and effective tests to measure how well you are breathing and how each part of the respiratory cycle is working.

PEAK EXPIRATORY FLOW RATE

The simplest test of breathing, the peak expiratory flow rate, has the advantage that the meter used is portable, so patients can monitor their own breathing. Peak expiratory flow is the maximum rate of breathing out after having taken in a full breath. The peak flow meter is a small tube with a mouthpiece, a dial, and a needle. The patient takes a breath in, then forces a fast hard breath out. The rate is measured in liters per minute, and varies according to age, sex, body weight, height, and ethnicity. It also varies from breath to breath and improves with practice.

Peak flow is useful in the diagnosis and monitoring of asthma. Airflow is reduced in an asthma attack because of airway obstruction, which restricts the speed at which air is emptied from the lungs. Peak flow monitoring may also be useful in the diagnosis of occupational asthma, because the meter can be used at work and at home.

SPIROMETRY

Using a spirometer is a more sophisticated method of measuring lung capacity and function. The spirometer measures not only the rate of breathing out but also the lung capacity at any one time. Taken together, these two measurements allow a doctor to differentiate between the two most basic classes of lung disease, obstructive and restrictive.

Obstructive diseases include asthma and COPD. In these diseases, there is impairment of air movement in the larger airways, typically worse when breathing out than when breathing in. When it is difficult to breathe out, air becomes trapped in the lungs, and they become hyperinflated, so lung volume increases, although the volume of air breathed out falls.

In contrast, restrictive diseases are usually caused by scarring within the lungs, such as pulmonary fibrosis, or, more rarely, diseases affecting the respiratory muscles or chest wall. In these diseases, the lungs effectively shrink, resulting in a small lung volume.

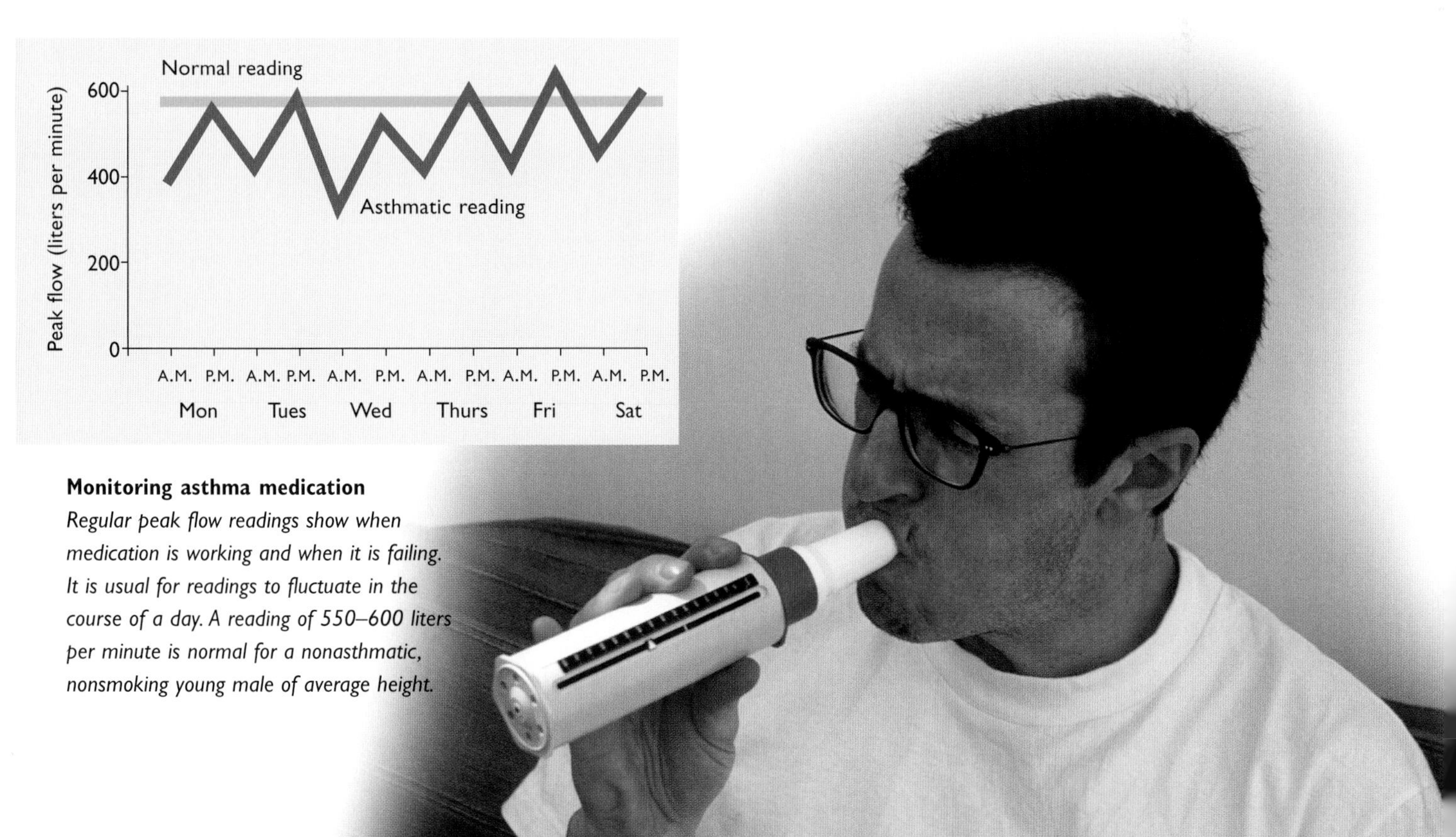

Monitoring asthma medication
Regular peak flow readings show when medication is working and when it is failing. It is usual for readings to fluctuate in the course of a day. A reading of 550–600 liters per minute is normal for a nonasthmatic, nonsmoking young male of average height.

The patient is asked to breathe out and continue to do so until there is no more air to exhale. You can try this yourself—take in a huge breath, and then breathe out hard with your throat open until you are "blue in the face." There are two significant measurements taken from this long breath. The first is the volume of air breathed out in the first second, and the second is the total amount of air breathed out. The ratio of one to the other is what defines the type of lung disease. In COPD, for example, there is a normal or even raised amount of air in the lungs, but it takes longer to breathe it all out. In restrictive lung disease, on the other hand, the relationship between the two measurements is normal, but both are reduced—the lungs are "smaller."

A flow-volume loop, so called because the curves produced by the readings make a loop shape, shows in- and out-breaths. This helps to establish if the obstruction is in the upper or lower airways, and whether it is within or outside the lung. Lung diseases have characteristic patterns of in- and out-breaths. From looking at a loop, a doctor can narrow down what the problem might be.

MEASURING RESIDUAL VOLUME

It is impossible to breathe out all the air in the lungs—a certain amount always remains. Known as the residual volume, this level is usually about 1.2 liters. If your lungs are compromised, however, residual volume can fluctuate. Residual volume can be calculated in two ways that involve breathing in a known concentration of an easily measured indicator gas. In the first, the inert gas, helium, is breathed in from a closed circuit for a few minutes, and it quickly becomes diluted by the air already in the lungs. Its concentration thus falls to a new level, which can be measured from the out-breath, and from this the residual volume is calculated.

In another method, known as nitrogen washout, the gases already present in the patient's lungs are measured. This is achieved by the patient breathing pure oxygen for 10 minutes and exhaling into a special bag. The residual volume of gas is calculated by measuring the nitrogen concentration of the expired gas.

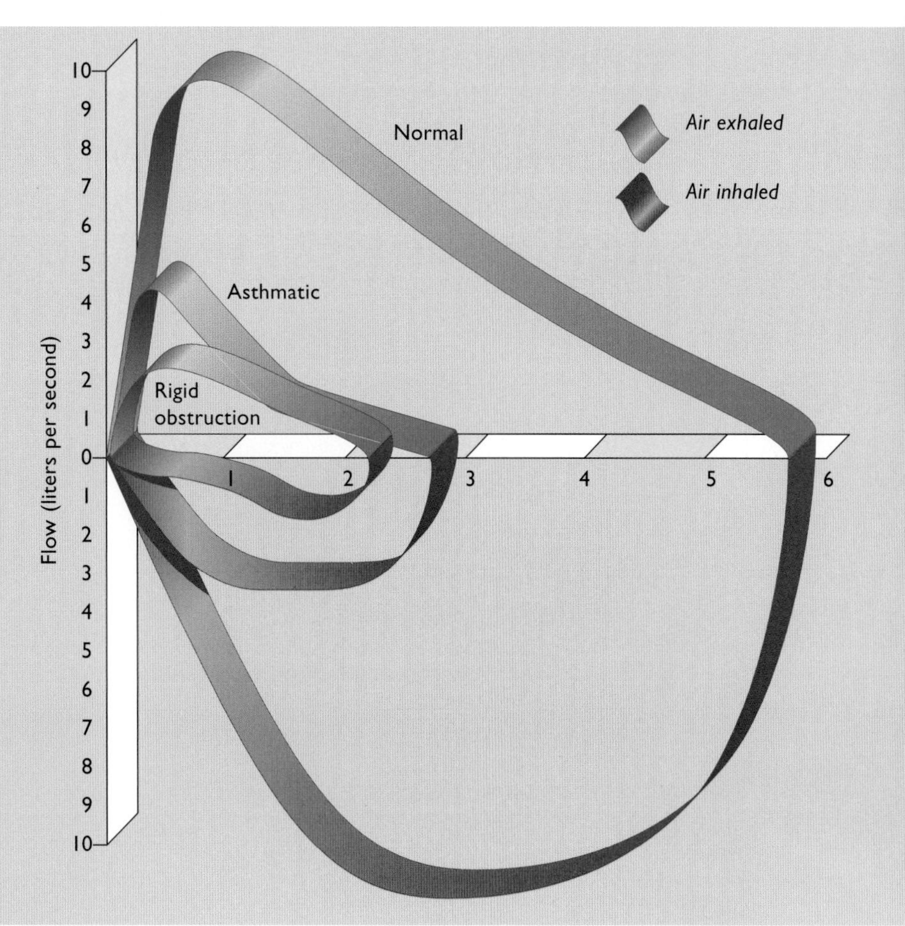

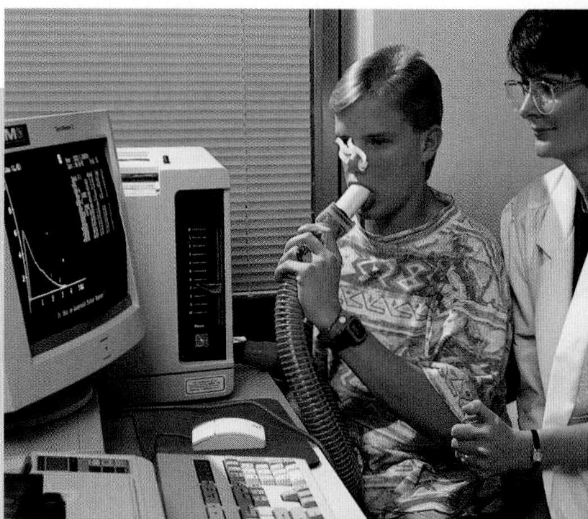

Flow-volume loops

A flow-volume loop gives the doctor three readings: (1) the amount of air exhaled in the first second after a full inhalation, (2) the total amount of air exhaled (top half of the loop), and (3) the amount of air inhaled (bottom half of the loop). Different conditions produce characteristic traces. In asthma and other obstructive diseases, the out-breath ends earlier than in someone with normal lungs, whereas rigid obstruction reduces both in- and out-breaths.

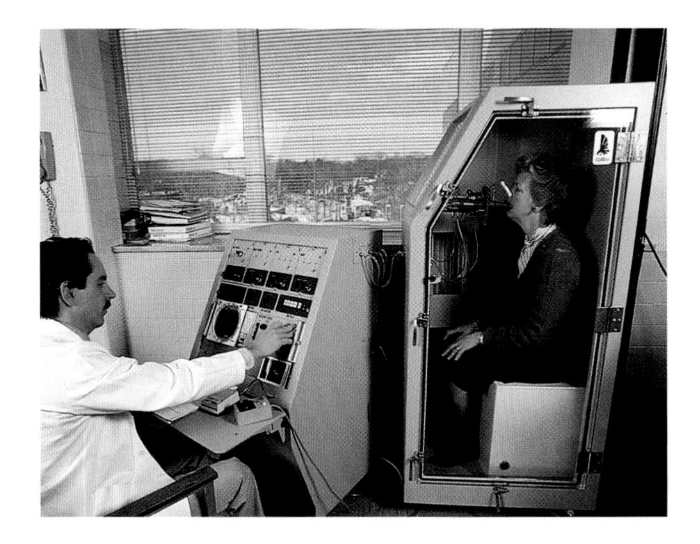

Testing residual volume and total lung capacity

To measure the residual volume, particularly in patients with asthma and COPD, the patient sits in a plethysmograph, an airtight cabinet. Changes in pressure within the lungs during breathing change the air pressure in the box, which is recorded by a sensitive measuring device. The box can also be used to gauge resistance in airflow.

DIFFUSION CAPACITY

Another important measure of lung health is how efficiently oxygen is transported across the alveolar membranes and into the blood. Called the lungs' diffusion capacity, this is measured by breathing in a small concentration of carbon monoxide (less than 0.3 percent) and holding the breath for exactly 10 seconds. Because hemoglobin has a very high affinity for carbon monoxide, the reduction in carbon monoxide in the exhaled air is wholly dependent on the diffusion rate across the alveolar membrane. This result is expressed as a percentage, known as the transfer factor.

As a general guide, doctors consider a transfer factor of more than 93 percent normal and healthy, whereas a factor of less than 90 percent may indicate a condition such as COPD or lung fibrosis, in which the alveolar membrane is damaged or thickened and therefore works less efficiently.

PULSE OXIMETRY

To measure the amount of oxygen in the blood, doctors often use a device known as a pulse oximeter, which is simply clipped onto a finger. It measures the saturation of hemoglobin molecules in the arteries, which should be fully oxygenated when leaving the lungs, making the blood look bright red. The saturation, expressed as a percentage, is usually well over 90 percent. (In contrast, blood in the veins will have already passed oxygen to the tissues, and the saturation falls to about 70 percent; this is what makes the veins appear blue.) An oxygen saturation of less than 93 percent is low for a healthy adult, although levels do fall slightly as you age. Cyanosis, or blueness of the lips and tongue, is not apparent until the oxygen saturation has fallen to about 85 percent.

A low oxygen saturation, known as hypoxia, may reflect decreased levels of oxygen in the air, for example, at high altitudes. It may also occur when hemoglobin is unable to transport oxygen around the body, which happens in cases of carbon monoxide poisoning. More commonly, however, it is seen in conditions where the oxygen transport across the alveolar membrane is impaired. This may be due to a discrepancy between the areas of lung filled with air and the areas supplied by blood, called a ventilation-perfusion mismatch. This is commonly seen in conditions like pulmonary embolism and pneumonia.

Decreased oxygen transfer may also occur because of thickening of the alveolar membrane, such as in pulmonary fibrosis. If breathing is simply not fast enough to keep up with the body's metabolic requirements, hypoxia may be the result.

How does a pulse oximeter work?

Pulse oximetry measures the oxygen saturation of the blood without the need for a sample to be taken. It is simple, painless, and noninvasive. The oximeter clips onto a finger, toe, or earlobe and emits light at two wavelengths. Hemoglobin, to which oxygen binds in the blood, absorbs the light by differing amounts, depending on whether it is saturated with oxygen or not: The darker the blood, the more light is absorbed and the lower the oxygen saturation. The oximeter compares readings from the two wavelengths to calculate the extent of oxygen saturation.

Laboratory tests

There is a wealth of information to be gleaned from every blood, fluid, or tissue sample from the body. Any unusual levels of chemicals, hemoglobin, antibodies, or infectious organisms can give doctors vital clues to working out what is wrong.

Several different tests can be carried out on a sample of blood, fluid, or tissue to enable the medical team to create the fullest possible picture of a condition.

BLOOD TESTS

A common way of finding out about an individual's health is to take a blood sample, and blood tests are routinely used to provide information about respiratory diseases. A blood test is a quick and simple procedure involving pricking a vein in the arm with a needle and drawing blood painlessly into small tubes through a syringe. A full blood count from the sample will give the doctor information about the hemoglobin level—which may be low in patients with chronic diseases or cancer—and the white cell count, which may be increased in infections such as pneumonia or low if cancer of the lung has affected the bone marrow. The blood test also acts as a guide to the quantity of inflammatory proteins in the blood, which helps to establish the presence of serious disease.

Measuring oxygen and carbon dioxide

An arterial blood gas test directly measures the amount of oxygen and carbon dioxide in the blood and their acidity or alkalinity (pH). This blood is usually taken with a needle placed into the radial artery, just under the skin at the wrist, where you can feel a pulse. The test can indicate a range of conditions that cause hypoxia (see page 101) and respiratory failure. It will show if oxygen therapy or urgent treatment such as mechanical ventilation is required, and it is also used to monitor the progress of these treatments.

Antibody levels

Serology tests are used to detect antibodies produced in reaction to infectious organisms. These include *Mycoplasma*, *Legionella*, and viruses such as Coxsackie B. The antibody level must be recorded twice at an interval of at least 3 weeks to confirm an acute rise, so these tests can only be used as a retrospective diagnostic tool.

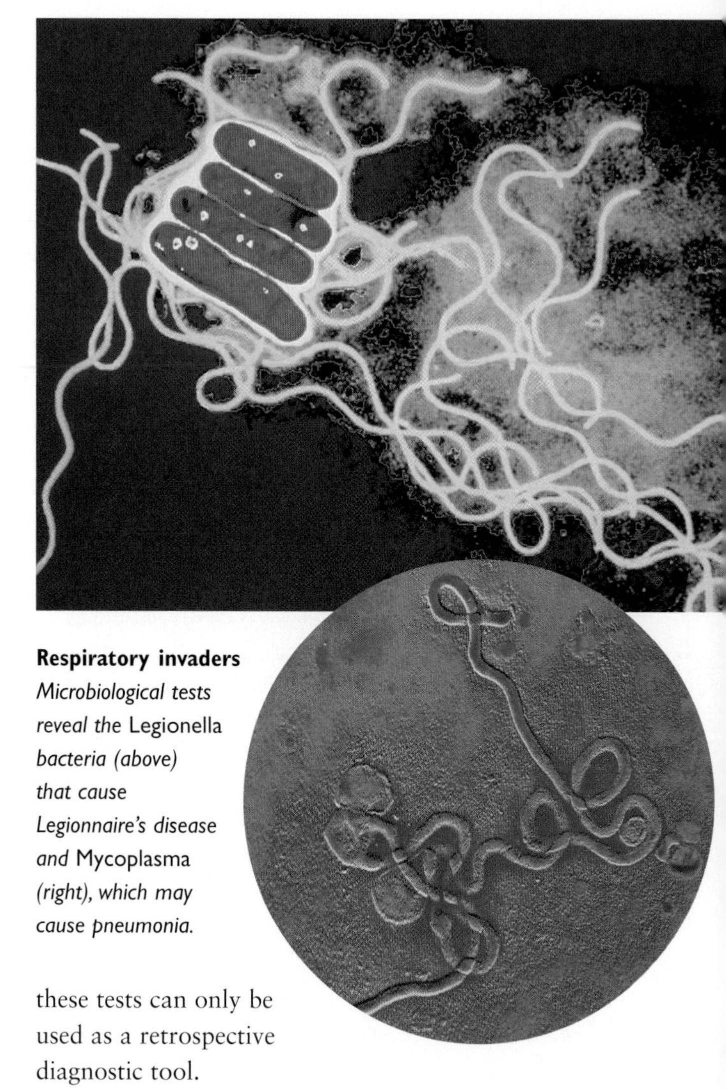

Respiratory invaders
Microbiological tests reveal the Legionella *bacteria (above) that cause Legionnaire's disease and* Mycoplasma *(right), which may cause pneumonia.*

An auto-antibody test measures antibodies that are directed at particular cell structures. Diseases for which these are useful markers include systemic lupus erythematosus, which can cause inflammation in the space surrounding the lung, and systemic sclerosis, which causes scarring in the lung tissue. Rheumatoid arthritis can also cause scarring and fluid in the pleura, and, if it is suspected, an auto-antibody test may confirm it.

Checking enzyme levels

Angiotensin-converting enzyme (ACE) is an enzyme released by the cells lining the alveolar walls. The level of this enzyme is often raised in the blood of patients with the lung disease sarcoidosis. Other diseases also cause a rise in this enzyme, so the measurement is not a useful diagnostic tool, but blood tests are often used to monitor the activity of a disease, once a diagnosis has been

EXPERIENCING A PLEURAL TAP AND BIOPSY

A physical examination and a chest x-ray detected a buildup of fluid in the pleural cavity. The doctor suspected the cause was a simple infection but, to be on the safe side, arranged for a surgeon to drain the fluid and take a sample of tissue from the pleura for analysis.

I was told that complications are rare but could include bleeding and pneumothorax. Therefore, my blood count was checked before the procedure, and a test was done to confirm that my blood was clotting normally.

I sat upright on a chair turned back-to-front, resting my arms on the bed. The doctor chose the most suitable site by looking at my x-ray and marked the spot on my back with a pen. The area was cleaned and dressed with sterile towels, and I felt the injection of local anesthetic under my skin. The doctor made a small incision in my skin, then he inserted an ordinary-sized needle between my ribs into the fluid. I could hear the suction as the fluid was withdrawn, but I didn't feel anything.

The doctor likened the biopsy to a hooking motion as he passed the cutting chamber of the needle across the inside of the chest wall to snip a piece of the pleura. The needle was withdrawn and the sample placed on a slide, and the doctor repeated the procedure a couple of times to be sure he had enough tissue to send to the lab. Although the doctor told me what he was doing, I didn't feel any of this. He then put a couple of stitches in the cut and bandaged the wound.

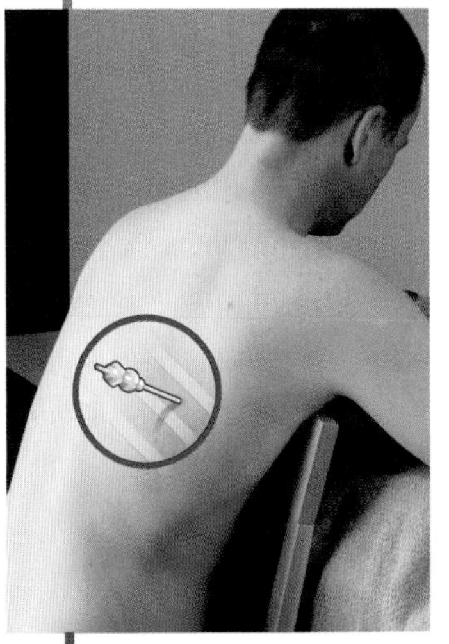

The site was sore once the anesthetic wore off, but I was given painkillers. I went home with more painkillers in case I needed them, but although my back stayed a bit tender, I found I could manage without them.

Too thick to shift
In cystic fibrosis, excess mucus (shown yellow in this false-color electron micrograph) accumulates in the bronchi. The hairlike cilia (orange and blue) are unable to clear this excess.

reached. If measured repeatedly for months and years, the enzyme level can indicate the need for or effectiveness of treatment such as steroid tablets.

MICROBIOLOGICAL TESTS

In infectious diseases such as bronchitis or pneumonia, it is vital to identify what has caused the problem to provide effective antibiotic treatment. This is done by obtaining samples of body fluids and examining them in a pathology laboratory. Sputum samples may be obtained by asking patients to cough into small pots, and small amounts of mucus may be taken from the nose or throat using a cotton swab.

Taking a fluid sample

Samples of fluid may also be obtained for examination from less accessible areas of the body. An example is pleural aspiration, in which fluid is taken from the space between the lungs and the chest wall. This can be done under local anesthetic. A small amount of fluid is usually sufficient for testing. If breathlessness is a problem, a tube known as a chest drain may be inserted and left to drain the fluid away completely to make breathing easier.

Samples of fluid may be taken from inside the lung, either through a bronchoscope (see page 110) or by inserting a needle directly into the lung from outside. This is a slightly more risky procedure because it can occasionally cause the lung to collapse from air entering the chest from outside (this happens in approximately 1 out of every 100 cases). It is performed in a computed tomography scanner (see page 108) or with ultrasound guidance.

Getting a tissue sample

In noninfectious disease, a key part of diagnosis in cases of doubt is obtaining a tissue sample. This can be examined under the microscope to see how tissue cells have been affected by the disease. Lung and pleural tissue may be obtained in a procedure called a biopsy. A pleural biopsy can be performed at the same time as a pleural aspiration, using a device about the thickness of a pencil called an Abram's needle. Lung tissue can be removed through a bronchoscope (see page 110) or in an open lung biopsy. The latter needs a general anesthetic and involves an incision in the back or side of the chest.

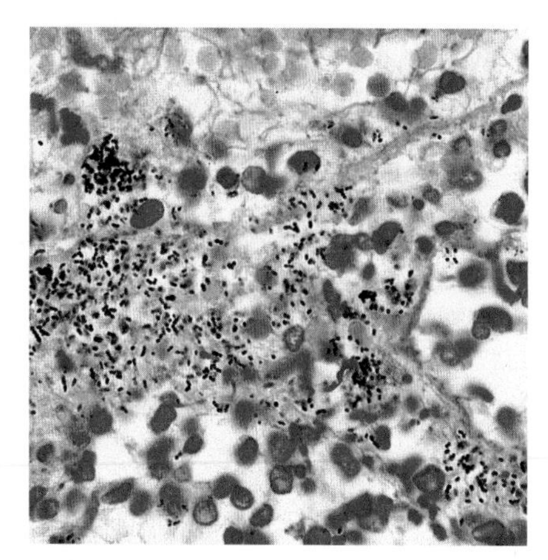

Blue bacterium

A gram stain reveals the presence of Staphylococcus aureus, *a baterium that may cause pneumonia. It shows up as blue on the gram stain.*

MICROSCOPIC EXAMINATION

If the doctor suspects that a patient has an infectious disease, samples of fluid or tissue can be taken and used to culture the infectious organisms—often bacteria—in order to identify them in the laboratory. The sample is spread onto glass or plastic plates coated with gels, providing a nutritious medium for the growth of bacteria. After 24–48 hours, bacterial colonies appear as pinhead-like blobs. These are removed and spread onto slides and, once they have dried, they are stained with one or more dyes and inspected under the microscope.

A number of factors help to identify different bacteria. These include the manner in which they take up dye, their shape, and their distribution. For example, one of the oldest and most frequently used dyes is Gram's stain, which allows the division of bacteria into those that stain blue (Gram-positive) or red (Gram-negative), helping to narrow which bacteria may be causing a problem. Another is the Ziehl-Neelsen stain, which is particularly effective in identifying the agents that cause tuberculosis.

The shape of the bacteria—for example, spherical or long thin rods—can also be a vital clue to identification, as can the way they are distributed. Staphylococci typically form clumps, for instance, whereas streptococci form chains.

Other organisms, such as protozoa, can also be identified using similar methods. For instance, *Pneumocystis carinii*, an important cause of pneumonia in AIDS patients, needs to be stained with silver to be seen. Viruses are much smaller than bacteria and can be identified only by looking at them under a much more powerful electron microscope.

Tissue specimens must first be placed in a preservative solution called formalin. They are fixed, usually in wax, before being sliced very thinly and placed on microscope slides. The tissue is then stained to make the cells visible. The standard stain is known as H-and-E, which stains the tissue pink-red. Many other stains are available; these emphasize different tissue components (such as the protein collagen present in diseases characterized by the formation of fibrous tissue) or types of cell (such as eosinophils in allergic diseases). An expert pathologist can identify the types and amounts of cells present and the processes occurring, such as cancer, inflammation, and the formation of granulomas, or inflammatory lesions.

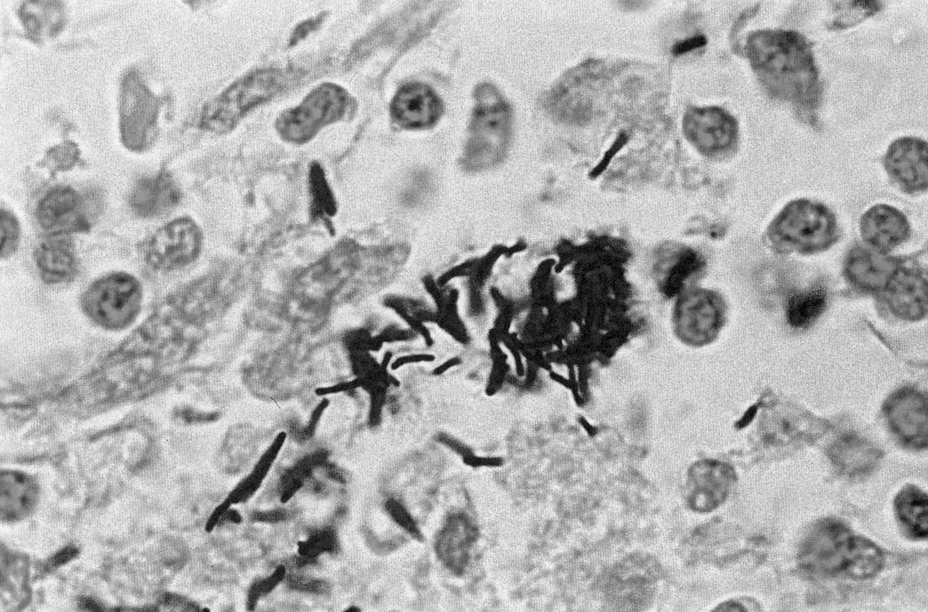

Signs of TB

Mycobacterium tuberculosis *appears red in a Ziehl-Neelsen stain. Macrophages—cells produced by the immune system to fight the infection—are the blue cells that surround the bacilli.*

SCREENING FOR TUBERCULOSIS

Screening for tuberculosis is done in high-risk individuals to protect them and their close contacts. These include health-care workers; immigrants from countries such as India, China, Mexico, and the Philippines; and nursing home residents. Screening involves injecting tiny amounts of tuberculin, a protein derived from the bacterium, under the skin. Forty-eight to 72 hours later the immune reaction is noted by measuring any swelling. A positive reaction is often visible at the site of the injection and a strong reaction is followed by a chest x-ray.

ALLERGY TESTING

The body's reaction to allergens plays an important role in certain respiratory diseases, particularly asthma. It is possible to assess an individual for allergies using skin prick, blood, or challenge tests. All have advantages and drawbacks, so a patient may have more than one test.

Skin prick tests

The most common allergy tests are skin prick tests. These are cheap, simple to perform, and give an easy answer quickly. Solutions of common allergens such as dust mites, animal dander (skin scales), and grasses are dabbed on the inner surface of the forearm. These are then pricked through the top layer of the skin using tiny needles, a process that is virtually painless. If an allergy is present, a welt-and-flare reaction—that is, an itchy blob of fluid under the skin, surrounded by redness—occurs within 15 minutes. The significance of the reaction is determined by comparing the size of this welt with those made by a positive control prick, using histamine, which always produces a weal, and a negative control, such as salt solution, which should not cause a reaction.

Blood tests

Skin prick tests are unreliable for food allergies, always negative when the patient is on antihistamine drugs, and carry a slight risk of provoking severe allergic responses. Therefore, blood tests are sometimes used to measure the levels of antibodies produced in response to an allergen. They are sometimes called RAST tests (radioallergosorbent) because they use a radioactive labeling method to detect the antibody.

TALKING POINT

Is my BCG vaccination still effective?

The effectiveness of the BCG vaccination is controversial. The policy of vaccinating all British schoolchildren was introduced in 1953 following a large trial that showed the BCG vaccine to reduce the incidence of TB by 80 percent. Subsequent trials in the UK and elsewhere have found it to be considerably less effective. In some countries, and these include the United States, it is given only to people at high risk of developing TB because of the low prevalence of the disease and the unclear benefit from the vaccine.

Ocher tests

There are many allergy tests available from pharmacies that claim to be able to diagnose food allergies. These tests are unreliable and expensive and have not fared well when subjected to serious scientific study.

Allergen challenge

In an allergen challenge, a patient is exposed, usually by inhaling or eating, to a suspected allergen under controlled conditions. This has the advantage of producing an allergic response in a natural situation but the disadvantage of possibly provoking a severe allergic reaction. Such procedures are not undertaken lightly and are only used when confirmation of a diagnosis of allergy is vital: for example, if a doctor suspects occupational asthma, where a person's job and right to compensation may be at stake, or if an individual is thought to have an allergy to drugs such as penicillin or anesthetics and is likely to require antibiotics or surgery in the future.

Testing is carried out in the hospital according to a strict protocol, starting with a tiny dose of the allergen and gradually increasing the dose. Resuscitation facilities must be available, and a doctor must be present. The patient cannot leave the hospital for an hour or two even after an apparently negative challenge, in case of a late reaction.

Imaging the lungs

The tried-and-tested method of using x-rays to image the chest and lungs has remained largely unchanged for almost a century. However, other more advanced techniques are now allowing doctors to pinpoint problems with more precision and flexibility.

Technological advances have revolutionized doctors' ability to take images of the lungs, and new developments are rapidly taking their place alongside more traditional methods in many hospitals.

CHEST X-RAY

Taking an x-ray of the chest is one of the oldest ways of investigating lung disease and is considered almost an extension of the physical examination. It is cheap, quick, and safe, using doses of radiation that are less than those found in an average urban environment.

How is it done?

X-ray beams are sent from a radiation source in a machine to penetrate the body and hit a photographic plate behind it. The patient may be positioned to face forward, backward, or sideways to the machine, each angle providing clear pictures of different parts of the chest. X-rays directed through the back have the advantage that they do not exaggerate the relative size of the heart, because it is up against the photographic plate, enabling the doctor to tell if it is enlarged, for example.

A good technique is vital when taking x-rays because too high a dose of radiation gives little contrast between the tissues, and too low a dose will not give enough penetration to record anything. X-rays can also be spoiled if the individual is not in exactly the right position. Patients are usually asked to take a big breath in to push the diaphragm down, which allows the base of the lungs to be seen. If the breath is not deep enough to inflate the lungs fully, the image is said to be "poorly inspired."

What does it show?

A chest x-ray demonstrates the anatomy of the lungs, heart, and bones and allows soft tissues such as breasts, lymph nodes, and blood vessels to be seen. The thinner the tissue, the less it absorbs the x-rays and the blacker the appearance on the film. Thus, the lungs appear black, whereas soft tissues and bones appear white.

Careful inspection of the chest x-ray will reveal many structures relevant to the lungs.

Healthy lungs
In a normal chest x-ray, the lungs are a regular shape, with no areas of unexpected shadowing or blurring, and the ribs, sternum, trachea, and spine are clearly visible and unbroken.

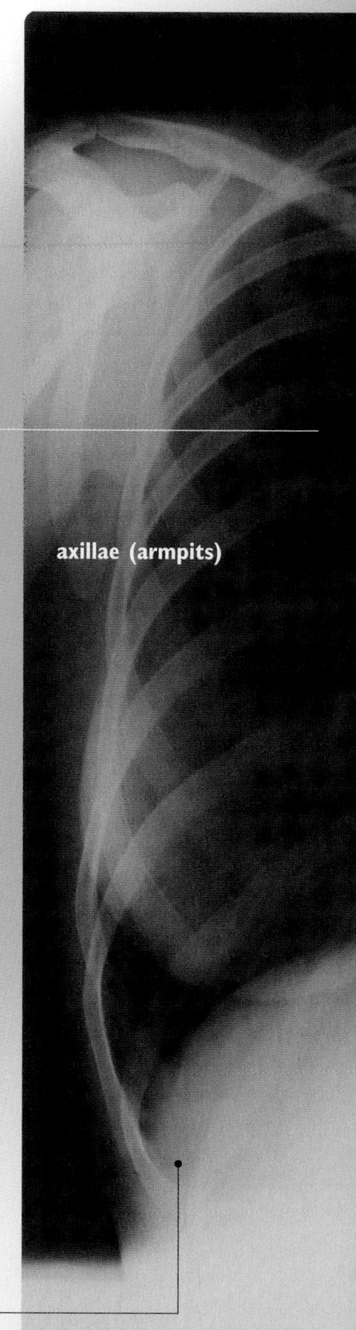

LUNG FIELDS
Any shadowing in the lungs, whether localized, as in the case of a tumor (below) or patch of pneumonia, or generalized, such as in diffuse fibrosis, is abnormal. The appearance and positioning of such dark marks may give clues as to the diagnosis; for instance, tumors have better defined borders than the inflammation of pneumonia, and tuberculosis characteristically causes shadowing in the top part (the apices) of the lungs.

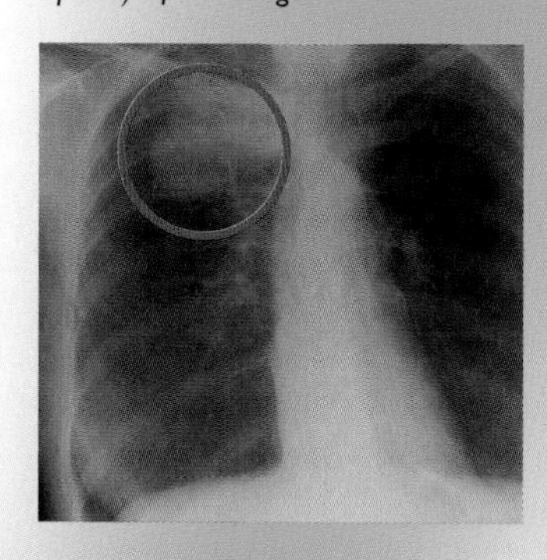

THE COSTOPHRENIC ANGLES
The areas where the diaphragm meets the chest wall are known as the costophrenic angles. These should be sharply defined; any blurring usually indicates the presence of a pleural effusion. Over half a liter of fluid must be present in the chest before it shows up on the chest x-ray. The same appearance may be seen with pleural thickening, which occurs after infections but also in tuberculosis and asbestosis (right).

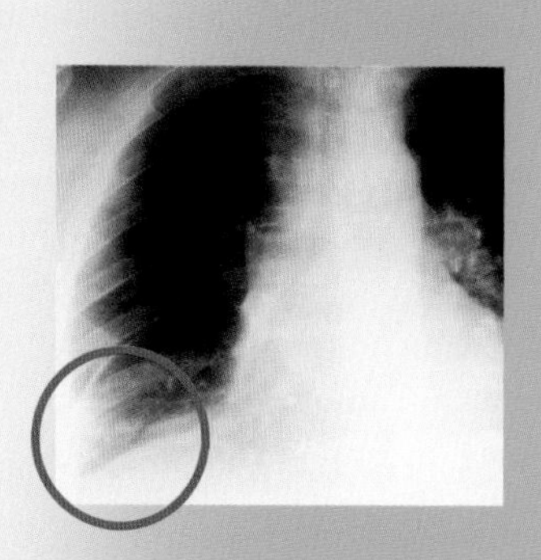

TRACHEA
Running down the center of the neck, the trachea and spine should be visible. The trachea may be narrowed by compression from outside or an obstruction, such as a tumor, within it. It may also be pushed or pulled to one side (see page 100).

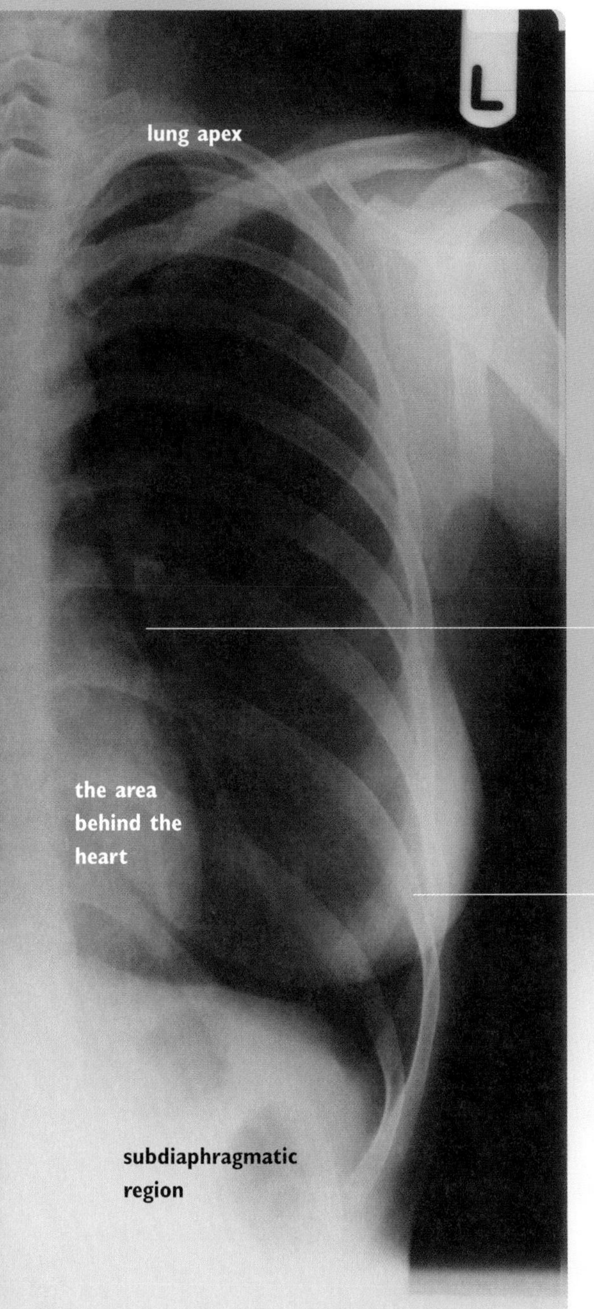

HIDDEN AREAS
There are areas on the x-ray where normal structures may obscure abnormal shadows, so the x-ray must be scrutinized so as not to miss anything important. These areas include the lung apices, the area behind the heart, the axillae (armpits), and the subdiaphragmatic region. The lungs extend below the diaphragm at the back, so a lateral chest x-ray is required to see this area properly.

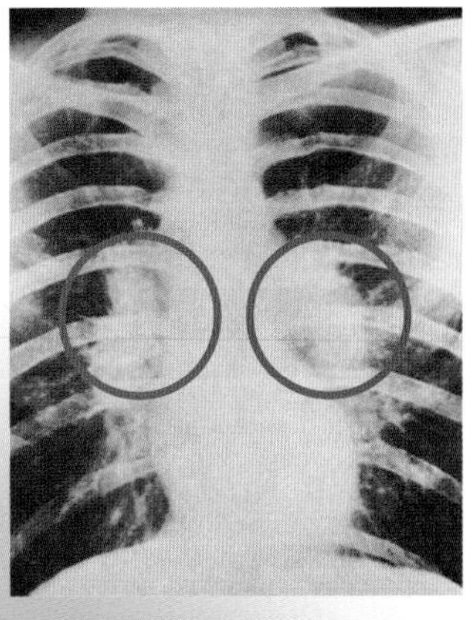

HILAR SHADOWS
The central area of each lung field (the hilum) is where the blood vessels emerge from the heart and contains lymph nodes to drain lymphatic fluid from the lungs. These areas may be abnormal if there is enlargement of lymph nodes (above) caused by diseases such as tuberculosis, sarcoidosis, or tumors, or if the blood vessels are enlarged because of pulmonary hypertension, for example.

RIBS
Conditions such as emphysema make the lungs appear barrel-shaped, so that the ribs appear widely spaced (below). In the absence of trauma, the ribs may be fractured if they are already weakened by a spreading tumor. This shows up as a black line interrupting the outline of a rib.

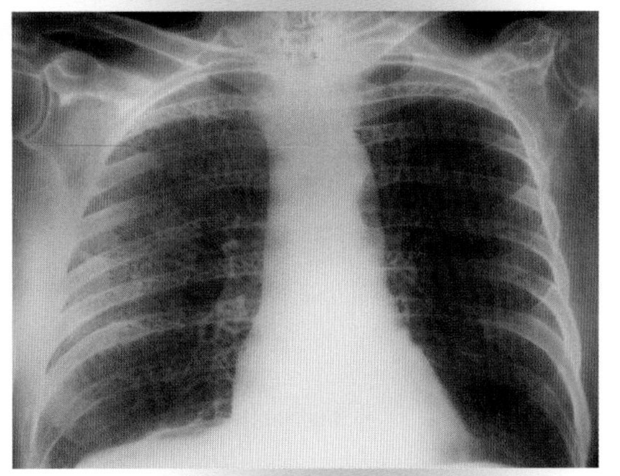

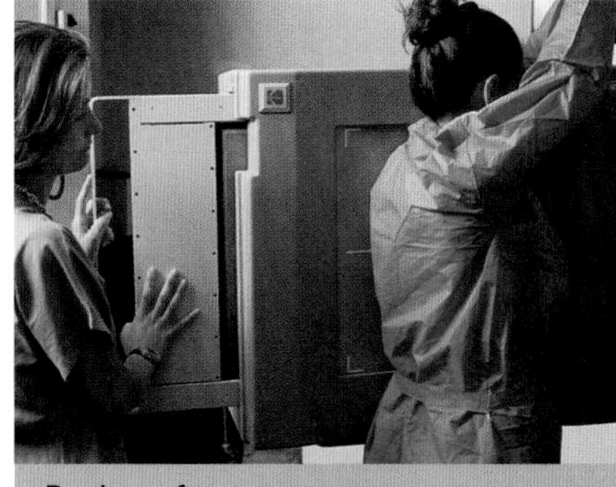

Back to front

The lungs and heart are often easier to see if the x-ray is taken from the back. If a patient raises and lowers the arms, the x-ray technician can get a good picture of inflated and deflated lungs.

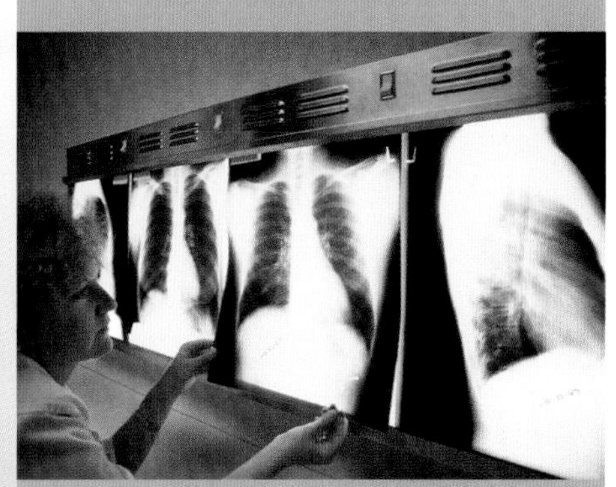

Unchanged technique

Although the technique of taking x-rays has hardly changed since it first came into general use about 90 years ago, the quality of the images obtained has increased dramatically.

EXPERIENCING A V-Q SCAN

I was told that these tests were nothing to be concerned about, and I was able to eat and drink normally before them. I went to the hospital in the morning for the first scan, then waited until the afternoon for the second.

The first scan took about an hour. I was assured that the amount of radioactivity was small and perfectly safe, although I was given a special bracelet to wear with a radiation hazard warning on it. For the ventilation scan, I was asked to breathe in gas through a mask. This did not seem or smell any different from normal air. For the actual scanning, I had to lie on a table while the machine—which looked like a trash-can lid—was passed over my body. I was asked to change position to lie on my front, back, and sides so that the technician could get a clear picture.

For the perfusion scan, I was given an injection in my arm. I felt the needle going in but nothing else. The scanning process was the same as in the morning, and this took about an hour, and I went home feeling fine.

VENTILATION-PERFUSION SCANS

A pulmonary embolus is a blood clot in one of the pulmonary arteries, which has usually broken off from a clot in a leg vein and entered the heart through the right atrium. It is transported into the right ventricle and along a pulmonary artery until it becomes wedged as the arteries get smaller and smaller. It then blocks the blood flow in that artery, resulting in pain, breathlessness, and sometimes low blood oxygen, or hypoxia. A chest x-ray is often not sensitive enough to pick up any abnormalities in the blood vessels. Therefore, other investigations are required.

A ventilation-perfusion (V-Q) scan is a routine investigation to establish the presence of a pulmonary embolus. The V-Q scan is based on the principle that although a blood clot disturbs the blood flowing to an area of lung, it does not disturb the air flowing in and out of the same area through the airways.

How is it done?

A V-Q scan has two parts. In the first part, known as a ventilation scan, a radioactive gas is added in small quantities to air and inhaled. A sensor passes over the chest to produce an image of the lungs, which should appear black if the gas has been distributed uniformly. In the second half of the procedure, called a perfusion scan, a radioactive dye is injected into a vein in the arm, and once again the sensor is passed over the chest to produce an image. If there is a pulmonary embolus, there will be a patch of white on the perfusion scan where the blood supply has been interrupted, stopping the radioactive dye from reaching that area. However, the ventilation scan will appear normal in the same area. This is known as ventilation-perfusion mismatch. In other diseases, such as pneumonia, both ventilation and perfusion are affected, and there will be matching defects on each scan.

Like all investigations, a V-Q scan does not allow a final diagnosis. It can only give a high, medium, or low probability of there being a pulmonary embolus. This possibility should be considered in conjunction with the patient's likelihood of having the disease as judged by their symptoms and history. If the result is in doubt and needs confirming, a special type of spiral computed tomography scan may be requested (see below).

CT SCANNING

The computed tomography or computed axial tomography (CT or CAT) scanner is a more sophisticated version of the x-ray machine. It looks like a large metal ring, with a table on which the patient lies and gradually

ON THE CUTTING EDGE

Spiral CT scanning

The new technique of spiral CT scanning allows scanning of the whole chest in fewer than 30 seconds. As a result, the image can be obtained in one breath-hold only, ensuring that the "slices" of the image really are contiguous. This results in a more accurate image and improves the detection rate of small lesions. Studies are under way to determine whether spiral CT scanning of smokers and former smokers would improve the early detection rates of lung cancer and, thereby, raise the 5-year survival rates for this disease.

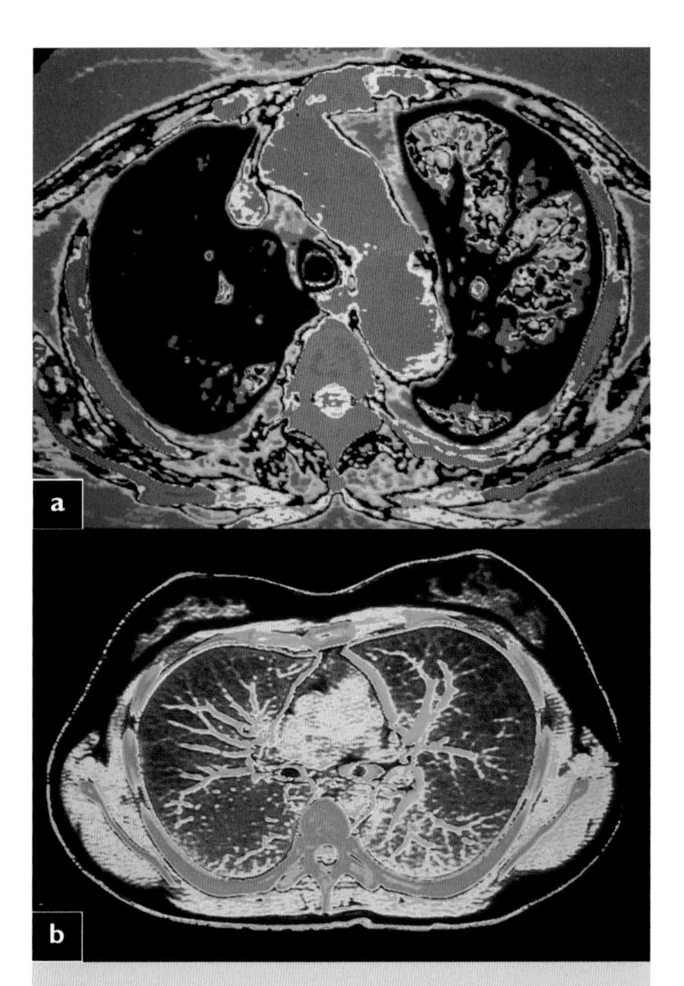

False-color CT scanning

a The lungs of a person suffering from emphysema appear shadowed in a CT scan. The left lung is relatively unaffected; in the right, however, areas of tissue damage appear blue-green.

b A CT scan of the normal lungs of a woman in her 20s, by contrast, shows healthy lung tissue, with the heart in between.

passes through. Inside the ring are an x-ray source and a detector, which slowly rotate around the patient, taking hundreds of pictures. These are built up using computer technology to create cross-sectional images through the body from top to bottom, each a few millimeters thick. Often, particular structures are outlined with a so-called contrast medium, either injected to show blood vessels, for example, or swallowed to highlight the digestive system.

A third dimension

The main advantage of CT scanning is that images have an extra dimension to aid diagnosis. Areas previously obscured by overlying tissue when looked for in chest x-rays can be seen clearly. Images are more detailed than normal x-rays, and soft tissues can be differentiated from fat and fluid. CT scan can pick up abnormalities such as small tumors and early scarring before they appear on x-rays. It can pinpoint lesions accurately, and some investigative procedures may even be performed while the patient is lying on the table: CT morphometry, for example, allows accurate and direct measurement of lung volumes.

MRI SCANNING

Magnetic resonance imaging (MRI) is a newer technique than CT scanning and works through a carefully controlled magnetic field rather than x-rays, so that it is much safer to use.

How does it work?

As well as cross-sectional scans similar to those of CT scanning, MRI is able to generate vertical slices through the body. It is a particularly useful technique for looking at "wet" tissues, and, because it is so sensitive, it can pick up possible tumors before they would appear on an x-ray.

MRI scanners look similar to CT scanners, but because the magnets must be very close to the region of interest, a scan of the chest is more claustrophobic.

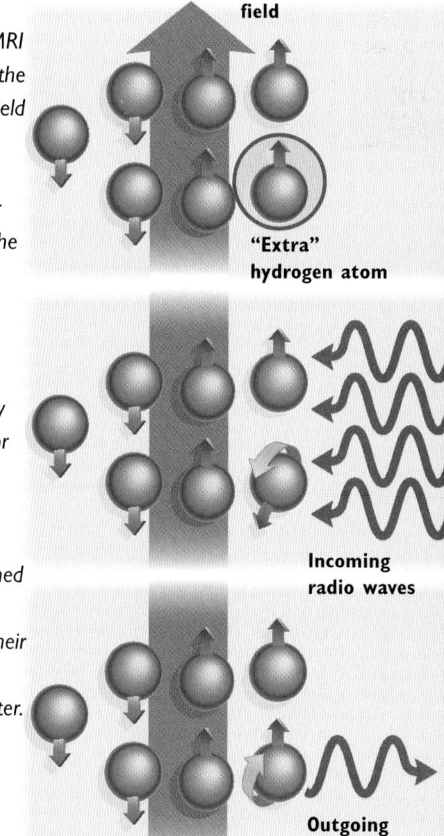

Creating magnetic images

a *When a patient enters an MRI scanner, the hydrogen atoms in the body align along the magnetic field to face either the head or feet. Most cancel each other out, but there are always one or two per million "extra" ones: These are the ones that create the image.*

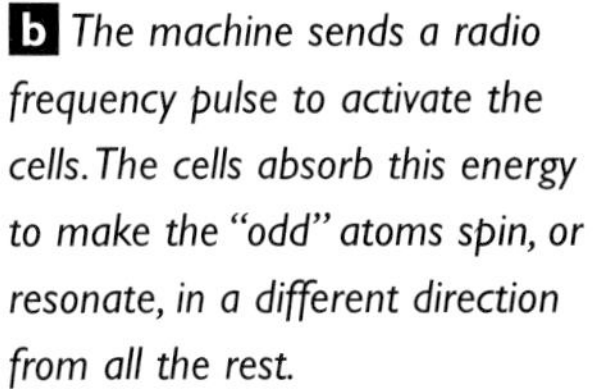

b *The machine sends a radio frequency pulse to activate the cells. The cells absorb this energy to make the "odd" atoms spin, or resonate, in a different direction from all the rest.*

c *When the radio pulse is turned off, the atoms return to their natural alignment and release their stored energy. This gives off a signal that is sent to the computer. The computer then translates these data into the image.*

Looking inside the lungs

Imaging techniques enable doctors to build up a good picture of what might be happening in the lungs, but there is nothing like actually passing a bronchoscope inside them and seeing what is there to help a doctor make an accurate diagnosis.

The development of the flexible fiber-optic bronchoscope in the late 1970s allowed direct vision into the airways of a living person for the first time. A cluster of fiber-optic cables is suspended inside a flexible, pencil-thick plastic tube and connected to an external light source. A tiny lens in the end of the bronchoscope relays images to a camera at the head of the instrument, which can also be connected to a screen. Using a small wheel at the head end of the bronchoscope, the last three centimeters can be bent to an angle of 90 degrees in two directions to give a sideways view of the airway. The bronchoscope can also be twisted to give a complete view of the airways.

Channels inside the bronchoscope allow fluid and local anesthetic to be introduced into the airways and allows the insertion of small tools to remove samples from the lung.

Taking fluid samples

Samples of lung fluid and cellular material can be collected by squirting fluid down a channel in the bronchoscope, then sucking it up again using a vacuum device. There are two types of fluid collection. In bronchial washing, fluid samples are collected from the small bronchi. In bronchioalveolar lavage, a tool is introduced into the bronchoscope, which is wedged as far down the bronchus as possible. From here it squirts fluid back up to be collected. The aim of this is to obtain samples from the alveoli themselves, to investigate unexplained alveolar shadowing.

The specimens can be inspected under the microscope for signs of abnormalities, such as cancer, or cultured in the laboratory to show up any infecting organisms, such as tuberculosis or other bacteria.

Taking tissue samples

A tiny set of forceps on the end of a wire can also be introduced through the bronchoscope into the lungs to take tissue samples from lesions in a procedure called a bronchial biopsy. Forceps are used to remove foreign bodies that are stuck in the airways.

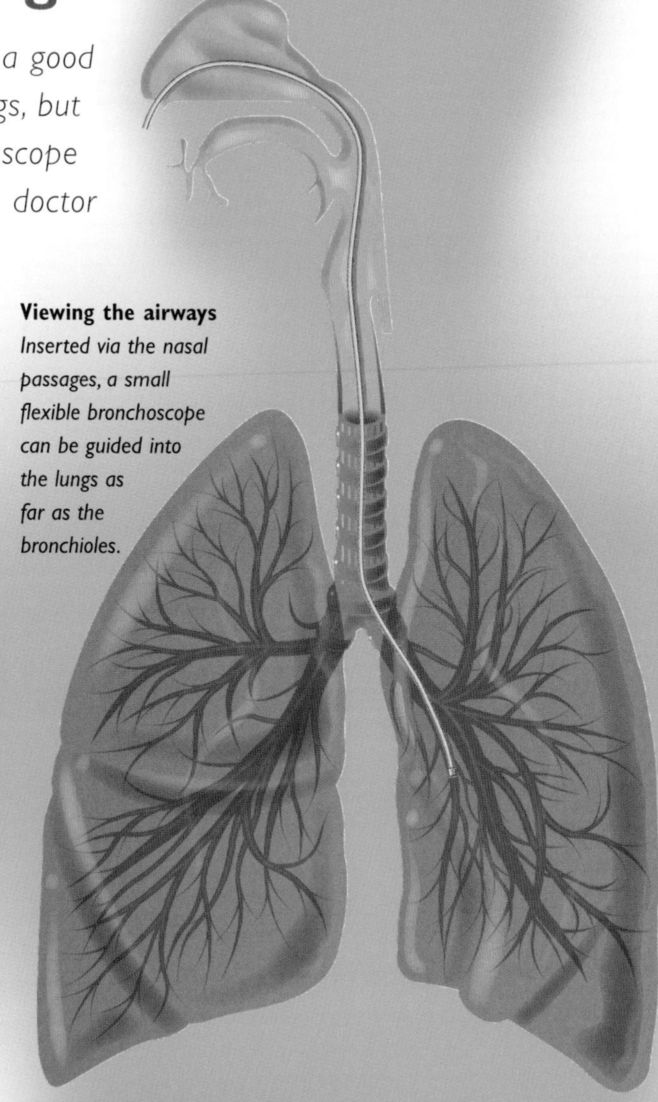

Viewing the airways
Inserted via the nasal passages, a small flexible bronchoscope can be guided into the lungs as far as the bronchioles.

Cutting edge
This false-color electron micrograph, magnified seven times, shows tiny endoscopic scissors cutting a lock of human hair.

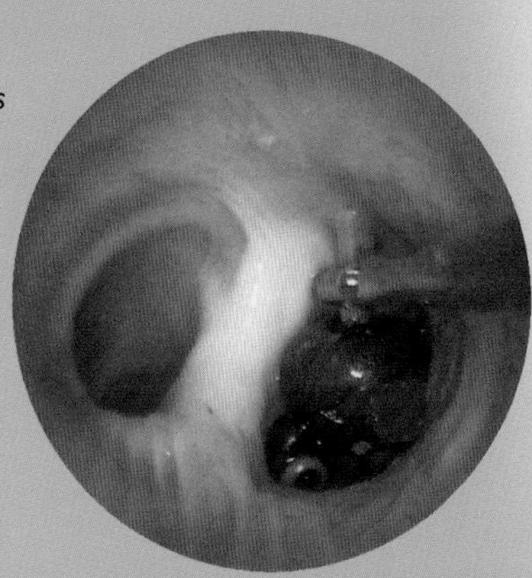

Microimages
An endoscope used for children is only 3 millimeters wide but still has room for a light, lens, and operating channel. This image from an endoscopic camera shows the removal of the top of a cocktail stirrer that was inhaled accidentally and became stuck in a bronchus.

REMOVING A FOREIGN BODY FROM THE LUNG BY BRONCHOSCOPY

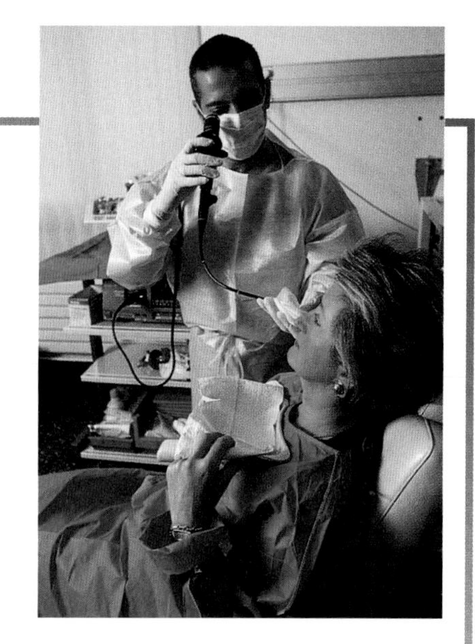

I was referred to a hospital for a chronic cough and bad breath. I remembered the cough starting after I had choked on some fish in a restaurant. A bronchoscopy was recommended.

I had been told not to eat or drink that morning. I was given an injection to make me feel drowsy, and a pulse oximeter was clipped to my finger. A nurse rubbed a smooth gel into and around my nostril to numb it, and the doctor put the bronchoscope into my nose. The instrument was coaxed into my nasal passages until it reached my throat, where I could see my vocal cords on the screen. The relaxant did its job, and I really couldn't feel anything.

The doctor explained that he was going to squirt some local anesthetic down the bronchoscope and onto my vocal cords and that it might make me cough. I felt the liquid hit and began coughing, but after a few minutes it subsided and the area felt numb.

Once I had recovered, he passed the instrument farther, into the trachea and right down to where the two major airways arise. The instrument went down one airway and all the smaller airways branching off it. Soon we could see a fishbone on the screen. Before removing it, however, the doctor checked the other bronchus and all its branches.

Going back to the fishbone, he introduced some tiny forceps into the bronchoscope, passing them down until they appeared on the screen. He opened them and snapped them shut around the fishbone. The bone was too big to go up the bronchoscope, so the whole apparatus was removed with it.

The process took about 15 minutes and was not uncomfortable. My blood pressure and oxygen saturation were checked in the recovery area. Once the anesthetic had worn off, I was able to have something to eat and drink, then I was driven home.

A different type of forceps is used to sample lung tissue adjacent to the airways. This involves puncturing a small hole in the airway as the biopsy sample is taken. Known as transbronchial biopsy, this carries a slight risk of bleeding or a collapsed lung. The amount of tissue is difficult to judge and is easily crushed during removal. As a result, transbronchial biopsy is not commonly performed, although it has become the investigation of choice for sarcoidosis, which affects lung tissue near the airway.

MEDIASTINOSCOPY

Often, when a patient has lung cancer, it can be difficult for doctors to tell whether it has spread to the lymph nodes, particularly because they may become inflamed and look suspiciously enlarged on scans. The decision whether to attempt surgery to cure lung cancer often rests on establishing the absence of such spread. This can be determined with a technique called mediastinoscopy, which involves inserting a bronchoscope-like instrument into the front of the chest, usually at the base of the neck. The aim is to explore the mediastinum, the area behind the breastbone that contains the lymph nodes, and to take samples from the nodes. The specimens are then examined in the pathology laboratory for evidence of any tumors. Mediastinoscopy is a very delicate procedure, as major blood vessels lie in the area, and it also requires a general anesthetic.

THORACOSCOPY

This procedure is generally used in the investigation and treatment of pleural effusions. If it is difficult to establish the cause of an effusion using standard investigations such as fluid examination and CT scans, a surgeon will sometimes insert a bronchoscope-like instrument through the side of the chest wall and into the area of the effusion. This procedure is known as a thoracoscopy, and it enables the surgeon to drain the area fully and see the surface of the lung and pleura and look for causes such as small pleural or lung tumours. A chest drain is left in for a few days after the procedure to remove any residual fluid. Like the mediastinoscopy, the thoracoscopy requires a general anesthetic.

CURRENT TREATMENTS

Medicine and surgery can go a long way in treating respiratory problems. Even patients with serious conditions can have their quality of life improved enormously by drugs, by additional oxygen, or by a physical therapist's detailed rehabilitation plan. Thousands of people monitor and manage their asthma daily through drug regimens. Surgery, too, has proved successful in treating many lung conditions that once were fatal.

Drug therapy

Drugs and the respiratory system have an uneasy relationship. Although the treatment and prevention of some conditions, such as asthma, rely on the use of drugs, the care of others is often best tackled by other means.

A doctor should always look at such factors as any other current medications, previous use of antibiotics, and any past adverse reactions to drugs before prescribing drugs for a respiratory patient.

ANTIBIOTICS

Viral respiratory infections affect hundreds of thousands of people every winter at great cost to the U.S. health system in terms of doctors' time and hospital admissions. Antibiotics are unnecessary because viruses do not respond to them.

Upper respiratory tract infections (URTIs)

The common cold is caused by a viral infection—usually a rhinovirus—and spreads easily and rapidly from person to person. There is no cure for the common cold. Sore throats, which often accompany common colds or flu-like illnesses, are also provoked largely by viral infection. An exception is a "strep" sore throat, which is caused by bacteria and treated with antibiotics. The best cure for URTIs is rest and plenty of fluids, although you can buy preparations to ease symptoms.

Acute sinusitis does not warrant antibiotic treatment in most cases, but patients with severe symptoms may be prescribed a short course in order to ease discomfort because they may also have a bacterial infection.

Influenza (flu) is also an acute viral infection in which virus particles invade cells in the back of the nose and

Influenza particles

A false-color electron micrograph of the flu virus shows the numerous virus particles (reddish-brown) that are attracted to mucous membranes.

Antibiotics and children

TALKING POINT

The overuse of antibiotics in early childhood is suggested as one of the reasons for the increasing prevalence of asthma and allergies. Early childhood infections work to build up resistance and are assumed to protect against the development of ailments, including asthma and allergies. The use of antibiotics at that sensitive age may inhibit this development and may lead to an increased risk of asthma and allergy. Many studies have been carried out on this subject, but the relationship remains ambiguous.

throat and use the host cell's chemical machinery to produce new virus particles. These invade new cells, and the process repeats itself at great speed. The influenza virus primarily attacks the respiratory tract, often causing coughing, but can also affect the muscles, joints, nerves, and the gastrointestinal tract as a result of the body's inflammatory response. In an average year in the U.S., the flu kills 20,000 people, but the 1918–1919 pandemic killed 500,000 in the United States alone. Health practitioners recommend that the elderly and vulnerable be vaccinated annually, although this is not a guarantee of health.

Antibiotics are not usually prescribed for flu, unless a secondary bacterial infection is suspected. Occasionally, an antiviral drug—generally zanamivir—is prescribed for at-risk adults who are able to start treatment within 30 to 48 hours of the onset of flu symptoms. Many preparations are available to treat flu symptoms, but plenty of rest and fluids are the best medicines.

Lower respiratory tract infections (LRTIs)

Acute infections of the lower respiratory tract are mostly viral, so antibiotics are rarely prescribed. There are two notable exceptions, however: COPD and community-acquired pneumonia.

COPD involves inflammation of the bronchi, which leads to coughing, sputum production, and breathlessness. Those who suffer from COPD are prone to regular and more severe chest infections than other people and should be treated with antibiotics. During infection, inflammation of the airways may be treated with a corticosteroid as well, and bronchodilators can be used to reduce breathlessness (see pages 51 and 114). Cough mixtures and expectorants can be helpful, but discuss taking these with a doctor first.

Community-acquired pneumonia is an inflammation of the lung caused by acute infection and is one of the main causes of death from infectious diseases. This infection can be caused by a variety of bacteria and viruses, although bacteria are the most common identifiable cause in hospitalized patients. A specific diagnosis can be difficult, so treatment commonly takes the form of a broad-spectrum antibiotic that will deal with the most likely bacteria. If pneumonia is suspected, treatment should not be delayed.

Problems with prescribing antibiotics

- **Side effects** Antibiotics are often considered safe despite direct and indirect side effects associated with their use. Allergic reactions, particularly to penicillin, can be a life-threatening emergency, but there are many indirect side effects that can be overlooked, especially because they may occur some time after the antibiotic has been taken. Antibiotics can interact with other drugs, making them more or less effective. They can also alter the types of microorganism present in the bowel, leading to overgrowths of—to take a common example—yeasts that cause vaginal thrush.

Side effects of penicillin

Penicillin is the most common cause of allergic drug reactions. Most are not serious—for example rashes, hives, itching of the skin, and wheezing—but in rare cases anaphylaxis can develop. This is an acute allergic reaction that can be fatal. Other side effects include abdominal pain, cramps, vomiting, and diarrhea.

SIDE EFFECTS	ALLERGIC REACTION
Respiratory	Swelling and constriction of the airways resulting in wheezing and shortness of breath. Fluid can also leak into the alveoli, causing pulmonary edema.
Circulatory	Rapid heart rate, lowered blood pressure, and fluid leaking from the bloodstream into the tissues, which lowers the blood volume. Prolonged anaphylaxis can cause heart arrhythmias (abnormal heart rhythm).
Dermatological	Rashes and hives. Sterile abscesses very occasionally occur at the site where the drug was injected.

- **Resistance** Bacteria are constantly evolving and developing ways to side-step antibiotics, either by adapting their growth and reproductive cycles or by producing enzymes that can neutralize the antibiotic. The problem is of such magnitude that some amount of bacterial resistance has been reported to most antibiotics currently available. Although the evidence that antibiotic use increases resistance is largely circumstantial, it is nonetheless plausible. Resistance tends to follow the introduction of new antibiotics closely and is greatest in countries and hospitals where antibiotic use is the heaviest. To try to prevent the development of resistance, antibiotics must be used only when they are needed, and sensitivity testing should be performed. This involves taking a sample, blood for example, from the patient and testing it against a selection of antibiotics in the laboratory to find out which will be most effective against a particular bacterium.

DRUGS FOR ASTHMA

Asthma is a chronic (long-term) illness, during which trouble-free periods alternate with times when symptoms are more severe. Sufferers do have numerous treatment options available to them, however. There are two main types of drug used to treat asthma: one that helps to prevent attacks (with anti-inflammatory agents) and the other that relieves them (especially short-acting bronchodilators). Both are usually inhaled.

How bronchodilators work

During an asthma attack, the muscles surrounding the bronchioles contract, the blood vessels widen, and the mucous lining swells. Bronchodilators relax the muscles, allowing the airway to open and narrow the blood vessels, although they have no effect on the mucous lining. Shown here is the same bronchiole during and after an attack, drawn to the same scale.

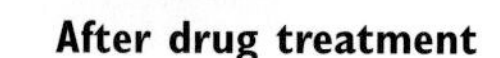

Relievers, or bronchodilators

The most important thing to do in an asthma attack is to open up and relax the narrowed airways. A number of drugs, called bronchodilators, help this process. In mild asthma, these drugs may be all that is needed, although they are also frequently prescribed alongside other medication. There are three main types of bronchodilator:

- **Beta-adrenoceptor stimulants (or beta$_2$-agonist)** The body produces chemicals, such as epinephrine, which prepare the body for activity. These act on receptor sites on the airway muscles—in the case of epinephrine, receptors called beta$_1$ and beta$_2$. One of the effects of this process is that the airways open up to allow more oxygen in. Albuterol and terbutaline, stimulate the beta$_2$ receptors only, in order to relax the bronchioles. When inhaled directly into the lungs, they give fast relief without other side effects.
- **Anti-muscarinic bronchodilator** These work by blocking nerve chemicals that control muscle contraction, allowing the air passages to open up again. They act more slowly than beta$_2$-agonists but continue to work for between 4 and 6 hours. An example includes ipratropium, which tends to be used for long-term relief and in COPD.
- **Theophylline preparations** The medication theophylline is used to relieve immediate asthma symptoms, causing direct relaxation of the muscles surrounding the air passages. It is especially effective if used in the evening to control night-time symptoms and early morning wheezing, and it is useful as a longer-acting or modified-release preparation. However, the margin between helpful and harmful dosages is small with these drugs, and regular blood tests may be needed to monitor levels of theophylline in the body.

Preventing asthma

Drugs to prevent asthma should be taken every day, even when the patient feels well and is free from symptoms. Preventive drugs work to protect the lining of the airways, reducing the sensitivity of the cells in the lungs to allergens. Drugs to prevent asthma fall into two broad groups: those that contain corticosteroids, and those that do not.

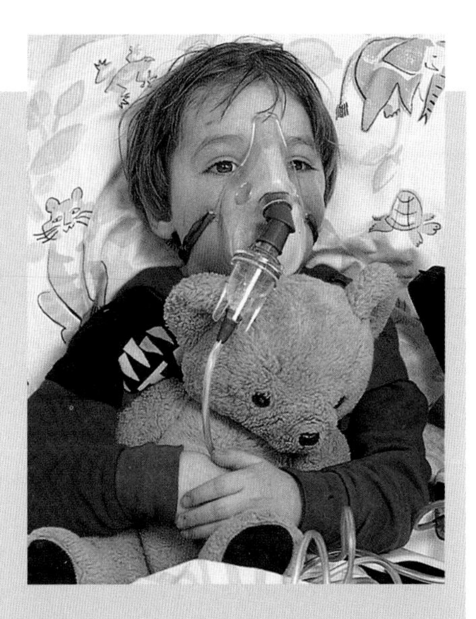

METHODS OF DRUG DELIVERY FOR ASTHMA

Drugs for asthma are almost always inhaled, which allows for high concentrations to be delivered directly to the airways. There are many variations on this method, and individuals should find a combination that works for them.

Aerosol devices Most asthma sufferers regularly use a pressurized aerosol inhaler. These devices deliver a measured amount of a drug carried by an aerosol propellant. Each time the canister is pressed, a dose is released, so you have to press and breathe in at the same time, which requires good coordination. Children, the elderly, and those with arthritic hands may find this a problem. Alternatively, breath-controlled devices fire a dose as you breathe in and may be useful for those who find inhalers difficult to use.

Spacers *(shown bottom left)* These are designed for those who find it hard to coordinate pressing and breathing in and are beneficial to those who find that the propellant causes irritation or the cold blast inhibits breathing in. The spacer extends the gap between the aerosol and the mouth and slows the speed at which the propellant and drug travel to the mouth. A spacer must fit the inhaler exactly, and with children the size should increase with age and lung capacity. Spacers also reduce the amount of medicine swallowed and absorbed at any given time, so side effects are minimized.

Dry-powder systems The main advantage of this method is that the patient does not need to rely on coordinating the dose with their breathing. Coughing may be a problem with these inhalers, however. Dry-powder devices require a breathing technique that may be difficult to produce during severe attacks and by children younger than 5.

Nebulizers *(shown above)* In this method, air or oxygen is forced through a drug solution and delivered through a mask or mouthpiece. Breathing need not be coordinated, so a nebulizer is useful for emergency treatment or for young children. Used in much the same way as a spacer, a nebulizer is more time- and labor-intensive than an inhaler.

- Corticosteroids Usually called steroids, these drugs reduce inflammation of the air passages and stop the production of extra fluid and mucus. The steroids most commonly used include beclomethasone, budesonide, and fluticasone. Preventers containing steroids tend to be more effective, especially in moderate-to-severe asthma. Inhaling steroids directly into the lungs is effective in small doses; little is absorbed into the rest of the body, and side effects are rare. These drugs must be used regularly as they take time to work and will not relieve sudden wheezing or breathlessness. Occasionally, short courses of high-dose steroid tablets may be necessary if symptoms are not controlled by the usual medicines, but even then they rarely cause side effects. Steroids left in the mouth and throat can worsen asthma and predispose the individual to infections in the throat and a hoarse voice. Rinsing the mouth and throat by gargling with water after inhalation can help prevent this, as can using a spacer with aerosol inhalers.
- Sodium cromoglycate (Intal) These nonsteroid preventers inhibit the release of histamine, the chemical produced by the body when it reacts to allergens, and are therefore most useful in cases with an allergy basis.

A survey has shown that half of all asthma patients do not use an inhaler properly, which means that a great many people are not getting the doses of medication they need.

Milestones IN MEDICINE

The French physiologist Charles Robert Richet, professor at the University of Paris from 1887 to 1927, was awarded the 1913 Nobel prize for medicine for his work on anaphylaxis. He coined the word to describe the reaction, then often fatal, of people on their second exposure to an organism to which they have previously become sensitized. He demonstrated that the first exposure permanently modified the chemical structure of the body's fluids. His work revolutionized the understanding of such conditions as asthma and hay fever.

They are not, however, useful for the immediate relief of symptoms. Nedocromil (Tilade) works in a similar way to sodium cromoglycate.

- **Leukotriene receptor antagonists** Available in tablet form, these nonsteroid medicines block the production of chemicals called leukotrienes, which are specifically involved in the development of asthma. Examples include montelukast and zafirlukast. They can be added when asthma is not well controlled with an inhaled steroid and bronchodilator; they can also be used to control exercise-induced asthma.

DRUGS FOR ALLERGIES

The body reacts to an allergen by releasing histamine, which acts on receptors in the skin, nose, eyes, and airways to produce symptoms such as itchy eyes and nose, headaches, and sneezing. Antihistamines either block the receptors where the released histamine acts or block the release of histamine in the first place.

Medicines to treat anaphylaxis

Occasionally, a patient can develop an extreme sensitivity to drugs and food, producing anaphylactic shock. In this state, the airways swell, breathing becomes difficult, and blood pressure falls. At its most extreme, anaphylaxis can be life-threatening, and symptoms require prompt treatment. First-line treatment is to restore the airway and blood pressure by laying the patient flat and raising the feet, then administering an epinephrine injection to stimulate heart activity and widen the airways. This rapidly restores normal functioning, making the blood vessels contract and relaxing the airways. Oxygen is essential, and an antihistamine is administered intravenously for 1 or 2 days to prevent relapse.

DRUGS FOR COUGHS

Cough medicines, or antitussives, can help to relieve a cough, although they are not always effective and may draw attention away from the primary problem. Some medication isn't suitable for everyone, so it's best to talk to the pharmacist before buying. It is important to seek medical advice for a cough that persists longer than a few days or one accompanied by fever or blood in the phlegm.

Expectorants

These are claimed to decrease the thickness and increase the volume of mucus in the respiratory tract. Often used for "chesty coughs," their aim is to thin the mucus while it is still in the lungs so that the phlegm can be coughed up easily. However, this effect probably only occurs at sufficiently high doses to make a patient vomit. A home-based alternative is to inhale the steam from a bowl of hot water with a drop or two of menthol or eucalyptus added to it. This will soothe the airways and loosen the phlegm; drinking plenty of fluids should thin it down.

Cough suppressants

Suppressing a cough can interfere when the body is trying to expel a harmful substance or excessive phlegm and is not always recommended. Mixtures for "dry coughs,"

Natural expectorant
Steam eucalyptus leaves in hot water and inhale the vapor to encourage the loosening of mucus.

however, can be useful in reducing symptoms if a patient is kept awake at night or the cough is interfering with everyday life. Medicines such as codeine and dextromethorphan suppress the cough reflex by acting on nerve centers in the brain. Cough suppressants do not treat or shorten the length of colds, coughs, and other respiratory infections; nor do they help people with bronchitis because they do not aid the removal of phlegm.

Soothing cough medicines

Also used to calm dry coughs and soothe any throat discomfort, mixtures containing syrup of glycerol (glycerine) protect and soothe mucous membranes, relieving irritation. They are available over the counter. Other remedies such as lemon, glycerol, and honey in hot water can be made at home.

Compound cough preparations

The ingredients in combination cough preparations are often present in too low a dose to be effective. Also, some mixtures contain ingredients that act in opposing ways to each other. Some include a sedating antihistamine, which dries phlegm, making it harder to cough it up from the lungs. These preparations may hinder the removal of carbon dioxide from the lungs in patients with COPD.

Mucus-thinning drugs

Also called mucolytics, these drugs contain enzymes that make mucus less sticky, so it should be easier to cough up. They are only prescribed for conditions of excessive mucus thickening or secretion, such as cystic fibrosis.

ANALGESICS

The most common type of chest pain encountered in respiratory disease is a sharp, localized pain, often referred to as pleuritic pain. Nonsteroidal anti-inflammatory drugs (NSAIDs) are the most effective treatment for pleuritic pain. Examples include aspirin and ibuprofen, as well as indomethacin, ketoprofen, and piroxicam. If taken regularly, NSAIDs reduce underlying inflammation by blocking prostaglandin production. Prostaglandins are body chemicals involved in the process of inflammation and the transmission of pain, in the body's immune response, and in tissue damage.
All NSAIDs have similar anti-inflammatory activity, but there is considerable variation in how individuals respond to any particular one. The main variables are the severity and frequency of side effects, such as upset stomach (this can be reduced by taking the medicine with or after food) and diarrhea. Occasionally, bleeding and ulceration occur in the stomach and duodenum, so patients with active peptic ulcers are advised to avoid these drugs. If the drugs are essential, the doctor will also prescribe something to protect the stomach or to prevent further injury to the stomach lining.

NSAIDS may, in rare cases, cause a hypersensitivity reaction. If a skin rash or wheeze develops after taking aspirin, an allergic reaction may occur on exposure to other NSAIDs as well. Similarly, if a patient has asthma and the condition worsens while taking an NSAID, the medicine should be stopped at once and medical attention sought. Over-the-counter painkillers often contain these substances, and it is important to know that two such preparations should never be taken at the same time.

Ointments containing NSAIDs, applied directly to the skin, may still trigger allergic reactions and asthma.

OTHER USEFUL DRUGS

Many other drugs may be useful in treating the symptoms of respiratory problems. Diuretics, for example, remove excess fluid from the body, which reduces the pressure in the heart, eases congestion in the lungs, and removes accumulated fluid from the ankles. Blood clots may form in various veins around the body; from there they may dislodge and travel to other areas, including the lungs. Anticoagulants, such as heparin, act rapidly in the body to prevent clots from forming and to dissolve existing clots.

Are NSAIDs always safe?

NSAIDs reduce inflammation and pain in many conditions, but they are powerful drugs—never use two preparations containing NSAIDs at the same time. NSAIDs should be taken with caution by elderly people and anyone with poor kidney, liver, or heart function. If long-term treatment is needed, regular checkups on kidney function should be performed, especially in those older than 65.

ASK THE EXPERT

Physical therapy

Physical therapy plays an important part in postoperative care and in treating conditions such as cystic fibrosis and chest problems. Physical therapists use many techniques to help loosen and expel mucus, keep airways clear, and improve breathing.

The most important responsibilities of the physical therapist dealing with patients with respiratory problems are teaching good breathing techniques and postural drainage.

BREATHING EXERCISES

Many people with respiratory problems breathe using too much energy for too little effect. Physical therapists teach relaxed, controlled, and efficient techniques. One of the most important is deep, or diaphragmatic, breathing to maximize the area of the lungs used, loosen secretions in the lobes, and aid relaxation.

Once diaphragmatic breathing has been learned, the physical therapist can apply pressure to specific congested areas of the lungs and ask the patient to push against the pressure while breathing. This helps to loosen any mucus.

POSTURAL DRAINAGE

This treatment technique relies on the force of gravity to help drain secretions from the lobes of the lungs, so the physical therapist places the patient in a different position for each area that needs to be worked on. If the posterior lower lobes of the lungs are to be drained, for example, the patient lies on the stomach; a pillow is placed under the hips, and the foot of the bed is raised at an angle so that the feet are 18 inches higher than the head. The physical therapist uses a variety of techniques to loosen the secretions and teaches the patient how to expel them efficiently. A 15-to-20 minute session is normally needed for each area to be cleared. The procedure can be tiring for the patient, and children may need lots of reassurance.

Patients who are short of breath or who have acute infections may find it painful to adopt a position for successful postural drainage, so nasal suction may be necessary. A tube is passed through the nose and back of the throat into the lungs, and secretions are sucked out.

Loosening secretions

Two techniques are used to loosen secretions: vibration and percussion. In vibration, the physical therapist's hands are placed over the area of the lungs to be cleared, and small, rapid, in-and-out movements are made in the direction of the main airways as the patient breathes out. This moves secretions up the respiratory tract to a position from which they can be coughed up more easily. Vibration over the breastbone is then used to stimulate the cough reflex to help this happen.

Percussion is more useful when the secretions are very

Breathing and postural drainage

a While the patient relaxes, the physical therapist's hands are placed over the lower ribs and base of the breastbone. The physical therapist exerts slight pressure as the patient breathes out.

b The patient breathes in slowly and deeply, using the abdominal muscles.

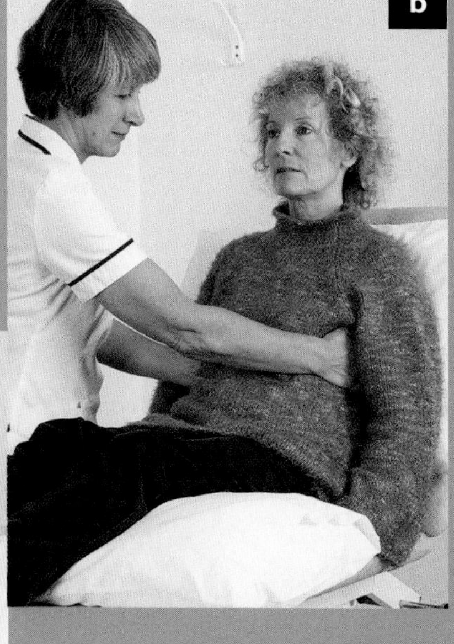

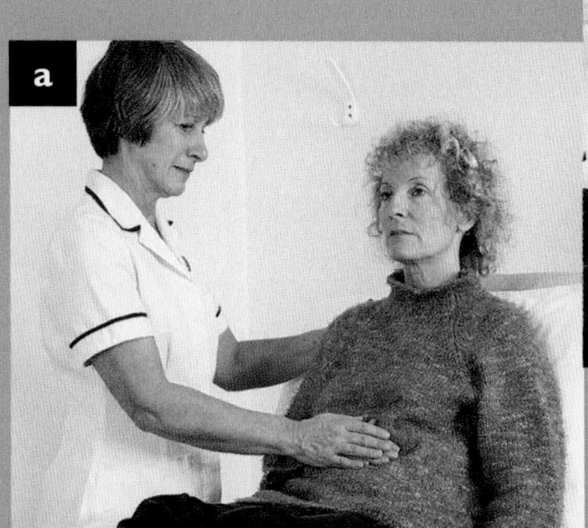

c A physical therapy session may last about 20 minutes for each area to be cleared. To loosen and expel sticky mucus from the lungs, the physical therapist works on each lobe in turn, placing the patient on the back, front, or side, as appropriate.

d The physical therapist uses quick movements of the hands as the patient breathes out to loosen the mucus.

e Gravity also helps, so the patient's head is below the level of the feet. This helps mucus expelled from the lungs back up the airways, where it can be coughed up. This technique is especially useful for people suffering from cystic fibrosis.

sticky and is especially helpful in cases of cystic fibrosis. The physical therapist uses cupped hands, bent at the wrist, to hit the chest wall alternately in the rhythm of a drum roll; contact is made primarily with the heel of the hand. The drum roll causes the airways to vibrate so that the secretions come away from the walls of the alveoli.

How are the secretions expelled?

The physical therapist teaches the patient two main techniques to remove secretions from the lungs: either huffing or coughing, or a combination of the two, and the forced expiratory technique (FET).

Huffing and coughing move secretions up the airways but narrow the airways, increasing the pressure gradient so that the pressure is higher at the base of the lungs than at the throat; this encourages secretions to move upward. However, a huff or cough expels only a certain amount of air, and if the lungs are full, this is the air in the main airways. To move the secretions in the lower part of the airways, the patient should take a light breath in.

Huffing and coughing are often combined with diaphragmatic breathing in the FET. In some conditions, such as asthma and emphysema, only FET is used because there is a danger that too much narrowing of the airways, caused by excessive huffing and coughing, will send them into spasm. In FET, the patient takes a breath in and then huffs twice, using the diaphragm and the muscles of the chest wall to expel the air, before taking three or four diaphragmatic breaths. When secretions are felt in the upper airways, a deep breath is taken so that they can be coughed out.

PHYSICAL THERAPY IN CYSTIC FIBROSIS

Although cystic fibrosis affects many glands, the most serious problems caused by the condition are those that have an impact on the lungs. Without regular physical therapy, large quantities of sticky, thick mucus build up, affecting respiratory function and making sufferers prone to infections such as pneumonia and bronchitis.

Health-care personnel and patients themselves can perform the treatment, which involves postural drainage twice a day, with vigorous percussion and FET. Each area of the lungs must be cleared in turn. Many children also require medication before treatment to help loosen the secretions.

POSTOPERATIVE PHYSICAL THERAPY

Surgery to the lungs inevitably has an effect on respiratory function. Postoperative pain and a lack of mobility of the trunk mean that breathing is shallow. Secretions build up, and patients are often reluctant to cough, both because of the pain and an unfounded but understandable fear that the wound will burst.

A physical therapist draws up an individual treatment plan for each patient. Before treatment, analgesia, usually gas and air, is given for the pain, and then the patient is taught breathing and other techniques so that self-treatment can continue after discharge from the hospital.

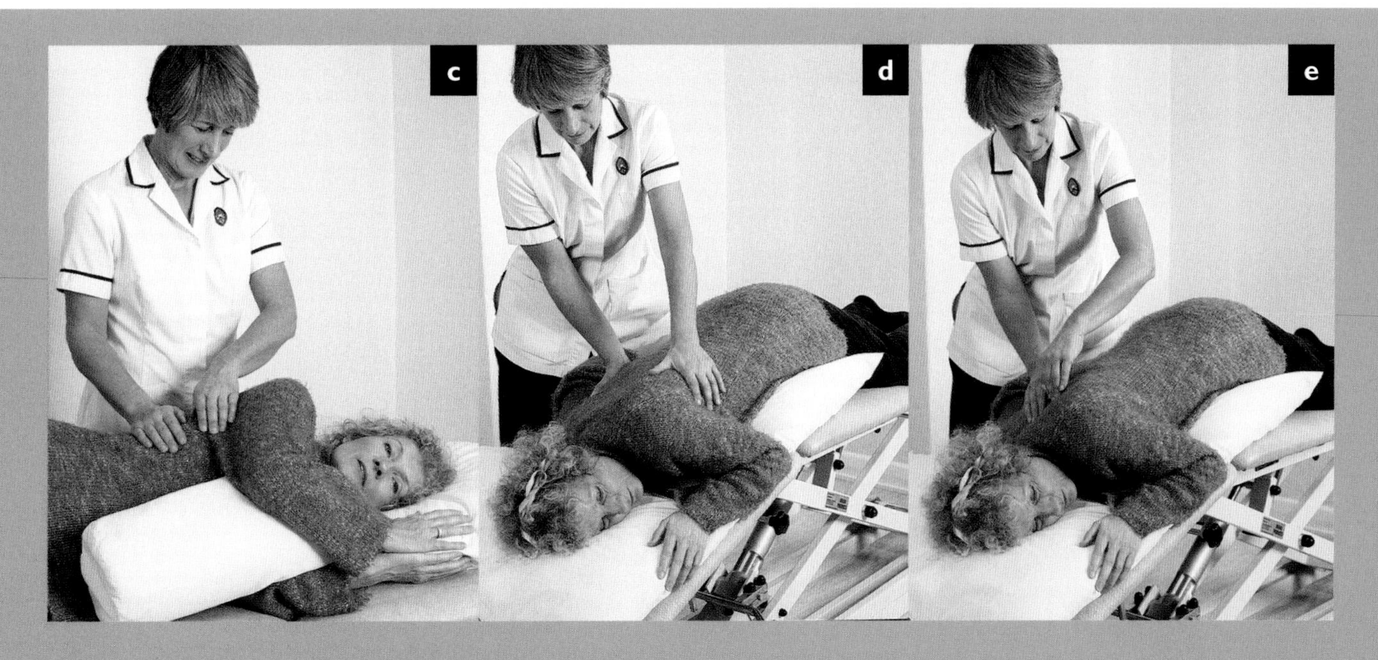

Oxygen therapy

Oxygen is vital for life: The brain dies after 3 minutes without it. When something interrupts or reduces the supply of oxygen to the tissues, oxygen therapy is started without delay. It is necessary in many instances, including cases of respiratory failure.

In hospitals, oxygen is stored in pressurized, liquid form and piped as a gas to operating rooms, intensive care units, and the bedsides of individual patients. It is given by mask, nasal prongs, or by means of a machine called a ventilator. There are many types of ventilator. Some take over the patient's breathing completely; others help a patient to breathe effectively without effort, taking over the process if insufficient oxygen is being received. All deliver oxygen and air to the lungs and allow carbon dioxide to be exhaled. To do this, the ventilator switches off between each push of air, allowing the lungs' recoil to push the air out. If this is not possible, a machine that sucks the air out of the lungs is used.

In order to determine the correct balance between oxygen and carbon dioxide in the patient's blood, a nurse takes frequent samples of blood that are sent through an autoanalyzer machine. Occasionally an electrode is placed beneath the skin to give a continuous reading. The action of the ventilator, and the level of oxygen in the air it supplies, is adjusted according to the results obtained.

Life-support ventilation

Life-support ventilation takes over a patient's breathing completely. An electric pump is linked to oxygen and air that are pushed into the patient's lungs by means of an endotracheal tube inserted into the throat, either through the nose, the mouth, or by tracheotomy.

Continuous positive pressure ventilation

Used when patients are seriously ill and cannot breathe unaided or have an endotracheal tube in place, this is also known as controlled ventilation because it overrides the patient's own breathing: The positive pressure is the pressure exerted by the pump, either to push air in or suck it out. The patient does not have to do anything, and any attempt to breathe independently is made impossible.

Intermittent positive pressure ventilation

Also known as patient-trigger ventilation, this procedure allows the patient to trigger when inspiration will occur: The ventilator senses the change in pressure when the

Types of ventilation

The amount of pure oxygen administered and the method of administration depend on the patient's condition. If a patient is experiencing severe respiratory failure, all the breathing functions may be transferred to a machine.

TYPE	HOW	WHEN USED
Life support	Endotracheal tube	Intensive care, operating room when a patient is unconscious
Continuous positive pressure	Endotracheal tube Tracheotomy	Seriously ill patient, unable to breathe alone or has a tracheotomy in place
Intermittent positive pressure	Endotracheal tube	Seriously ill patient, unable to take in adequate breaths alone, pale and exhausted
Noninvasive	Nasal prongs Face mask	Acute or chronic respiratory failure when patient is conscious and cooperative

Breathing by machine

A seriously ill patient may need 100 percent oxygen saturation for up to 24 hours and help from a ventilator to breathe in and out.

patient tries to take a breath and supplies oxygenated air by positive pressure. The technique allows the patient some control over breathing but reduces the effort involved to a minimum. It is used when patients are in pain and tired, as well as postoperatively, and to help clear sputum from the lungs in respiratory diseases.

Noninvasive positive pressure breathing

This type of ventilation does not require an endotracheal tube, hence the term noninvasive. Instead, it employs intermittent positive pressure ventilation by means of a mask covering the mouth or the nose.

The most common type of mask is known as a Venturi mask or air entrapment mask. This fits snugly over the face and is made up of two parts: a jet nozzle that delivers oxygen, and apertures, called portholes, that suck air into the mask. The ratio of air to oxygen can be changed by altering the flow of oxygen through the jet or by changing the size of the portholes. This means that the patient can easily and accurately be given the amount of oxygen required, whatever the pattern or rate of breathing.

HOME OXYGEN THERAPY

People with respiratory conditions such as severe chronic bronchitis, congestive heart failure, emphysema, cystic fibrosis, lung cancer, asbestosis, and other occupational lung diseases do not always need hospitalization. Instead, they can give themselves oxygen at home to improve sleep, mental alertness, memory, and physical abilities. Safety precautions are vital in storage and handling, however, because pressurized oxygen is volatile.

How it works

Oxygen can be supplied from a cylinder, in which it is stored in liquid or pressurized gas form, or it can be drawn from the air by an electrically powered device that concentrates and stores it. People using electrical devices must also have a cylinder as back up, in case of a power outage. Portable models are also available, which allow a patient greater freedom of movement.

Using nasal prongs
Nasal prongs are preferred by many oxygen users because they allow normal speech and eating. Prolonged use, however, may cause irritation of the nostrils, with the result that a mask may be a more suitable method of delivery.

Can you ever have too much oxygen?

Breathing high levels of oxygen for long periods can be dangerous because it leads to a condition called oxygen toxicity. It is thought that excess oxygen releases chemicals called free radicals that can damage organs and cells. The most susceptible organs are the lungs, eyes, intestines, and central nervous system. Newborn babies are especially vulnerable to damage to the eyes—in particular, a condition called retrolental fibroplasias, in which new blood vessels develop in the eye and cause the retina to become detached—and to the central nervous system, resulting in fits. For this reason, oxygen levels are always monitored closely.

ASK THE EXPERT

VENTILATION OF PREMATURE BABIES

Babies born before the 36th week of pregnancy often have underdeveloped lungs. One problem is that they do not get enough surfactant (see page 28). Without it, a baby becomes exhausted with the effort of breathing. In addition, a baby's diaphragm is underdeveloped, so more effort and more oxygen are needed to breathe. Premature babies need ventilation until their lungs are sufficiently mature to breathe alone.

Because full-term babies breathe quickly, high-frequency oscillating ventilation is now used in many neonatal special care units for premature babies. This provides oxygen in tiny doses at a rate of as much as 150 breaths per minute. The almost constant supply of oxygen saves the baby's energy resources and protects the immature lung tissue from damage. This high-pressure oxygen delivery can cause problems with exhaling. To break this cycle, two small-bore prongs deliver oxygen into the nose during inspiration, but during expiration the air is passed out through a wide-bore tube that has a lower resistance, making expiration easier.

Cancer treatments

Carcinomas of the lungs are the result of abnormal cell growth and the development of malignant tumors within the body. These cells are able to divide rapidly and can result in metastasis—a process in which the cancer spreads from a primary tumor to a second site.

Lung cancer can be divided into two main types: small-cell lung cancer and non-small-cell lung cancer. These types spread differently and can be treated in a variety of ways. Small-cell lung cancer affects fewer people and spreads quickly, initially with few symptoms. Non-small-cell lung cancer is more common and grows more slowly. All forms of lung cancer may involve metastasis, with varying degrees of speed.

Currently, there are three approaches to treating cancer: chemotherapy, radiotherapy, and surgical excision. The role of each depends on the tumor type and the stage of its development. Some cancers can be detected early and can often be cured by surgery alone. Others can't be excised successfully because the tumor is already invading local tissue or has spread to distant sites. The extent of spread of the primary tumor is established by means of CT, MRI, and bone scans. This is known as staging and determines the best treatment for each individual.

CHEMOTHERAPY

Chemotherapy is the most effective treatment for cancer that has already spread to other parts of the body, primarily small-cell lung cancer, although it is also used to slow down the progress of non-small-cell lung cancer. About 35 different drugs are currently used, all of which are cytotoxic: that is, they kill cells. They do this by damaging the cells' DNA, which prevents them from dividing. Unfortunately, some normal cells, particularly those in the bone marrow, skin, and genitals, are also susceptible to chemotherapy drugs. The best way to administer chemotherapy is in short courses, with gaps between treatments to allow the normal cells to recover.

Chemotherapy can be given as tablets or as an injection into a vein, either by using a syringe or a drip. A combination of different types of drugs is often more effective without necessarily increasing the toxic effects. It may also reduce the risk of the tumor cells becoming

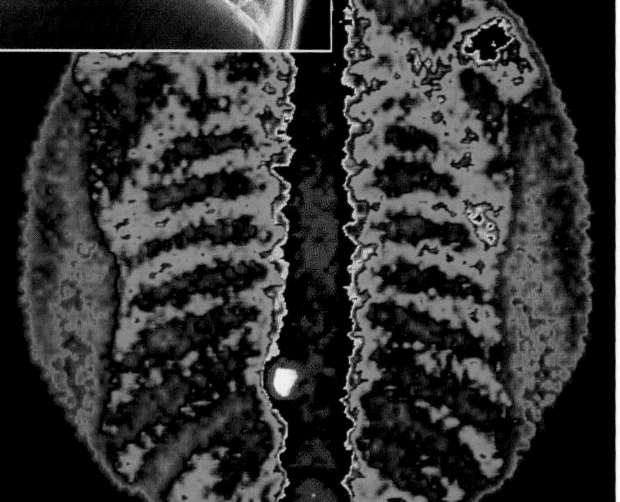

Imaging a tumor
Left: a colored chest x-ray clearly shows a primary cancer of the lung in red and yellow. Below: a false-color bone scintigram—also of the spine and ribs—identifies as a white "hot spot" a secondary bone cancer tumor affecting the dorsal spine.

Does chemotherapy always cause hair loss?

Contrary to common belief, not all chemotherapy drugs cause hair loss. They cause temporary damage to all cells that grow and divide, including hair follicles, and hair can be lost from any part of the body. This is generally noticeable within a few weeks of starting treatment, but the amount can vary from negligible amounts to total hair loss. Regrowth usually starts within 4–6 weeks of completing the treatment and may take 3–6 months. Initially, hair may be curlier, finer, or even a different color. Scalp cooling using a "cold cap" during treatment may help to prevent hair loss. By temporarily constricting the blood vessels in the scalp, it reduces the amount of chemotherapy reaching the hair follicles. Other practical steps include cutting hair short, using conditioner, and brushing hair gently. It is advisable not to use rollers and "hood" hair dryers.

ASK THE EXPERT

HAVING A RADIATION SESSION

My doctor explained that the radiation sessions would be similar to having a series of x-rays. She also told me that the course of sessions would be designed individually to target my particular tumor.

I had to go to the center for an initial visit to enable the radiologist to map out the area he would be treating; he called this a "simulation" session and referred to my x-rays and CT scan as he was doing this. My skin was marked with colored pens and a special dye and tiny pinprick, although it didn't hurt at all. The technician explained that this was so that he could be sure he was targeting the same area at each session.

I was surprised to find at the first session that the radiation was entirely painless—I had expected at least some discomfort. Plates to direct the beams were moved close to my body. I suffer from claustrophobia in certain situations, and so I was a little concerned about this, but actually I didn't feel as nearly shut in as I had feared, and the technician was very reassuring. I had to lie still during the session, but as it lasted only about 10 minutes, this wasn't too difficult. I had a new type of radiation that involved 3 sessions a day over 12 days, including weekends.

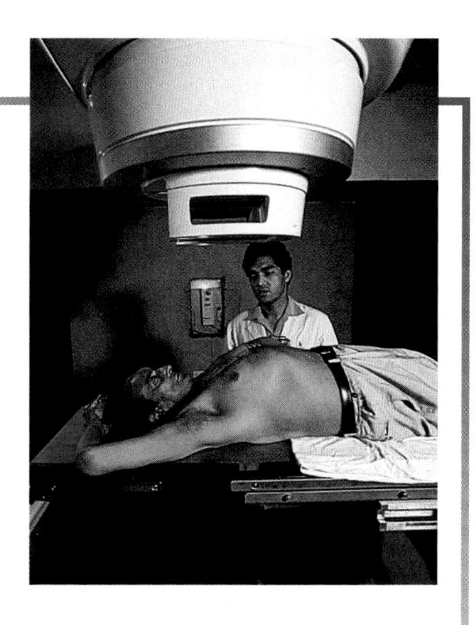

resistant to a particular drug. There are four broad groups of chemotherapy drugs, each of which target DNA in a slightly different way.

- Alkylating agents These include cyclophosphamides and chlorambucil; these form strong bonds with nucleotides, the building blocks of DNA, preventing its replication.
- Antimetabolites These drugs interfere with substances such as folic acid, which are required to make nucleotides. Examples include methotrexate, used in the treatment of breast, lung, and bladder cancers.
- Cytotoxic antibiotics By inserting themselves between nucleotides, these drugs also disrupt DNA function. They include bleomycin, used in testicular cancer.
- Spindle poisons These drugs interfere with the process of cell division.

Side effects of chemotherapy

The drugs used for chemotherapy are toxic not only to cancer cells but also to other cells in the body. There are several unwelcome side effects of this treatment:

- Bone marrow suppression Chemotherapy temporarily destroys the cells produced in the bone marrow. This includes white cells necessary to fight infection, platelets required to clot the blood, and red cells carrying oxygen around the body. Any infection, suspected by a rise in the patient's temperature, is treated promptly with antibiotics. For bleeding gums or skin bruising, platelets can be given. Lack of red blood cells causes anemia, which can lead to fatigue and sometimes to shortness of breath.
- Skin problems Certain drugs may cause dryness, rashes, and discoloration along the veins.
- Digestive problems Soreness of the mouth can occur; it is important to keep the mouth clean. Nausea and sickness are not inevitable and may be treated effectively. Diarrhea and constipation can both occur.
- Fertility problems Some drugs can cause temporary or, occasionally, permanent infertility. Sperm storage for men may be advisable. Women may experience irregular periods and in some cases premature menopause.

RADIOTHERAPY

Radiation therapy is effective in the treatment of localized non-small-cell lung cancer, particularly squamous carcinoma, which tends to be discovered earlier than other lung cancers. The aim is to prevent each cell of a tumor mass from dividing while preserving the integrity of healthy tissue surrounding it. There are several methods of delivering radiotherapy.

External beam radiation

This involves the use of high-energy x-rays and gamma rays, which penetrate tissue and damage DNA. Both are photon beams—tiny "packets" of invisible types of light. The beam from gamma rays is produced by the nuclear decay of cobalt. X-rays produce the photon beam by firing electrons at a metal target (usually tungsten) in a linear accelerator—an x-ray machine that concentrates a narrow, high-power beam. In each case, the beam is aimed at the tumor within a radiation field, marked on the patient's body to ensure the radiation targets the tumor accurately while avoiding, as much as possible, surrounding structures. Identifying the field is a highly complex procedure, involving multiple scans.

Brachytherapy

This is the placement of a radioactive source directly into a tumor or an adjacent body cavity, which minimizes the radiation exposure of the surrounding normal tissue. Commonly used materials include cesium, iridium, and iodine. Tumors of the prostate, cervix, thyroid, and oral cavity are particularly receptive to this treatment.

Photodynamic therapy

This is a more accurately targeted form of radiotherapy in which a light-absorbing substance is injected into the body and is taken up selectively by tumor cells. The tumor is exposed to light at the appropriate wavelength, which activates the substance, killing the cells. This approach is used for tumors of the lung and pleural surfaces, which are easily accessible to the light source.

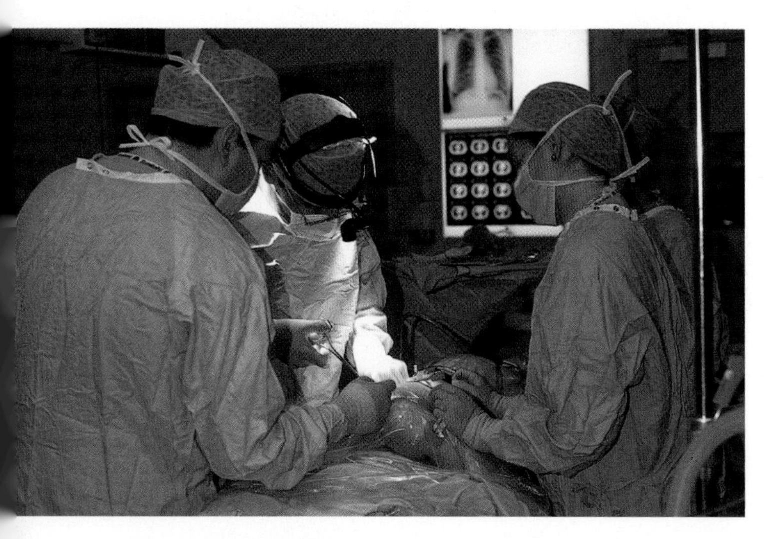

Team of professionals

Surgery on the lungs involves a specialist surgeon and assistants: an anesthetist and operating room nurses. CT images and x-rays are taken into the operating room so that they can be referred to throughout the operation.

Can you live a normal life with only one lung?

Recovery from surgery to remove a lung can take up to a year, but if the operation is successful, patients should be well enough to live normally and exercise—some even return to work. Five-year survival rates are up to 40 percent in some areas. However, the removal of a lung is appropriate only when the cancer has not spread outside the lung. Even if there is no spread, it is not suitable for patients with serious heart or other lung problems. Breathing function tests are usual before surgery, but a patient who has no breathing difficulties before surgery should not experience them after. Chemotherapy may be advised to eradicate remaining cancerous cells.

ASK THE EXPERT

Side effects of radiotherapy

The skin is often affected because this is the tissue that is hit as the beams enter the body. The skin can become red and inflamed or can peel as if sunburned. Although radiotherapy is planned and delivered to minimize damage to surrounding tissues, some damage does occur. Organs that are particularly sensitive include the bowel, bladder, gonads, and nervous system.

SURGICAL TREATMENT

Surgery is the oldest form of cancer therapy and is the most likely treatment for non-small-cell lung cancer. It also remains the only potentially curative treatment for many patients. There are three main reasons for surgery: prevention, treatment, and palliative.

Certain cancers have a premalignant stage, and tests can detect changes in cells before they transform into cancer, allowing surgical removal of the abnormal cells. In other cases, it is possible to remove a tumor and effect a cure. Many operations are performed to improve a patient's quality of life. Some tumors can become painful or block structures such as the gullet. It may be helpful to remove a tumor even if the cancer has spread elsewhere.

Surgical solutions for lung problems

Lung surgery has become routine practice. Good preoperative assessment, safe anesthetic techniques, postoperative care, and advances in surgical technology enable lung operations to be performed safely, and many patients make a complete recovery.

Lung surgery is performed in special thoracic surgical units. Before being admitted, a patient will already have seen other doctors, including their own doctor, a pulmonologist, or an oncologist, and will have undergone tests to establish the underlying condition causing respiratory symptoms. This is an anxious time for patients and their families. By the time of admission to a thoracic unit, however, a patient will have met the consultant surgeon, a likely diagnosis will have been established, and a personalized treatment plan will have been drawn up.

PREPARING FOR A LUNG OPERATION

Most people are admitted to the hospital the day before an operation. Those who are particularly unwell may be admitted earlier. Routine blood tests, chest x-ray, electrocardiogram (ECG), and any other appropriate investigations will be performed. The entire team caring for a patient in the hospital, including doctors (surgical and the anesthetic team), nurses, and therapists, will carry out a full examination, observation, and assessment of each particular case. It is important that a patient continues to take any regular medication until the doctors specifically advise that it should be stopped.

Before surgery, a patient may have any body hair in the region of the incision shaved—typically the side of the chest. The anesthetist sees the patient and explains the options for pain relief during and after surgery, and the patient is asked to sign a consent form (see page 126). On the day of the operation, a period of fasting is needed so that the stomach is empty at the time of surgery.

All these preparations and planning help ensure that the operation and recovery period are as smooth as possible.

Anesthetics

Premedication, either an injection or a tablet, is usually given to relax the patient in readiness for the anesthetic. The patient is then taken to the operating suite, initially to the anesthetic room, where a number of monitoring devices are attached. These include an ECG to monitor the heart and a pulse oxymeter to record the level of oxygen in the blood. A face mask is placed over the nose and mouth to deliver oxygen. The anesthetist will then insert a number of drips, including one in the hand to record blood pressure and one in the hand and one in the neck to give fluids, blood, and drugs. Some of these drips are inserted after the patient is asleep.

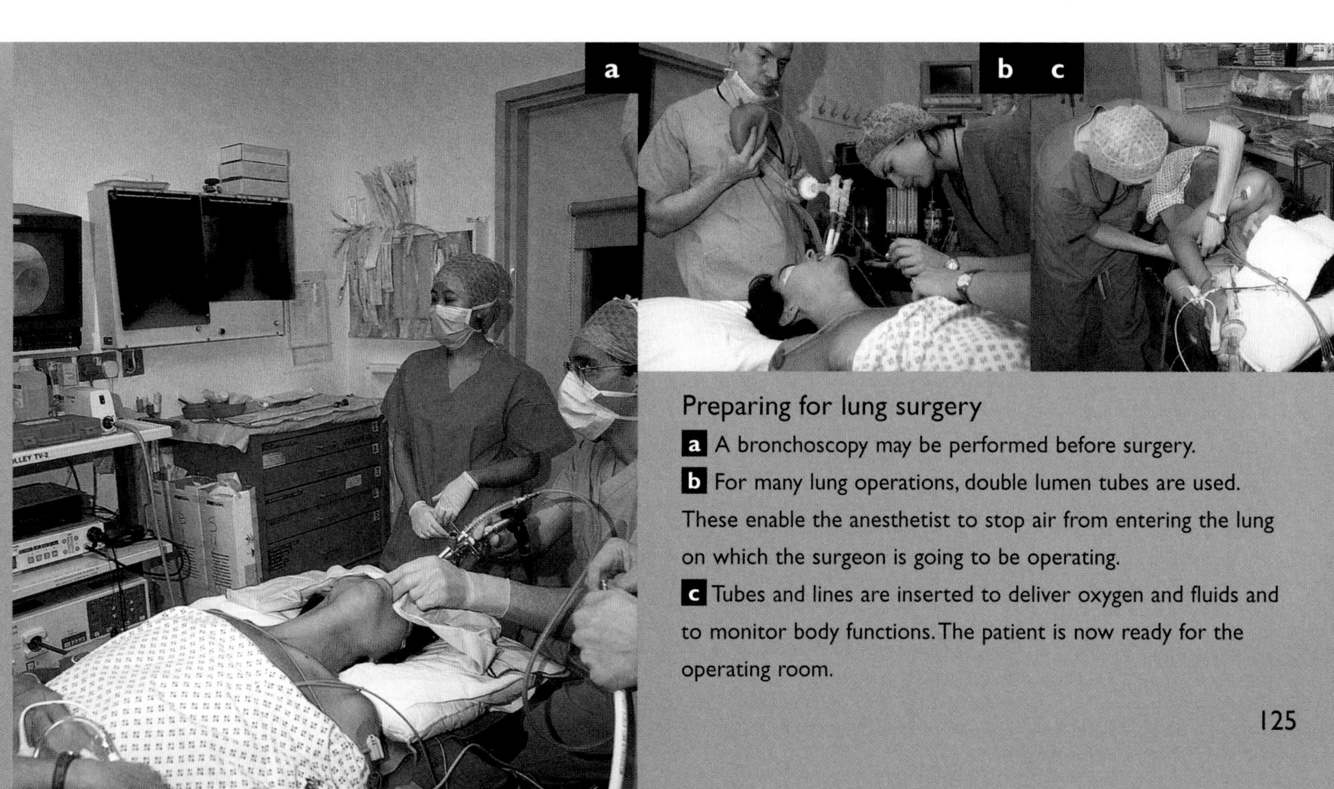

Preparing for lung surgery

a A bronchoscopy may be performed before surgery.

b For many lung operations, double lumen tubes are used. These enable the anesthetist to stop air from entering the lung on which the surgeon is going to be operating.

c Tubes and lines are inserted to deliver oxygen and fluids and to monitor body functions. The patient is now ready for the operating room.

Why do patients sign a consent form?

Before surgery, a doctor will explain the nature of the procedure and its risks and benefits. The consent form is a document that states that a patient has agreed to undergo the proposed operation and is fully aware of the doctors' explanation of the surgery and the risks and benefits involved. A patient is also seen by an anesthetist, who explains the types of anesthetic available for the particular operation. The patient also consents to the anesthetic.

ASK THE EXPERT

The anesthesia begins with an injection in one of the drips to send the patient slowly to sleep. The anesthetist places a tube in the trachea (windpipe) and attaches it to a ventilator that will breathe for the patient during the operation. An epidural for postoperative pain relief is inserted in patients who have chosen this option.

REVEALING THE LUNGS

Once the patient is fully prepared, the surgeon has three principal ways of gaining access to the lungs: thoracotomy, midline sternotomy, and the "keyhole" alternative of video-assisted thoracoscopic surgery (VATS). The method the surgeon selects depends on the operation.

Thoracotomy

Most lung operations are carried out through an incision in the patient's side, a thoracotomy. The size and position of the incision depend on the type of operation and the surgeon's preference. After making the skin incision, the surgeon divides the deeper tissues such as the muscles on the side of the chest using a diathermy needle. This small electric device divides muscle, and heat seals the cut ends of the blood vessels to stop bleeding. Finally, the muscles between the ribs are divided, and the ribs are spread using retractors to reveal the lungs inside the chest cavity. At the end of the operation, the ribs are brought together using sutures, the muscle layers are stitched back together, and the skin is closed. Following most operations requiring a thoracotomy, the recovery period is a week.

Midline sternotomy

Operations involving work on both lungs may be performed through a vertical incision in the front of the chest known as a midline sternotomy. The breastbone is split in half using a special saw; at the end of the procedure, it is put back together using wires.

TRACHEOTOMY

The trachea connects the larynx to the smaller airway leading to the lung. A tracheotomy is an operation to make a small hole in the trachea into which a special tube is inserted. The aim of this procedure is to help with

Video-assisted thoracoscopic surgery (VATS)

1 For this procedure the patient is placed on the side opposite to the lung requiring surgery and covered with sterile drapes.
2 The incisions (or ports) made by the surgeon are only 10–20 millimeters long. Three cuts are usually made, one to take the camera and two—sometimes more—for instruments. The incisions are made using a diathermy needle: This seals the blood vessels as they are cut, so there is no blood in the incisions.
3 For a VATS procedure, the patient must be positioned so that the surgeon, assistant, and nurse can all see the monitor clearly. The surgeon manipulates the surgical instruments according to the video view of the inside of the chest.
4 This operation was carried out to remove blebs—pockets where air was leaking out of the lung. This involved passing a stapler through one of the incisions to seal the abnormal part of

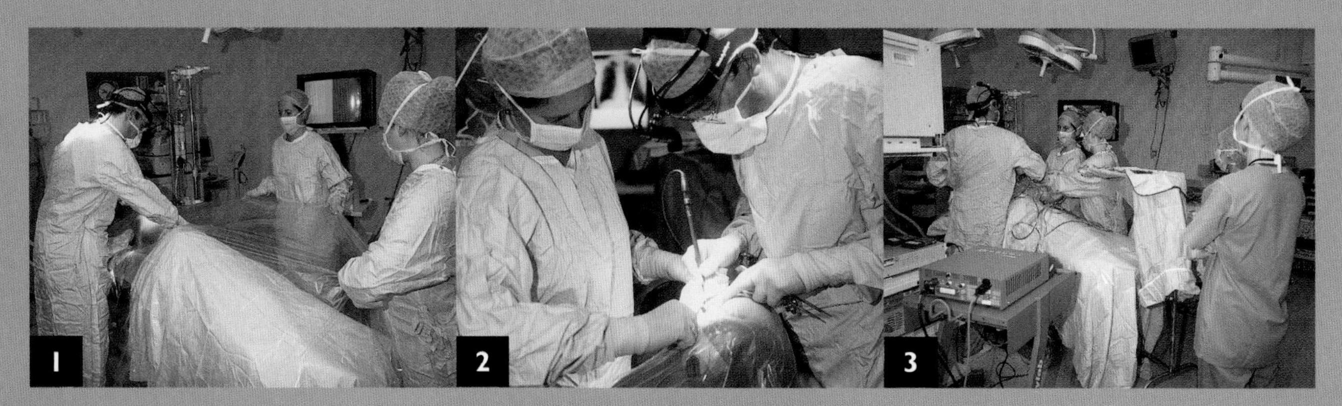

breathing. Most tracheotomies are performed to overcome obstruction of the airway above the trachea, to facilitate weaning from a ventilator, or for prolonged mechanical ventilation. A tracheotomy may also be performed after a laryngectomy, the removal of the voice box.

Surgically planned tracheotomies are performed under general anesthetic. A small incision is made on the front of the neck between the larynx and the breastbone. Deeper tissues are divided to reveal the trachea. An incision is then made in the trachea, and a tracheotomy tube is inserted and secured. The tube is then connected to the ventilator. Tracheotomy reduces the effort required to breathe, which means that some patients with a tracheotomy are able to breathe on their own.

REINFLATING A COLLAPSED LUNG

A two-layered membrane called the pleura normally encloses the lungs. The inner layer covers the lungs, and the outer layer lines the chest wall. The space between, the pleural space, is lubricated, allowing the lungs to move freely. The air that we normally breathe is contained within the lungs. However, occasionally air escapes from the lungs into the pleural space, and the lung collapses. People with asthma and tall, thin men are more prone to a collapsed lung, or pneumothorax. A diagnosis is confirmed on a chest x-ray. The aim of treatment is to remove the air from the chest cavity; treatment is stepped, with the simplest procedures tried first.

- **Aspiration** Under local anaesthetic, a needle and a syringe are used to aspirate the air from around the lung, allowing it to reexpand.
- **Intercostal drain** If aspiration is unsuccessful, a chest drain can be inserted under local anesthetic. If the drain bubbles, this indicates that the air leak from the lung that caused the collapse is persistent. Most air leaks stop with time, usually about a week; failure of a leak to stop is an indication for surgical intervention by pleurectomy, and the source of the air leak needs to be identified and sealed.
- **Pleurodesis** To prevent a lung from collapsing in patients who have had one or more episodes of pneumothorax, it must be made to stick to the inside of the chest wall. This can be achieved by introducing a substance, such as iodized talcum powder, into the pleural space to create an inflammatory response, causing the layers of the pleura to stick together.
- **Pleurectomy** Alternatively, the pleura lining the chest wall, that is, the outer of the two layers of pleura, is stripped away from the chest wall. The absence of the pleura causes the lung to stick to the chest wall, thereby preventing the lung from collapsing in the future. This operation is called a pleurectomy and is performed under a general anesthetic, either through a small thoracotomy incision or using VATS keyhole surgery. The recovery time from this operation is usually between 3 and 5 days in the hospital.

the lung before removing part of the pleura and the intercostal muscles: This tissue can be rolled and extracted through one of the ports. Diathermy is used to stop any bleeding in the lungs.
5 After most lung operations, chest drains are placed in the chest cavity, brought out through the chest wall in between the ribs, and connected to a bottle. Drains allow the air, fluid, or blood that always accumulate after surgery to come out of the chest cavity. After a VATS procedure, the drains are inserted into the same incisions made for the camera and instruments.
6 With drains in place, the patient is given a local anesthetic for postoperative pain relief. The drains stay in place for up to 5 days. Under local anesthetic, the patient is asked to breathe out; at the height of the out-breath, the surgeon removes the drain and stitches the wound.

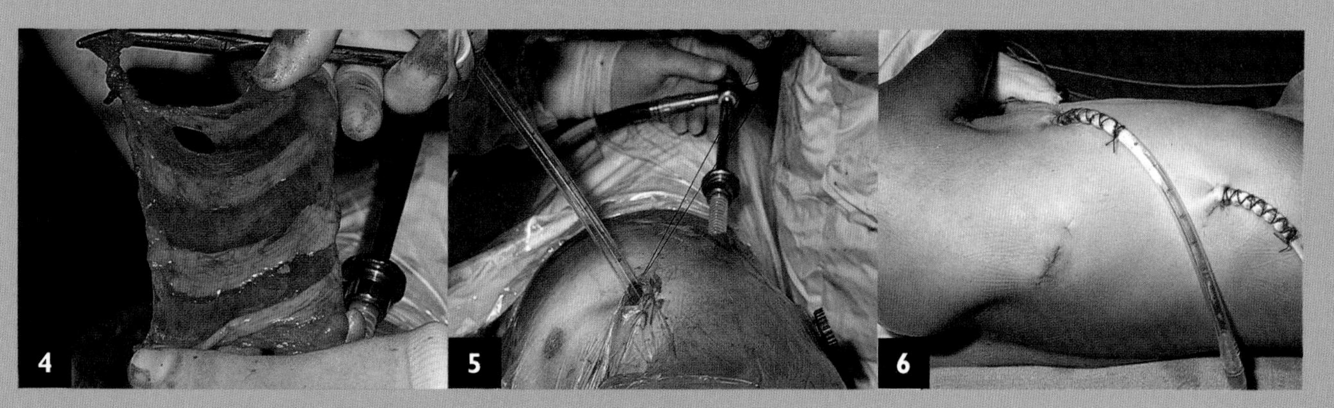

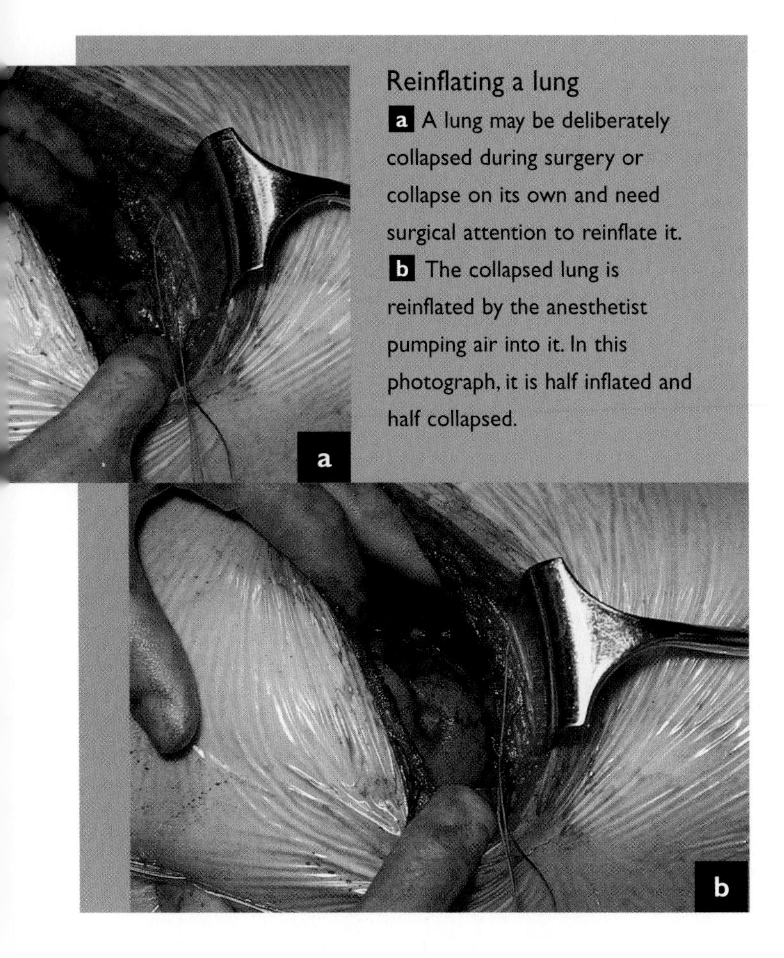

Reinflating a lung

a A lung may be deliberately collapsed during surgery or collapse on its own and need surgical attention to reinflate it.
b The collapsed lung is reinflated by the anesthetist pumping air into it. In this photograph, it is half inflated and half collapsed.

PROBLEMS IN THE PLEURAL SPACE

A number of conditions cause fluid to accumulate in the pleural space. These include many types of cancer, chest infection, and heart failure. Fluid can be removed using pleural aspiration or by a chest drain. Pleurodesis can also be performed to prevent fluid from building up again. Pleurodesis can be performed by introducing a so-called pleurodesing agent into the space through a chest drain. Depending on the fitness of the patient and the exact nature of the illness, this can be done in the ward or under a general anesthesic in the operating room.

In rare situations, the fluid can become infected so that pus surrounds the lung—the condition referred to as empyema. If empyema is diagnosed early and a chest drain is used to eliminate the pus, no further intervention is necessary. If, however, there is a delay in treating the empyema, the pus can thicken and start to encase the lungs with a thick layer of fibrous tissue. In this situation, a thoracotomy is usually necessary to remove all the infected matter from within the chest and the thick lining encasing the lungs. This operation is called decortication, after which the lung expands to fill the available space.

BIOPSY PROCEDURES

A biopsy is performed to allow for further investigation of any abnormality discovered by a scan or x-ray.

Biopsy of the abnormal areas of the lung can be performed through a small thoracotomy or using VATS. A small piece of the abnormal area is removed and sent to the pathologist to examine under the microscope so that a final diagnosis can be made and appropriate treatment started. Sometimes the biopsy is performed by the radiologist using CT scanning to guide a large needle to the abnormal site. Some lymph nodes in the center of the chest can be biopsied by an operation called mediastinoscopy, performed through a small incision just above the breastbone at the bottom of the neck: A keyhole telescope is passed to the center of the chest to take a biopsy of the lymph nodes.

Biopsies of other areas in the center of the chest can be performed by making a small incision at the side of the breastbone. Although most biopsy procedures on lung and lymph nodes in the chest are performed under general anesthesic, these are considered minor operations: The usual recovery time in the hospital is 1–3 days.

TRAUMA

Lungs are well protected, but in high-impact injuries such as a traffic accident, a fall from a height, or a penetrating wound by a sharp object like a knife, the lungs can be injured. In the majority of cases, trauma to the lungs results in air leaking from the lung into the pleural space, leading to a pneumothorax, usually treated by a chest drain. Injury to a major blood vessel, when there is internal bleeding, with blood accumulating in the chest cavity—a condition referred to as hemothorax—is also treated by a chest drain to remove the blood and monitor the amount and rate of blood loss. As a result of such injury, the lungs can be severely bruised, and mechanical ventilation may be necessary (see page 120).

BULLECTOMY

A bulla is an abnormal area of lung tissue that has blown up like a balloon and is occupying a large portion of the chest, preventing good parts of the lung from functioning well. If the bullae are removed, the lung reexpands to fill the space. Depending on the nature, number, and size of the bullae, the surgeon may choose to remove them either by VATS or a thoracotomy. Recovery time is 2–7 days in the hospital.

LUNG-VOLUME REDUCTION SURGERY

This surgical option is offered to some patients with severe emphysema, with the aim of treating their breathlessness. Although the operation is fairly new and not widely available, it has proved an exciting area of development. By removing the most severely diseased parts of the lung, there is more room within the chest cavity for the remainder of the lung, which is able to function better. This also improves the mechanics of breathing by reducing the trapped air, which causes the characteristic barrel chest of emphysema.

REMOVING A LUNG OR PART OF A LUNG

Most lung resections are performed for cancer, but they can also be the treatment of choice when chronic infection is leading to destruction of the lung and in some cases of trauma.

The goal of lung resection is to remove all diseased parts of the lung, with minimal amounts of healthy lung tissue. The extent depends on a number of factors. The removal may involve a localized part of the lung only (local wedge resection), one segment of the lung (segmentectomy), one lobe of the lung (lobectomy), two lobes of the lung (bilobectomy), or the whole of one lung (pneumonectomy).

LUNG TRANSPLANT

During the last 20 years, lung transplantation has become an accepted form of treatment for some conditions that irreversibly damage the lungs. However, the availability of organs hampers this type of surgery: The number of potential recipients always exceeds available organs. Common indications for lung transplantation include cystic fibrosis, emphysema, pulmonary fibrosis, and pulmonary hypertension. Whether a single or a double lung transplant is offered depends on the type of disease.

The diseased lung is removed, and the donor lung is transplanted in its place by connecting the pulmonary artery, pulmonary vein, and the bronchus. The operation is usually performed through a thoracotomy, although other incisions may be used if a double transplant is performed. Following a transplant, a patient has to take immunosuppressant drugs for life to prevent the immune system from rejecting the transplanted lung. Recovery is slow, and careful monitoring of the transplanted organ and recipient are necessary. Success rates range from 70 percent after 1 year to 50 percent after 5 years.

Transplant most often fails for one of two reasons: There was an underlying problem with the transplanted lung or the patient suffers problems relating to the immunosuppressant drugs.

AT THE LEADING EDGE

Da Vinci and Zeus systems

One of the drawbacks of VATS surgery is that the surgeon has to work with images on a flat, two-dimensional screen that represents a three-dimensional space. Improving technology and developments in robotics, however, have led to two new operating systems: da Vinci and Zeus. Through a series of small incisions, cameras and instruments can be introduced inside the chest to create a three-dimensional picture. The surgeon views this image sitting at a computer console and manipulates the surgical instruments from there, while precision robots make the actual movements. This gives a more precise and reliable result, which is less prone to human error. At present this is an area of evolving technology, but this sort of robotic surgery is likely to have a major impact on "keyhole" surgery in the future.

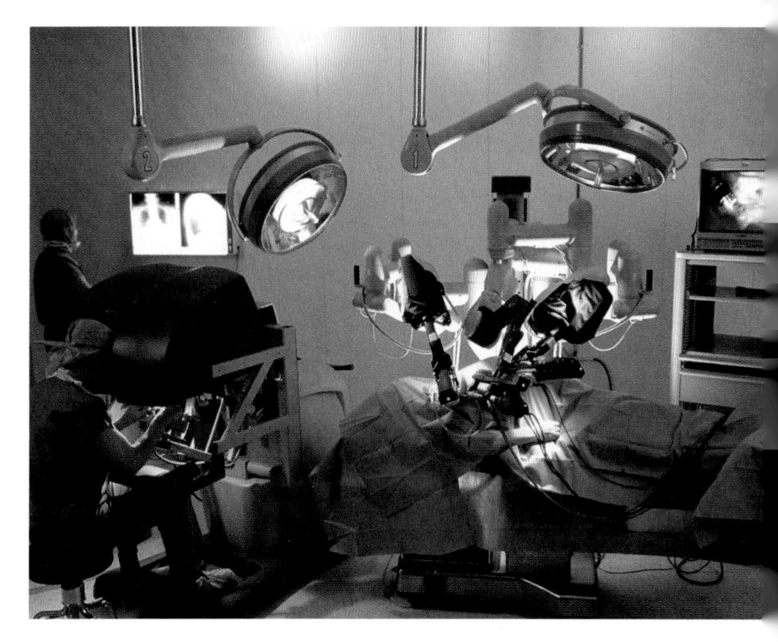

Robotic surgeons

Robotic eyes can magnify a stitch 16 times, hold a long instrument rock-steady, and fine-tune a movement to one millionth of an inch. The surgeon at the console directs the surgery, but the robots do the work.

Resection for lung cancer

Lung cancer is a common condition: There are about 160,000 new cases in the U.S. each year. The exact treatment offered depends on the type of cancer, but surgery in the early stage of lung cancer offers the only prospect of a cure.

Only 15 percent of lung cancer cases are diagnosed at the localized early stage, making them suitable for resection—the removal of an area including the tumor. By the time a diagnosis is made in the majority of cases, the lung cancer is at an advanced stage, and surgery is inappropriate. Other forms of treatment, such as chemotherapy or radiotherapy, may be offered.

Lung resection for lung cancer is a major operation requiring the whole team to function as a unit. The surgical team is led by a thoracic surgeon and assistants. During the operation, the anesthetist will give the general anesthetic. Before surgery, the patient is thoroughly investigated and well prepared.

THE PROCEDURE

Most lung resections are performed using a thoracotomy. Once the patient is fully anesthetised with all monitoring lines and devices attached, the patient is placed on the side and transferred from the anesthetic room to the operating room. The decision whether to remove one lobe, two lobes, or the whole lung is made in the operating room, after examination of the lymph nodes.

After surgery, the patient is taken to a recovery room and monitored until the anesthetic has worn off, before being transferred to the ward.

Imaging and removing a tumor

Some lung tumors are so large when diagnosed that they are inoperable. This tumor of the left lung (below left, on CT scan) was invading the fat of the mediastinum and the pleura. The patient was referred for chemotherapy, which shrunk the tumor, allowing the surgeon to perform a lobectomy, removing the whole upper lobe of the left lung, including the tumor (below right). The area of lung removed measured 6.3 x 4.1 x 2.0 inches. The yellow areas on the lung are areas of tumor tissue killed by the chemotherapy.

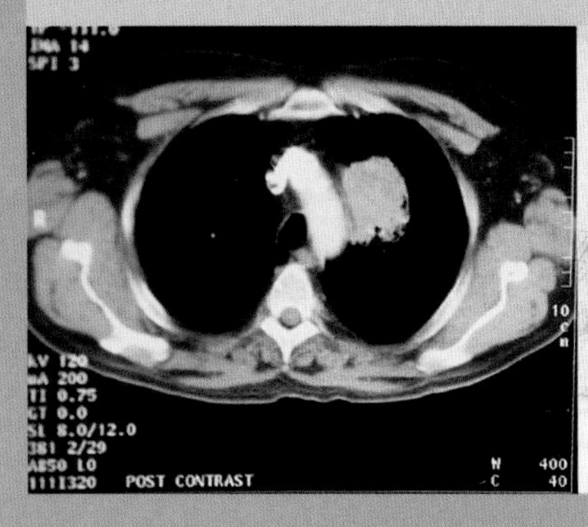

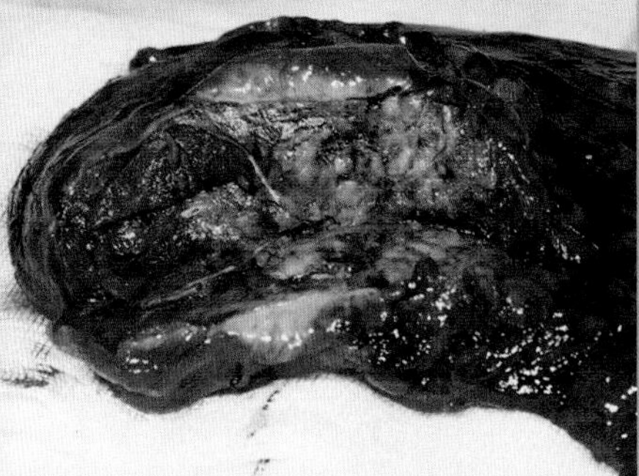

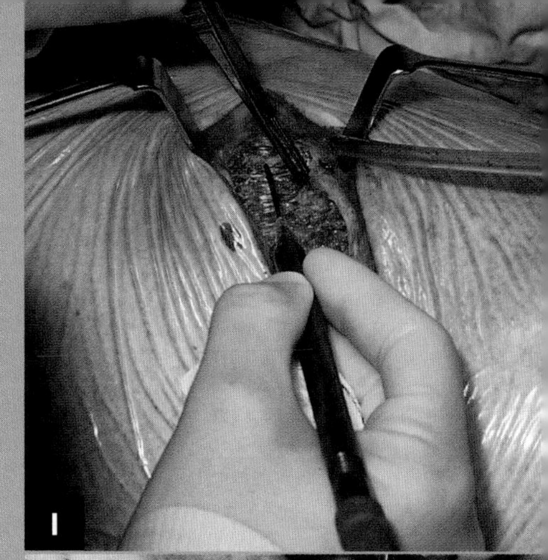

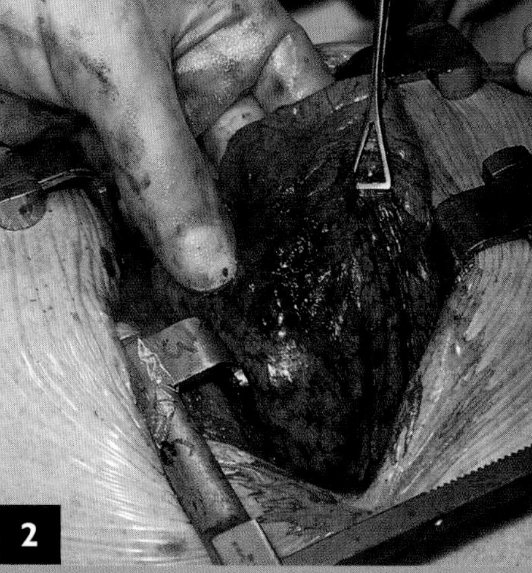

The surgical procedure

1 The area of the incision is cleaned with a special solution to decontaminate it as much possible, then the patient is covered with sterile plastic drapes, and the operation can begin. The surgeon makes a skin incision and continues through the deeper tissues, using a diathermy needle to divide the muscle layers at the side of the chest.

2 The pleura is opened and held back with forceps. Retractors hold back the ribs. The anesthetist collapses the lung that is to be worked on.

3 The surgeon uses a hand to make a space between the chest wall and pleura so that the lung can be reached. The pleura and fat are left attached to the lung to ensure that all cancerous tissue is removed.

4 Lymph glands are removed from designated areas of the mediastinum, hilum, and fissures between the lobes for analysis; this is termed a frozen section.

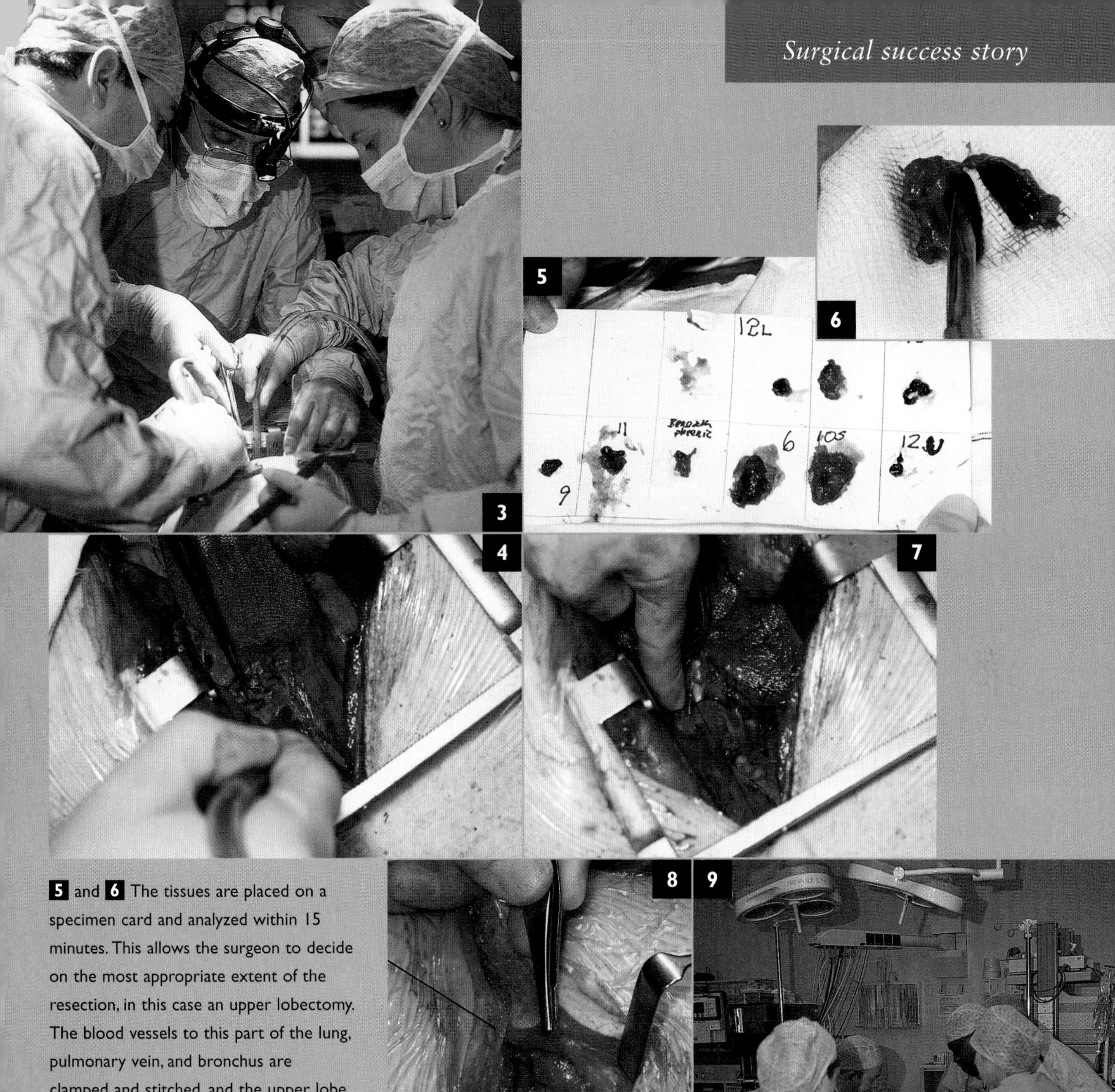

5 and **6** The tissues are placed on a specimen card and analyzed within 15 minutes. This allows the surgeon to decide on the most appropriate extent of the resection, in this case an upper lobectomy. The blood vessels to this part of the lung, pulmonary vein, and bronchus are clamped and stitched, and the upper lobe is removed and sent for analysis.

7 Water is used to wash out the pleural space and ensure that the closure of the bronchus is watertight; then chest drains are inserted. The remaining lower lobe of the left lung is reinflated.

8 The ribs are brought together again using stitches, and layers of tissue, muscle, and skin are stitched.

9 The patient is given a long-acting local anesthetic for postoperative pain relief, then moved to a bed in the recovery room.

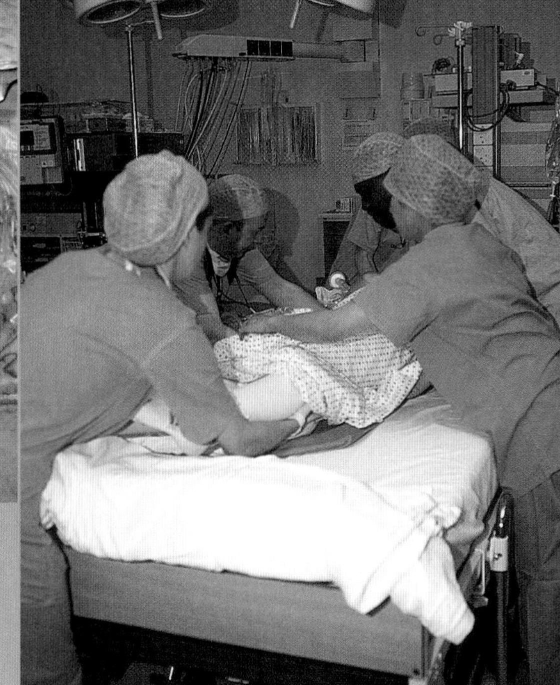

Palliative care

Palliative care as a speciality in its own right originated with the development of the hospice movement in the 1960s. The movement's aim was to "provide total care of the patients whose disease is no longer responsive to curative treatment."

Palliative care is a successful part of hospice care for those with cancer and other incurable conditions, with death seen as "a final stage of growth." Effective pain management is a key component of palliative care.

PAIN MANAGEMENT

Pain is a complex symptom, and often physical pain is increased by emotional factors such as anxiety, anger, or fear. The quality or type of pain helps to determine the appropriate treatment. Somatic pain—the type that arises from skin, joints, tendons, and teeth—is usually localized. By contrast, visceral pain, which arises from damage to internal organs such as the gut, liver, lungs, or heart, is often poorly localized and "referred" to distant sites. Neuropathic pain arises from damaged nerve tissue and is often described as burning, stinging, or stabbing.

The use of drugs

Analgesic drugs are the mainstay of managing pain, particularly somatic pain. They are introduced in a stepwise fashion starting with mild painkillers and building up to stronger opium-related drugs (opioids). Mild pain is controlled with paracetamol or NSAIDs. Moderate-to-severe pain requires the use of opioid analgesics. These drugs act in a way similar to that of the naturally occurring endorphins that are released by the body in response to pain. With repeated use of opioids, progressively larger doses are required to produce the same pain relief. This is known as tolerance to the drugs.

The milder opioids, such as codeine, can be given as tablets. Severe pain is treated with morphine, either liquid or tablets, or by injection. Alternatively, an adhesive patch or an automated release mechanism allows continuous release of drugs through the skin. Neuropathic pain responds better to antidepressants and antiepileptics.

OTHER ASPECTS OF CARE

- Cachexia Progressive, involuntary weight loss is thought to be caused, in part, to substances produced by the immune system in an attempt to eradicate the tumor. Nutrition may be improved by giving a patient high-calorie, high-protein drinks and foods.
- Dehydration As patients approach death, appetite and thirst diminish. Clinical studies show fasting to help rather than cause discomfort by increasing the level of endorphins in the body. Dryness of the mouth caused by thirst may be relieved with ice chips.
- Confusion Changing levels of consciousness, defects in memory, and disturbances in the sleep/wake cycle are all common and may upset the patient and family. Causes may include disease in the brain, the use of morphine, and disturbances in the electrolytes of the body. Knowledge of these mechanisms and correction where possible may help to ease distress.
- Spiritual care A holistic approach to dying, with the participation of religious representatives, may assist patients in finding meaning and purpose in the final stage of illness and life.

TALKING POINT

Do complementary therapies have a role in palliative care?

Complementary therapies cannot replace conventional treatments for cancer or other life-threatening diseases, but they can support them, either to control symptoms or to improve a patient's quality of life and well-being. Some therapies are relaxing, which can lessen the perception of pain: these include meditation and visualization. Aromatherapy oils can be both relaxing and stimulating, depending on the oils chosen. Many patients benefit from the one-to-one relationship built up during a course of massage or reflexology sessions and may feel calmed or invigorated afterward. Others find peace and solace in the so-called talking therapies and through sessions with a counselor may find themselves able to come to terms with their situation. A doctor or nurse can offer advice on therapists in the hospital, hospice, or local community.

A TO Z OF DISEASES AND DISORDERS

This section gives information on the main illnesses and medical conditions that affect the lungs and respiratory system.

This index is divided into two sections: Symptoms, and Diseases and disorders. Within these sections, entries are arranged alphabetically, and each is structured in a similar way:

What are the causes?

What are the symptoms?

How is it diagnosed?

What are the treatment options?

What is the outlook?

SYMPTOMS

BREATHLESSNESS

All of us have experienced breathlessness—the sensation of the effort of breathing. Most of the time it is a normal reaction to exertion, but occasionally it is indicative of respiratory or lung disease.

Breathlessness is natural when it occurs during or immediately after strenuous exertion or at an altitude where there is less oxygen in the air. Some people become breathless when anxious, and people who do not get regular exercise or are overweight experience breathlessness even with minor exertion. This can lead to a mistaken belief that serious illness is responsible. Clinical examination and investigations such as chest x-rays and electrocardiograms can rule this out. However, breathlessness can be a result of disease, particularly of the lungs or heart.

What diseases cause breathlessness?

The onset and pattern of breathlessness, together with other symptoms and risk factors, give clues to the cause:

- Pneumothorax (p. 149) This condition causes sudden breathlessness at rest, often with pain in the pleura, the membrane lining the thorax and covering the lung. The pain is sharp and worse on breathing in.
- Pulmonary embolism (p. 150) A condition that can occur after surgery or a long journey or in those taking a contraceptive pill; it may also cause breathlessness.
- Pulmonary edema (p. 150) This failure of the left ventricle of the heart to pump effectively causes breathlessness, which is worse when lying down. Patients may have to sleep propped up on pillows and often have other health risks such as high blood pressure, smoking, a previous heart attack, or angina.

Other illnesses that cause breathlessness include pneumonia (p. 149), usually accompanied by a cough, fever, and sometimes excess sputum. In asthma (p. 139) and chronic obstructive pulmonary disease (COPD, p. 142), breathlessness may be worse at night, typically with a cough, wheeze and, in COPD, sputum. Breathlessness caused by pulmonary fibrosis (p. 151) tends to develop over a period of months and may be associated with certain occupations. Lung cancer by itself may not initially cause breathlessness, but as it progresses, it can do so for a number of reasons, including obstruction of a large airway, an associated pleural effusion, or by causing anemia. Weight loss would usually also be observed.

CHOKING

Choking is the complete obstruction of the larynx, either by the tongue or a foreign body.

Usually caused by a lump of food, choking may also result from any object that is put in the mouth, such as chewing gum or an eraser from the end of a pencil, or from being sick. Food is transferred during swallowing from the front of the throat, over the airway, to the esophagus, which lies behind the larynx. Normally, the larynx is protected by the epiglottis. This mechanism may go wrong, and food gets under the epiglottis and enters the larynx. Choking is the coughing spasm and spluttering that result. If choking is not remedied, the inability to breathe starves the brain of oxygen in as few as 3 minutes.

Choking on food often happens when trying to talk and eat simultaneously, especially if coordination is impaired by excess alcohol—one reason why it often occurs in restaurants. It is also more common in people who have suffered epileptic seizures or neurological problems, such as stroke, or after surgery for throat cancer, which may damage the swallowing muscles. When people are unconscious, the tongue may fall back and obstruct the larynx. This occurs under general anesthetic, when the anesthetist monitors the airway. It may also happen in cases of alcohol or drug overdose and with a concussion, for example, following a sporting injury.

COUGH

The most common respiratory symptom, coughing is the body's attempt to maintain clear airways.

The entire lining of the respiratory tract contains sensory receptors. When these are stimulated, for instance by the presence of a foreign body, a reflex is triggered involving a "cough center" in the brain stem. This reflex leads to coordinated movement of the diaphragm and larynx, forcing air out of the lungs, which is heard as a cough.

What causes a cough?

Among the most common causes of coughing are infections, from pharyngitis and bronchitis to pneumonia. These cause inflammation, leading to the release of irritant chemicals from immune system cells, and sputum production, which both cause coughing. Cigarette smoke contains many different irritant chemicals, and sooner or later all smokers will develop a persistent cough.

How can you best help someone who is choking?

If the person is still conscious, sharp thrusts with the heel of your hand between the shoulder blades may help. If this does not work, use the Heimlich maneuver. Stand behind the person with your arms around the waist. Wrap one of your hands around your other fist to form a ball, then sharply dig your fist under the ribs, pulling upward and inward. This increases the pressure in the chest and should force the object out of the larynx.

If the person is already unconscious, you will not hear the choking but should suspect it if you cannot see regular chest movements. Look in the mouth and remove any obvious objects or vomit. Make sure the tongue is not in the way by putting your fingers behind the angles of the jaw and thrusting the tongue forward: be careful not to move the head so you will not exacerbate any spinal injury.

ASK THE EXPERT

In asthma, chronic inflammation of the lung lining not only causes a cough but also makes the lungs irritable and more likely to respond to other stimuli—such as cold air, exercise, pollen, and dust—by producing a cough or wheeze. In severe asthma, the lining of the lung becomes damaged, exposing the underlying nerve endings and making a cough even more easily provoked.

Many other lung and heart diseases, including cancer, pulmonary fibrosis, and heart failure, may cause a cough. It may also result from drugs such as angiotensin-converting enzyme (ACE) inhibitors, which cause an increase in the production of the natural irritant bradykinin. Weakness of the laryngeal muscles, which control the epiglottis, may cause chronic aspiration, in which saliva and food "go down the wrong way." This is common after a stroke and may pass unrecognized other than by coughing after meals.

Severe prolonged coughing may even result in fainting. Known as cough syncope, this is due to sudden changes in pressure in the chest, preventing oxygenated blood from reaching the brain. Fortunately, the fainting usually stops the cough and allows recovery.

Treating a cough

Many cough medicines are available in pharmacies. These medicines either coat the throat to reduce its irritability or contain codeine, a mild opium-based drug that reduces coughing by acting on the cough center in the brain. This treatment may be effective for short-term infections, but prolonged coughing should be medically investigated.

CYANOSIS

This is the blue color of tissues when they are deprived of oxygen. There are two types of cyanosis.

Peripheral cyanosis refers to blueness of the extremities, such as the fingers, toes, and tip of the nose, because of the constriction of blood vessels. This may be normal, for instance in cold weather, or it could be a sign of central cyanosis, which is always abnormal. This is also indicated by blueness around the lips and tongue. Central cyanosis signals a decrease in blood oxygen to less than 85 percent, which is dangerously low—it is normally above 95 percent.

Any severe respiratory disease may cause central cyanosis. In abnormally functioning lungs, the amount of oxygen in the lungs becomes patchy. Blood is diverted to areas where there is less oxygen, with the result that areas with normal oxygen levels receive little blood to oxygenate. This is known as ventilation-perfusion mismatch and results in lower levels of oxygen being carried away in the pulmonary veins back to the heart and the rest of the body.

The underlying cause must be treated, and oxygen is given through a mask. In severe cases, patients may need a ventilating machine to breathe for them.

HEMOPTYSIS

Hemoptysis is the medical term for coughing up blood. It should always be discussed with a doctor.

Coughing up blood indicates damage to blood vessels in the lining of the lung. Sometimes it is difficult to be sure if blood has come from the nose and dripped into the back of the throat, or even if it has been vomited up from the stomach, but investigation is warranted whatever the cause. Usually, the airways are examined with a bronchoscope.

Blood coughed up with sputum usually indicates an infection, such as bacterial pneumonia, tuberculosis, or bronchiectasis. If blood is coughed up alone, the main concern is a possible tumor. Trauma to the chest, bleeding disorders such as hemophilia, large pulmonary emboli, and vasculitis (inflammation of blood vessels) may also be responsible. Rarely, a major artery may be affected and cause massive hemoptysis, which can be fatal.

HICCUPS

Spasms or irritation of the diaphragm.

What is the cause?

Although hiccups are usually harmless, if difficult to alleviate, they can occasionally be a sign of an abscess of the diaphragm or an even more serious disease, such as lung cancer when it has invaded the diaphragm.

What are the treatment options?

The various "folk cures" for hiccups, such as holding one's breath, work by changing the pattern of breathing, which in turn alters the flow of nervous impulses from the diaphragm to break the cycle. Continued hiccups can be unpleasant, and treatment is unsatisfactory (other than removal of any underlying cause, such as surgery for an abscess that fails to clear). Sedative drugs such as chlorpromazine are used to reduce anxiety.

HYPERVENTILATION

An increased rate of breathing resulting in a decrease in the amount of carbon dioxide in the blood.

Hyperventilation usually occurs in people who are tense, nervous, or under stress, but it may also be a symptom of an underlying respiratory problem such as asthma, bronchiolitis, pleurisy, and pulmonary fibrosis. It may occur on its own, but it can also be accompanied by further symptoms such as cyanosis, pain, and shortness of breath.

How is it treated?

Hyperventilation can be treated at home by breathing into a paper bag (p. 43): This returns some carbon dioxide to the bloodstream, helping to normalize levels. This may take anywhere from 5 to 15 minutes, during which it is important to reassure the patient that hyperventilation is a symptom, not a disease. Usually, once the panic subsides, normal breathing is resumed. Repeated attacks, particularly if accompanied by pain, should be investigated by a doctor to rule out a more serious underlying condition. Stress management may be useful.

HYPOVENTILATION

A reduction in the rate and depth of breathing that causes a drop in blood oxygen and a rise in blood carbon dioxide.

Hypoventilation occurs when the "respiratory center" in the brain stem, which controls respiration, is not functioning properly. The most common causes of this malfunction are sedatives such as alcohol and drugs, including morphine-based painkillers and sleeping pills taken therapeutically or in overdose. Severe brain disease such as stroke or brain hemorrhage may also produce the effect. Hypoventilation may be caused if chest movement is impaired; this may be a result of obesity, weakness of the respiratory muscles (for instance, in motor neuron disease), or diseases affecting the rib cage, such as tuberculosis of the spine during childhood or congenital scoliosis (bending of the spine). Acute hypoventilation, for instance with a morphine overdose, may be fatal. Chronic hypoventilation, for instance in obesity, is usually mild but does place extra strain on the heart, which after months or years may lead to heart failure.

How is it treated?

Treatment of hypoventilation depends on its cause. Mild hypoventilation caused by being overweight can be remedied by losing weight. In severe cases, treatment may include breathing apparatus such as a noninvasive ventilator, in which inadequate breathing at night is aided by a mask attached to a machine.

SPUTUM

Sputum (or "phlegm") is excess mucus produced by the respiratory tract.

Under normal circumstances, the cells lining the airways produce a thin layer of clear fluid—mucus. This prevents the airways from drying out and enables foreign particles, including bacteria, to be removed by the coordinated beating action of the cilia, or tiny hairs, on the surface of the lining. When the mucus reaches the top of the airways, it spills over into the pharynx and is harmlessly swallowed.

The lungs respond to any irritant, such as cigarette smoke, by increasing the production of mucus, which stimulates coughing; this extra mucus is coughed up as sputum or phlegm. During infections, the sputum captures bacterial debris, together with immune cells such as neutrophils and macrophages attempting to engulf the bacteria. This makes the sputum thicker and green-yellow in color. Sputum may also contain blood if blood vessels are damaged, as in tuberculosis and lung cancer (see Hemoptysis).

As an aid to diagnosis, sputum samples may be examined under the microscope for the presence of bacteria or cancer cells. Sputum can also be cultured in nutrients in an agar gel to grow any bacterial colonies that may not have been visible under the microscope. This takes up to 6 weeks.

STRIDOR

Stridor is a noise heard when breathing in. It is caused by severe narrowing of the upper airways.

The difference between stridor and wheezing is that a wheeze is heard when breathing out, whereas stridor occurs when breathing in. Wheezing is caused by narrowing in the lower airways; stridor is a medical emergency because of the risk that the upper airway could become completely obstructed and cause respiratory failure.

What causes stridor?

Stridor may occur suddenly after accidental inhalation of a foreign body associated with choking (p. 134), or it may occur gradually over several hours, such as in viral croup and epiglottitis. Both these conditions cause swelling and excess secretions of the upper airways, but epiglottitis, a bacterial infection of the epiglottis caused by *Haemophilus influenzae* type B, carries a much greater risk of obstruction of the airway. The stridor may be audible to the ear or amplified by placing a stethoscope over the throat. In viral croup, the stridor is usually harsh-sounding, whereas in epiglottitis it is soft and blowing, reflecting the more severe narrowing. Occasionally, stridor is slow in onset and is the result of tumors of the upper respiratory tract or of compression of the airway by an enlarged thyroid gland. Tests including computed tomography scans, and flow-volume loops (p. 100) can be used to confirm the severity and cause of the stridor.

How is it treated?

The management of stridor depends on the underlying cause. Choking must be treated immediately to remove the foreign body (p. 134). In a child with viral croup or epiglottitis, it is important to avoid examining the throat directly with instruments or mirrors because this can precipitate complete obstruction. Close monitoring in the hospital is important, with appropriate, usually penicillin-based, antibiotics to combat *Haemophilus* and intravenous fluids if swallowing is difficult. If complete obstruction is believed to be imminent, an anesthetist is called to sedate the patient before passing an endotracheal tube past the obstruction into the airway to ensure that adequate respiration is maintained to supply vital organs. The patient needs to be ventilated mechanically in an intensive care unit. All other causes of stridor are treated by surgery or radiation.

WHEEZE

A wheeze is a high-pitched whistling sound from the lungs. It is audible when breathing out and, if severe, sometimes when breathing in.

A wheeze is the result of air being forced through narrowed airways. If the narrowing occurs in the small airways, the resulting sound, when heard through a stethoscope, seems to have many pitches and is termed a polyphonic wheeze. Less commonly, wheezing may be caused by obstruction of a single large airway, in which case it has only one pitch and is termed monophonic. This may be heard on one side of the chest only. Wheezing is not harmful, but because it narrows the airways, the lungs have to work harder, and shortness of breath usually results. Also, the air becomes trapped in the lungs, causing them to hyperinflate, which makes breathing harder still.

What causes wheezing?

Polyphonic wheezing is most commonly the result of asthma, although it can occur in severe left ventricular failure. The airways are narrowed because of inflammation, which causes swelling of the airway lining, increased mucus, and constriction or spasm of the smooth muscle surrounding the airway. The severity of the narrowing may be gauged by the use of a peak flow meter (p. 99). The more severe the narrowing, the lower the peak flow rate.

How is it treated?

A wheeze is best treated by anti-inflammatory drugs, such as inhaled steroids, but in the short term it can be treated with drugs such as albuterol and salmetrol, which reduce muscle spasm. In severe heart failure, the wheeze is a result of fluid in the small airways, which can be reversed with diuretic treatment. Monophonic wheeze may be caused by narrowing of a large airway by a tumor such as cancer in the lung. It may eventually block the airway completely, leading to collapse of the lung. The wheeze will not improve unless the underlying cause is treated.

DISEASES AND DISORDERS

ABSCESS

A mass of dead tissue, fluid, bacteria, and living and dead white blood cells.

What are the causes?

Lung abscesses are always caused by pus-forming bacteria, some of which are more commonly found in alcoholics and drug users. If the bacteria survive and multiply, the abscess can enlarge, and the pus-filled cells are gradually replaced by scar tissue, forming a chronic abscess.

Only two ingredients are needed to make an abscess, an area of dead tissue and some bacteria, so lung abscesses can occur as a complication of many lung conditions, including infections, tumors, and emboli.

What are the symptoms?

The symptoms of an abscess depend on its underlying cause. A patient suffering from a respiratory tract infection complicated by the formation of an abscess will be very unwell, coughing up foul, bloodstained phlegm.

How is it diagnosed?

An x-ray of the chest will show a round shadow containing fluid. A CT scan can help to better define the abscess. Sometimes it is necessary to retrieve a sample of bacteria-filled fluid from inside the abscess (p. 103) for analysis.

What are the treatment options?

Treatment usually involves an intensive course of antibiotics and physical therapy. If there is an underlying tumor or if the abscess fails to resolve, surgery is required to remove it.

ACUTE RESPIRATORY DISTRESS SYNDROME (ARDS)

ARDS is not a disease in itself but a product of many different serious illnesses.

ARDS occurs because of extensive damage to the air sacs (alveoli) in the lungs. These sacs are lined by a membrane that is designed to allow oxygen to pass into the blood and to allow carbon dioxide to be breathed out (gaseous exchange). If alveoli are damaged, fluid leaks into them from the blood vessels, making gaseous exchange increasingly difficult. It is as if the lungs are drowning in their own fluid.

What are the causes?

Illnesses associated with ARDS include major injury to the brain; infections, such as pneumonia, that have spread to the blood; major burns; near-drowning; inhaling toxic fumes; and the effects of some anticancer drugs. The tissue damage caused by these conditions releases chemicals that spread via the blood and damage the lungs.

What are the symptoms?

Symptoms occur 12–24 hours after the event and include breathlessness, coughing, and, because oxygen does not reach the body tissues in adequate quantities, cyanosis.

How is it diagnosed?

The diagnosis is suspected by the presence of a known causal factor as listed above, by low blood oxygen levels, and from evidence of widespread damage on a chest x-ray. The hallmark of the condition is lung "stiffness" because of loss of elasticity of the damaged alveoli. The stiffness means that very high pressure is required to force air into the lungs.

What are the treatment options?

In addition to treating the precipitating event, it is often necessary to manage the patient in intensive care with the help of a life-support machine. This allows oxygen to be delivered efficiently to the lungs, either using a mask or a tube passed into the trachea while the patient is sedated. Other organs, such as the heart and kidneys, may be affected by the inflammatory chemicals generated in the lung as a response to the injury, leading to multiorgan failure.

What is the outlook?

Prognosis is generally poor. ARDS kills more than 40 percent of those affected, despite intensive care. Those who survive the acute phase are at risk of the lungs becoming scarred, resulting in breathlessness on physical effort.

ALLERGY

An exaggerated reaction of the immune system to a variety of molecules, or allergens. The inherited tendency to develop allergies is known as atopy.

What are the causes?

Common allergens include grass pollen; the feces of the dust mite; the saliva and dander of cats and dogs; foods such as shellfish, peanuts, and fruits; medications such as penicillin; insect stings; and latex.

Hygiene and allergies

TALKING POINT

The incidence of allergies and allergic diseases has increased dramatically in the last 30 years, particularly in the Western world. More than 10 percent of children now develop asthma and eczema. One theory to explain this increase is known as the hygiene hypothesis. With improved standards of living and the widespread use of antibiotics, our infants and children are much less exposed to bacteria and parasites. At the same time, they spend much more time indoors, where their exposure to allergens can be high, particularly those from dust mites, which inhabit our carpets, curtains, and bedding, and from domestic animals. This may lead to faulty "programming" of the immune system in early life, activating an inherited tendency to atopy, which then produces allergic disease.

What are the symptoms?

There are two main types of allergic disease. The first is a group of sudden severe reactions, such as urticaria (acute skin rash), angioedema (swelling in the mouth and throat), and anaphylactic shock (collapse with low blood pressure). These reactions are most frequently provoked by certain foods and medications. The second type includes chronic diseases such as hay fever, perennial rhinitis (blocked or runny nose with sneezing), and childhood-onset asthma and eczema, which have an allergic component among other factors.

The allergic reaction proceeds in two stages. The first exposure to an allergen results in "sensitization," which involves the production of large amounts of a type of antibody known as IgE. This binds to a type of immune cell known as a mast cell and acts as the body's "memory" of the allergen. The next time that the body comes into contact with the allergen, the IgE antibody recognizes it, triggering the mast cell to produce substances that attract other immune cells, including T cells and eosinophils. Unfortunately, these substances, which include histamine and leukotrienes, provoke symptoms, such as swelling of mucous membranes, causing, for example, nasal blockage; constriction of the smooth muscle of the airways, which in turn causes wheezing; and in severe cases, a rapid drop in blood pressure, leading to collapse or anaphylaxis.

Available on prescription, an EpiPen is an easy-to-use, self-administered injection device that contains a dose of epinephrine. Anyone who has ever suffered anaphylactic shock should carry one.

What are the treatment options?

Where possible, allergens should be avoided. Treatments include anti-inflammatory drugs such as corticosteroids. Severe reactions may need emergency treatments such as epinephrine, which can be injected by patients into their thigh muscles.

ASTHMA

A common condition, asthma affects 5 percent of the American population, and the incidence is increasing.

When an asthma sufferer is exposed to certain stimuli, an attack occurs that makes the muscles wrapped around the airways spasm, causing narrowing of the airways and difficulty in breathing. At the same time, in response to the invader, the cells of the airways secrete more mucus, further narrowing the airways. Asthma is a chronic condition; most attacks are mild and easily treated, but asthma still kills about 4,500–5,000 people in the U.S. each year.

What are the causes?

There are many well-known asthma triggers. Unfortunately, it is not always possible to discover which one is responsible for an attack in a particular individual.

Common nonspecific factors that can bring on an attack include cold air, exercise, strong emotion, infections of the airways, smoke, and even laughter. In certain industries there is contact with material known to cause asthma: examples include soldering flux in the engineering industry, cotton dust encountered in textiles, flour and grain, and the dander of animals. The house dust mite, grass, and pollen are also common asthma triggers. A tendency to atopy, which may show itself as asthma, runs in families and may begin at an early age; in addition to asthma, atopy may cause eczema or hay fever.

What are the symptoms?

An asthma patient experiences periods with no symptoms at all and can lead a normal active life. During an attack, however, symptoms include shortness of breath, coughing, and wheezing as the air whistles through the tight airways. In a severe attack, the sufferer uses extra muscles to help with the action of breathing.

How is it diagnosed?

A first asthma attack can be frightening, especially for a young child. Anyone who experiences breathing difficulties following a respiratory infection should visit his or her doctor; many hospitals now have specialist asthma clinics. A peak flow meter (p. 99) is a method of measuring if and to what extent the airways are narrowed. Patients are taught to keep diaries of measurements. Given the variability of asthma, serial measurements help in monitoring the disease. Usually, asthma is worst at night or in the early morning; this is demonstrated by dips in flow readings in the morning.

What are the treatment options?

In some cases it is possible to identify specific triggers involved in a patient's asthma. By avoiding these triggers, the patient can avoid attacks.

Chronic asthma One of the most important steps in the management of the disease is education of the patient. This helps prevent severe attacks because patients use their medication at the first sign of difficulties, and it encourages patients to seek early advice if their treatment is failing. The drugs are usually delivered by means of an inhaler, which directly targets the inflammation in the walls of the airways and the hyperactivity of the surrounding muscles.

- Bronchodilators dilate the airways by relaxing the muscles that are in spasm. These drugs act immediately, giving fast relief of symptoms. It is not necessary to use them regularly. Bronchodilators include albuterol, atrovent, and theophylline, a caffeine derivative.
- Steroids such as beclomethasone act on the inflammatory cells, which are present even during a symptom-free period, and these drugs therefore need to be taken regularly to help prevent symptoms. Steroids are known to cause many unwanted side effects, including thinning of the bones, but inhalers minimize these effects by delivering the drugs locally.

Acute severe asthma An attack that does not respond to bronchodilators is a life-threatening medical emergency. Doctors use indicators such as a patient's inability to complete sentences and the speed of breathing and heartbeat to assess the severity of an attack. The extent of airway narrowing can be measured using a peak flow meter. A blood test is taken in the hospital or ambulance to determine how much oxygen is being delivered to the tissues and how much carbon dioxide is being expelled. The lower the oxygen level and the higher the carbon dioxide level, the more the respiratory system is failing. Oxygen treatment may be necessary. In this situation, bronchodilator drugs are usually delivered via a nebulizer, a "cloud-forming" device that allows the drug to be dissolved in a solution and delivered via a mask in the form of a vapor at a time when the patient is struggling to breathe. Some patients fail to respond to this treatment, however, and need to be ventilated in an intensive care unit.

What is the outlook?

About half of all children with asthma do not experience attacks as adults: the bigger they grow, the larger their airways, which helps some asthma sufferers. For those who continue to have attacks, a management plan involving regular peak flow readings and medication should keep the condition well controlled.

BRONCHIAL CARCINOMA

Lung cancer is the leading cause of death from cancer among men and women in the U.S.

What are the causes?

Smoking is responsible for the majority of lung cancer cases, and increased smoking among young women is responsible for the increase in lung cancer incidence in women. Passive smoking causes about 3,000 deaths each year. Atmospheric pollution and industrial exposure to dusts, especially asbestos, are implicated in some cases of lung cancer.

What are the symptoms?

In the early stages, cancer may not cause any symptoms. The main symptoms include a cough, in which mucus can be bloodstained, and breathlessness. As the tumor grows, the air whistles through increasingly narrow airways, causing both a wheeze and stridor. As the tumor expands, it squashes surrounding structures, such as the laryngeal nerve controlling the movement of the voice box, causing hoarseness. A tumor growing high in the lung can press against a mass of nerves under the collarbone, causing the eyelid to droop, a condition known as Horner's syndrome.

One type of bronchial carcinoma known as small-cell carcinoma has the unusual capacity to form hormones that normally regulate the levels of certain electrolytes such as sodium and calcium in the body. This can lead to additional symptoms, such as depression, because of a high calcium level; confusion, the result of a low sodium level; or obesity, because of an excess of steroids.

The most common sites of distant cancer spread (metastasis) are the bones, brain, and liver. By this stage, symptoms such as lethargy and weight loss are common. Other poorly understood signs include darkening of the skin in the armpits and changes in the nails.

How is it diagnosed?

Diagnosis is aided by scans and confirmed by obtaining a piece of the tumor and looking at it under the microscope. There are four main types of tumor, each with a slightly different behavior and sensitivity to treatment.

What are the treatment options?

Surgery is the only possible cure. The chances of success depend on the lack of spread and rely on whether the patient's health is otherwise good. Part of the problem is late diagnosis; by the time lung cancer is diagnosed, 85 percent of cases are inoperable.

Lung cancer has a 5-year survival rate of just 14 percent.

Chemotherapy, involving three to four drugs in combination, can improve survival rates by several months. Radiation is used mainly for the relief of symptoms, particularly of secondary cancers in the bones.

BRONCHIECTASIS

An abnormal dilation of the airways (bronchi) usually associated with problems in clearing mucus and other secretions from the lung.

What are the causes?

There are two main predisposing factors:

- Diseases such as cystic fibrosis in which abnormalities in the viscosity of bronchial mucus make secretions more difficult to clear. Kartagener's syndrome is a rare disease caused by an abnormality in the cilia. Recurrent infections such as measles and whooping cough in childhood may weaken the bronchial walls, and when there is a shortage of immune cells, infections are more frequent.
- Interference with the drainage of bronchial secretions. Obstruction by a foreign body, such as a peanut, a tumor, enlarged lymph gland, or a mucus plug that can form in a person with asthma, can lead to the accumulation of secretions that stagnate and become infected, causing damage to the bronchial wall.

In many cases no cause is ever found, and the bronchiectasis is described as idiopathic.

What are the symptoms?

Patients have a constant cough and produce lots of infected phlegm, which can become bloodstained. In severe cases, large amounts of blood can be coughed up, and the patient can lose weight and feel breathless and tired.

How is it diagnosed?

Characteristic patterns, including shadows resembling train lines, are visible on a chest x-ray. These shadows represent thickened, damaged bronchi. On a (CT) scan it is possible to see the dilated bronchi.

What are the treatment options?

If it is not treated promptly, complications can arise. These include pneumonia (p. 149) and abscesses (p. 138). Antibiotics are the mainstay of treatment. The danger is in the frequent use of antibiotics, because recurrent antibiotics make bacteria resistant and may diminish the effectiveness of future courses of treatment.

Long-term management of bronchiectasis includes physical therapy and postural drainage (p. 118). If the disease is very localized, surgery may be appropriate.

BRONCHIOLITIS

The name of this disease means "inflammation of the bronchioles"—the small airways of the lungs. It is the most common lung infection during infancy.

What are the causes?

In more than 75 percent of cases, the cause is a virus known as the respiratory syncytial virus, or RSV, so called because when grown in culture, it forms clumps (syncytia). RSV bronchiolitis occurs in annual winter epidemics, making it the number one cause of hospitalization for children under 1. The younger the infant, the higher the risk.

What are the symptoms?

The illness usually starts with the symptoms of a cold—such as sneezing, sniffles, and a runny nose. These develop into a dry cough, low-grade fever, and increasing breathlessness. The infant loses interest in feeding. In more severe cases, there may be wheezing and signs of distressed breathing, such as recession of the intercostal and subcostal muscles—the spaces between and below the ribs are sucked in by the increased effort to

Increasing maturity of the lungs and the immune system make bronchiolitis rare after the age of 1 year.

inhale. Finally, there may be short periods when the infant stops breathing altogether, accompanied by cyanosis around the lips and extremities caused by lack of oxygen.

How is it diagnosed?

The diagnosis may be confirmed by an immunofluoresence test of nasal secretions, in which the virus particles are "lit" by a fluorescent antibody. A chest x-ray will show if the lungs are overinflated and trapping air because of obstruction of the airways, which is caused by inflammation and swelling. In more severe cases, a blood sample is taken from an artery and checked for low levels of oxygen and elevated levels of carbon dioxide—the classic signs of respiratory failure.

What are the treatment options?

Treatment of the infection is largely "supportive" and includes giving humidified oxygen in an incubator and intravenous fluids. In severe cases, mechanical ventilation (a life-support machine) may be necessary to deliver oxygen effectively. Antibiotics are sometimes given to prevent additional bacterial infection. The antiviral drug ribavirin makes only a slight difference and may even have adverse effects, so it is used only in cases of the highest risk from infection, such as infants with underlying diseases of the heart, lungs, or immune system. Up to one third of these infants die from bronchiolitis, but only 1 percent of healthy infants succumbs.

BRONCHITIS

Inflammation of the large airways below the trachea, but not affecting the lungs themselves.

What are the causes?

Acute bronchitis is a self-limiting disease, usually caused by infection, either viral or bacterial. It affects healthy people, but more often it affects smokers, for two reasons. First, the delicate lining of the airways, the epithelium, is damaged and admits infecting organisms more readily. Second, the cilia (the tiny hairs lining the airways) do not function effectively to remove the organisms and mucus, allowing the organisms to multiply more easily.

What are the symptoms?

The main symptoms of acute bronchitis are fever and a cough, the body's usual reflex attempts to expel the infective organisms.

How is it diagnosed?

The cough may be dry or purulent with green–yellow mucus, indicating the presence of neutrophils—the immune cells responsible for first-line defenses that engulf the organisms. The sputum may be bloodstained because of inflammatory damage to the delicate blood vessels lining the airways. There may also be soreness over the front of the chest. Breathlessness is not usually a feature; if it is present, it generally indicates progression of the infection to the lungs (Pneumonia, p. 149).

What are the treatment options?

Acute bronchitis In otherwise healthy persons, rest and drinking plenty of fluids (3–4 quarts per day) are all the treatment required. Acetaminophen may be taken if the fever causes discomfort or is dangerously high (especially in infants prone to febrile, or feverish, convulsions), but it is important to remember that fevers are the body's natural response to infection and help the immune system work better. Tampering with this mechanism should be avoided as much as possible. If symptoms do not resolve after a few days, or if there is underlying disease of the lungs or heart, an antibiotic, usually penicillin, may be prescribed to kill the infection.

Chronic bronchitis This is not caused by infection but is a disease exclusively of smokers and is part of the spectrum of chronic obstructive pulmonary disease (COPD). Chronic bronchitis refers to the daily coughing up of sputum, provoked by the toxic effects of cigarette smoke. A prominent feature is the increased number of mucus-producing goblet cells lining the airways. The extra mucus is a perfect food source for viruses and bacteria, and episodes of acute bronchitis are common, known as acute exacerbations of COPD. These can be serious and even fatal. The most effective treatment for the condition is to stop smoking.

CHRONIC OBSTRUCTIVE PULMONARY DISEASE (COPD)

A chronic, slowly progressive disease of the lungs because of obstruction of the airways.

The diminished function of the lungs in COPD is largely irreversible. It is a major cause of illness and death in adults and is estimated to cost approximately $15 billion per year in healthcare expenditures. More people die from COPD than from asthma.

What are the causes?

Cigarette smoking is the main risk factor for developing COPD. Approximately 15 percent of smokers will develop the disease. It is thought that smoking probably damages the lungs by releasing enzymes that "eat away" at the walls of the alveoli. Pollution is less of a factor in the development of the disease, although death rates among people with COPD do increase in times of heavy atmospheric pollution. Urban living, social class, and occupation may play a part, but it is difficult to separate these effects from the effect of smoking.

What are the symptoms?

COPD develops over many years, and patients are usually older than 40 by the time symptoms occur. Initially, there may simply be a cough that produces phlegm, perhaps in the morning, akin to the smoker's cough. Later, a patient will begin to feel breathless, initially only accompanying exertion, but gradually exercise capacity declines. The problem is limitation of airflow when breathing out. The lungs become hyperinflated as more and more air becomes trapped inside. The symptoms of those with severe disease regularly become worse, particularly in winter, and the longer a patient has the disease, the worse the symptoms become. There is increasing breathlessness, chest tightness, and a change in the cough, usually with more pus-infused phlegm.

COPD is the fourth leading cause of death in the U.S., causing 120,000 deaths per year.

How is it diagnosed?

Lung function tests are performed to check for airflow limitation and hyperinflation of the lungs. A biopsy of lung tissue may be taken to examine microscopically for destruction of lung tissue, particularly of the alveoli. This affects the exchange of oxygen and carbon dioxide into and out of the circulation and impairs the elastic recoil of the lung.

What are the treatment options?

It is possible to slow the progression of the disease by the following:

- **Quitting smoking** This is central to altering the course of COPD. Withdrawal symptoms can now be reduced by nicotine replacement therapy with patches, inhalers, or gum. New drugs, for instance Zyban (p. 63), are being developed to increase the number of people who quit.
- **Oxygen therapy** In patients with advanced disease who are unable to maintain adequate levels of oxygen circulating to tissues, long-term oxygen therapy improves survival. Because oxygen is highly flammable, this therapy is only offered to people who have stopped smoking.
- **Vaccination** Acute episodes of infection superimposed on COPD can cause worsening breathlessness. For this reason, an influenza vaccine is advisable. Pneumococcal vaccine (against the microorganism that most commonly causes pneumonia) is also recommended.
- **Bronchodilators** Most patients find bronchodilators, such as albuterol and salmetrol, beneficial. They can be used regularly, either via an inhaler or a nebulizer in more severe cases.
- **Steroids** Steroids such as beclomethasone improve symptoms in about 10 percent of cases.

What is the outlook?

Pulmonary rehabilitation includes individually tailored exercises, education, and nutritional advice. The programs are of proven efficacy, improving exercise capability and quality of life.

Surgical options are increasingly being considered, but are appropriate in fewer than 1 percent of patients. The procedures include a reduction of the volume of the lung, lung resection, and lung transplant.

CROUP

A viral infection of early childhood that affects the larynx and the trachea. It usually occurs in a child's second year.

What are the causes?

The most common cause of croup is a virus of the parainfluenza family.

Does steam help relieve croup?

For a mild attack of stridor in a child who has croup, breathing moist air may be beneficial, although clinical trials have yet to support this. There are two ways you can do this. Simply wet a washcloth with warm water and use it to cover the child's nose and mouth. The child breathes in and out through the cloth. Alternatively, run a hot shower or bath with the bathroom door shut. When the room is steamy, sit in there with your child. If the breathing does not sound better after about 10 minutes, you should call your doctor.

ASK THE EXPERT

What are the symptoms?

Croup begins with symptoms of a cold accompanied by a fever. This is followed by a severe cough that sounds like a dog's bark. This is alarming for both the child and parents, but the most potentially dangerous feature is not the cough but the narrowing of the trachea just below its origin at the glottis. This results in a hoarse voice and a harsh noise, or stridor, during inspiration (breathing in).

Young children have narrow tracheas. During an infection, the inflammation causes swelling of the tracheal lining and an increased amount of secretions. This partially obstructs the trachea, causing stridor, and in severe cases may block it completely; this requires emergency treatment to reestablish breathing. In older children and adults, the trachea is wider, so they are not prone to this complication.

Another danger is the potential confusion of croup with a similar but more severe bacterial infection, epiglottitis, caused by *Haemophilus influenzae* type B (Hib). This has a quicker onset, does not cause a cough, and is more likely to cause respiratory obstruction. The child usually has a softer stridor, looks unwell, has a high fever, and is unable to swallow saliva. The incidence of this disease has been much reduced by the introduction of the Hib vaccine.

How is it diagnosed?

Because of the possible confusion with epiglottitis, the doctor should be seen to confirm the diagnosis. Close observation is required to check for increasing sickness, worsening stridor, or increasing recession of the sternum (breastbone), intercostal muscles, and subcostal margin (bronchiolitis, p. 141).

What are the treatment options?

Severe cases, particularly in infants, require hospital admission. No specific treatments are available, although steroids may help some children. Monitoring is continued in the hospital, and a tube can be inserted temporarily into the trachea if necessary. Ventilation on a life-support machine is necessary in up to 5 percent of children.

CRYPTOGENIC FIBROSING ALVEOLITIS

One of a group of conditions known as interstitial lung disease, affecting twice as many men as women.

The inflammation starts in the interstitium (the connective tissue between the alveoli), but the alveoli themselves soon fill up with inflammatory cells and fluid (alveolitis). This acute phase gives way to a more chronic phase in which the inflammatory debris gradually heals, leaving scar tissue that hinders respiration (fibrosis). In some people, both chronic and acute forms of the condition are present at the same time.

What is the cause?

The cause is unknown, hence the description cryptogenic (mysterious). A similar lung disease occurs in association with so-called autoimmune diseases, such as rheumatoid arthritis, systemic lupus erythematosus, and systemic sclerosis, in which the body produces antibodies that then attack it. However, there is no evidence of an autoimmune reaction in fibrosing alveolitis. Some doctors think that a viral infection may trigger the disease, but again, there is no evidence of infection in tissue samples taken from diseased lungs.

What are the symptoms?

A gradual onset of breathlessness, first with exertion but in severe cases even when at rest, is the initial symptom. Sometimes there is a dry cough. Cyanosis around the lips and fingernails may develop, caused by lack of oxygen in the blood.

How is it diagnosed?

An open lung biopsy under general anesthetic is usually needed. The disease mainly affects the lower lobes of the lungs and starts on the surface, gradually progressing inward. On a chest x-ray and CT scan, the shadowing of alveolitis often looks like ground glass. The fibrous tissue separating the air spaces resembles a net and is known as reticular shadowing. Eventually, the process may end in "honeycomb" lung (see Pulmonary fibrosis, p. 151).

What are the treatment options?

Treatment is unsatisfactory and consists of trying to suppress the inflammation with anti-inflammatory drugs such as corticosteroid tablets. Only about 20 percent of patients respond to treatment, because in most cases, irreversible scarring has already occurred. Even in patients who do respond, it is not clear whether treatment makes any difference to the final outcome.

What is the outlook?

In about half the cases, the disease remains stable; in the rest, it tends to progress. Many in the latter group of patients eventually require oxygen for large parts of the day to help with breathing, and death may occur from respiratory failure.

CYSTIC FIBROSIS

A multisystem disease characterized by recurrent infections of the lower respiratory tract, inadequate functioning of the pancreas, high salt content of sweat, and male infertility.

What is the cause?

Cystic fibrosis is the most common inherited disease among white people. The abnormal gene responsible is carried by as many as 12 million people and affects about 2,500 live births in the U.S. each year. For a baby to be affected, both the mother and father must pass on the abnormal gene. Genetic testing can reveal the presence of the gene and is offered to couples with a family history of the condition. The gene holds a code for the formation of a protein involved in regulating the viscosity of mucus. This mucus is usually secreted in the respiratory tract; the digestive system, including the pancreas; and the male genital tract. A mutation (change within the gene) causes the formation of abnormally viscid mucus in the lungs, bowel, and main ducts of the pancreas. More than 800 different mutations are known.

The gene that causes cystic fibrosis was isolated as recently as 1989 by teams at the Hospital for Sick Children in Toronto and at the University of Michigan.

What are the symptoms?

Symptoms differ according to age at the onset of the disease. Newborns fail to thrive and suffer complete blockage of the bowels. In adults, the following occur:

- Accumulation and stagnation of mucus in the airways forms a favorable medium in which bacteria can multiply, causing recurrent respiratory tract infections.
- Difficulty clearing the mucus causes the main airways to dilate to up to five times their normal diameter, a condition known as bronchiectasis. This in turn causes a cough in which excess amounts of mucus are produced and that can be bloodstained.
- Blockage of the pancreatic ducts impairs the digestion of food, particularly of proteins and fats by enzymes, and causes loss of weight and foul-smelling stools that are difficult to flush because of their high content of undigested fat.
- Damage to the pancreas can cause diabetes because the pancreas also controls insulin secretion. In addition, the liver can become shrunken and scarred, similar to the effects of cirrhosis.
- Mucus blockage in the vas deferens and the genital tract can lead to fertility problems in men.

ON THE CUTTING EDGE

Gene therapy for cystic fibrosis

Scientists are currently researching whether it is possible to use a copy of the gene responsible for cystic fibrosis as a drug in its treatment. They have succeeded in creating a copy of the gene with no defects in the laboratory and are now looking at the best way to deliver it into the lungs. Methods being tested include binding it to a virus or to liposomes (fat droplets). These can then be administered as nose drops or dripped through a bronchoscope into the lungs. These cells fuse with those of the lung lining and then manufacture the protein they are lacking. So far, results have not been lasting, and not all damaged cells have "taken up" the missing protein, but trials are under way to improve on these results.

How is it diagnosed?

The most important test available is the sweat test, which measures the concentration of sodium in sweat secretions. The genetic defect causes an increase in sodium content. A diagnosis can be achieved in the womb by measuring the levels of specific enzymes in the amniotic fluid.

What are the treatment options?

The most important treatment available for respiratory problems is physical therapy for the chest. This improves the drainage of the extra secretions in the airways. Severe infections, often with bacteria not normally found in the respiratory tract, require antibiotics injected directly into the veins. Infections can occur frequently, and in these situations it is possible to form permanent access into one of the veins in the neck. This allows patients to be cared for at home, administering their own antibiotics. Poor digestion is aided by supplements of enzymes normally found in the pancreas.

What is the outlook?

Significant improvements in early diagnosis and treatment have increased life expectancy enormously: about 39 percent of those with cyctic fibrosis in the United States are 18 years or older. Some patients are now treated with lung transplants, so even greater improvements in survival may be seen. Developments are under way to try to produce a drug that will modify the effects of the gene defect (see box), and eventually gene replacement therapy may be possible.

EMPYEMA

An accumulation of pus inside the chest.

What are the causes?

Pus is liquefied matter consisting of bacteria; cells that produce inflammation, such as neutrophils; damaged tissue; and clotted blood products. It can accumulate in the chest following an attack of pneumonia; it can follow trauma to the chest, which restricts breathing or leads to an accumulation of blood; and it can be a part of other infections, particularly tuberculosis.

Empyema was much more common in the days before antibiotics became available, when pneumonia was more prolonged and recovery was often partial rather than complete. Today, empyema can occur in a healthy person with pneumonia, but it is more likely if pneumonia has been partially treated. This may happen if, for instance, an antibiotic course is not completed. Empyema is also more likely if there is an underlying lung, heart, or immune system disease preventing complete recovery.

What are the symptoms?

Symptoms and signs of empyema may include increased breathlessness, prolonged fever not responding to antibiotics, weight loss, and an area of reduced movement on one side of the chest when breathing. To a doctor, the chest will sound "dull" on percussion, and breathing will sound quiet through a stethoscope.

How is it diagnosed?

A chest x-ray may indicate an area of increased opacity (whiteness of fluid), typically over the lower part of a lung, and an ultrasound scan of the chest can easily identify fluid and quantify the amount. The diagnosis may be confirmed by using a needle to remove a small amount of the fluid, which reveals yellow–green pus. This is cultured in order to determine the type of bacteria involved. Usually the result is available within a few days, but in the case of tuberculosis, it may take up to 6 weeks to identify.

What are the treatment options?

The basic principle of treatment is "if there is pus, let it out!" For healing to occur, the pus must be drained, either through a plastic tube or by surgical removal. A recent innovation involves introducing a substance called streptokinase through the tube, which breaks down clotted blood and allows better liquefaction and removal of pus. This has prevented the need for surgery in many cases.

HONEYCOMB LUNG

See Pulmonary fibrosis, p. 151.

HYPERSENSITIVITY PNEUMONITIS

Reactions to fungi or animal proteins present in organic dusts that are inhaled in the course of various occupations or hobbies.

Hypersensitivity reactions are more commonly known by names such as farmer's lung, malt worker's lung, bird-breeder's disease, and so on. The diseases share many features.

What is the cause?

On first inhaling the dust, the body becomes sensitized to one or more proteins and produces IgG antibodies; this is the most common type of antibodies. For instance, farmers inhaling dust from moldy hay become sensitized to the spores of a fungus, *Micropolyspora faeni.* On subsequent exposure, the antibodies bind to the spores, activating a series of proteins called complements, which attract other important immune cells such as T cells and neutrophils, leading to an inflammatory reaction.

What are the symptoms?

Attacks may start with flulike symptoms, coughing, and shortness of breath 6 or more hours after exposure; these settle down after 1–2 days. However, in many cases, individual attacks are not severe enough to warrant seeing a doctor. In addition, because of the delay between each exposure and the appearance of symptoms, the connection with the patient's occupation may not be noticed.

Unfortunately, recurrent attacks may eventually cause progressive, chronic disease in which there is permanent damage to the lung tissue in the form of granulomas (clumps of inflammatory cells surrounding dust particles) and fibrosis (scarring). This results in a chronic cough and increasing breathlessness, which eventually leads the sufferer to seek medical attention.

How is it diagnosed?

The disease may be initially suspected because of a relevant occupation or hobby. Crackles may be heard in the lungs with a stethoscope. A chest x-ray typically shows shadowing and shrinkage, caused by scarring, in the upper lobes (the site of inhalation). Lung function tests may show a reduction in the efficiency of gaseous exchange, and antibodies are often detectable in the blood.

What are the treatment options?

Like that of any allergy, the initial treatment is to prevent further exposure to the allergen. This may be achieved by wearing an efficient face mask or by changing jobs; in severe cases, retirement on the grounds of ill health may be the only option. Medical treatment such as corticosteroids may help. In severe cases, chronic oxygen therapy or even lung transplant may be necessary.

LEGIONNAIRES' DISEASE

A type of pneumonia caused by an unusual organism.

The bacteria that causes Legionnaires' disease is now called *Legionella pneumophilia*. Infection is acquired from contaminated water, often in air-conditioning systems and showers in hotels. It does not spread from person to person.

What are the symptoms?

Infected patients are often very ill compared with patients infected with common pneumonias. In addition, there is fever, vomiting, abdominal pain, and diarrhea. Often the salt levels in the blood are disturbed, causing confusion.

The first recorded outbreak of Legionnaires' disease was in 1976 in Philadelphia during an American Legion Convention, hence its name; 34 people died.

How is it diagnosed?

The diagnosis can be confirmed by a blood test; this will show a high level of antibodies that the body has formed as a defense against the bacteria.

What are the treatment options?

Treatment is with antibiotics and intravenous fluids. Despite best treatment, about 5–30 percent of patients die.

LUNG CANCER

See Bronchial carcinoma, p. 140.

OCCUPATIONAL LUNG DISEASE

Injury to the lungs caused by dusts and toxins inhaled in the workplace.

In the U.S., there are strict criteria for the diagnosis of occupational lung diseases to determine the level of compensation paid to sufferers.

ASBESTOS-RELATED DISEASE

Asbestos fibers persist in the lungs long after inhalation. At-risk groups include demolition workers and boilermakers. Several well-recognized syndromes are caused by asbestos inhalation:

- **Asbestosis** This results in progressive breathlessness and coughing, together with changes in the fingernails (clubbing). The asbestos fibers release enzymes that eat away at the lungs, producing a "honeycomb" effect on a chest x-ray.
- **Plaques** These form on the lining of the lung. They are not dangerous but indicate previous exposure to asbestos.
- **Bronchial carcinoma** This is the most common tumor caused by exposure to asbestos.
- **Mesothelioma** A tumor of the lung lining (pleura), which spreads over the pleural surface until the lung becomes encased. The patient has usually been exposed to asbestos for some 30 years before the tumor becomes apparent. No treatment has been shown to prolong life.

COAL MINER'S PNEUMOCONIOSIS

Inhalation of coal dust over prolonged periods can damage the lung. Certain types of coal—for instance, anthracite—are more likely to cause harm than others. The diagnosis is made by chest x-ray, which shows small nodules. If the nodules are less than 1.5 millimeters in diameter, the disease is in its early stages and is referred to as simple pneumoconiosis. The nodules can enlarge and merge with one another: this more severe stage is called complicated pneumoconiosis.

SILICOSIS

Resulting from the inhalation of silicon dioxide crystals, silicosis affects those involved in mining, quarrying, metal casting, sandblasting, and pottery. The illness can occur abruptly, causing fever, shortness of breath, and even death. Most people, however, experience a more chronic form of the disease, with symptoms developing gradually. Silicosis may progress even if exposure stops. A chest x-ray reveals areas of calcification with an "eggshell-like" appearance.

What are the treatment options?

These diseases are irreversible. Treatment of symptoms includes painkillers, oxygen therapy, and diuretics.

What is the outlook?

These occupational diseases cause permanent damage resulting in progressive loss of lung function and shortened life expectancy. The number of cases will rise until 2010, when the last people to have been exposed may develop symptoms.

PERTUSSIS

See Whooping cough, p. 155.

PLEURAL EFFUSION

A collection of fluid between the outer surface of the lung, lined by the visceral pleura, and the chest wall, lined by the parietal pleura.

Various disease conditions cause fluid to be secreted from the pleura in large quantities, resulting in an effusion. This compresses the lung, making breathing more difficult.

What are the causes?

The main causes are the spread of infection from pneumonia in the lung, and malignant conditions, such as lung cancer or mesothelioma (a primary cancer of the pleura). Conditions causing increased fluid retention or low blood protein (which normally "holds" fluid in the blood vessels) result in loss of fluid into the pleural space. These include liver failure, heart failure, and nephrotic syndrome (loss of protein through damaged kidneys).

What are the symptoms?

Breathlessness is the main symptom. It causes the chest to sound "dull" when it is percussed and obscures the normal breath sounds heard by a stethoscope. On chest x-rays it appears as a white shadow with a concave upper margin.

How is it diagnosed?

A sample of fluid can be withdrawn through a small needle (see p. 103) without damaging the lung, because the fluid lies immediately under the chest wall, pushing the lung away from it. This can be analyzed for the presence of bacteria or tumor cells. Its protein content will be high if an infection is present and low if there is a tumor.

What are the treatment options?

Breathlessness can be relieved by draining the fluid through a plastic tube inserted into the chest and connected to a seal to prevent air entering the pleural space. This is known as a chest drain. However, the fluid will soon return unless the underlying cause is dealt with. In incurable secondary malignant disease, the pleural space can be sealed after draining by injecting an irritant substance (such as talcum powder). This sets up an inflammatory reaction between the pleural membranes, making them stick together. This is successful in up to 70 percent of cases.

PLEURISY

A disease caused by inflammation of the pleura, the membranes that line the lung and the chest wall.

In normal circumstances, as the lung expands and shrinks with breathing in and out, the visceral pleura—the membranes that line the lung—and the parietal pleura that line the chest wall glide past each other, lubricated by a thin layer of fluid. Inflammation causes friction between the two membranes.

What are the causes?

The cause of the inflammation is usually an infection in the lungs, such as pneumonia, which has spread to involve the pleura. This type of infection is caused mainly by the bacterium *Streptococcus pneumoniae*, which may affect healthy young people. In the past, when this organism caused pneumonia predominantly affecting one lobe of the lung (lobar pneumonia), pleurisy was more common. Today, probably because of the widespread use of antibiotics, the types of pneumonia tend to be more diffuse, and pleurisy is fairly uncommon.

Pleurisy may also be caused by:

- other types of bacterial and viral pneumonias;
- inflammatory autoimmune diseases, such as systemic lupus erythematosis and rheumatoid arthritis;
- physical or chemical injury to the lungs, such as radiation treatment or inhalation of irritant chemicals.

Pleurisy may be deliberately induced by introducing an irritant substance onto the pleura or by surgical trauma in order to make the membranes stick together. This is done to prevent fluid or air accumulating in conditions such as pneumothorax or pleural effusion.

What are the symptoms?

The parietal pleura is richly supplied with nerve fibers, and the friction is felt as a sharp pain, worse when breathing in. The sufferer may take shallow breaths and hold the chest in an attempt to restrict its movement and so reduce the pain. The inflammation may also cause secretion of fluid from the pleura, resulting in a pleural effusion.

How is it diagnosed?

Diagnosis may be made from a description of the pain. When pain is referred, usually to the abdomen, the absence of symptoms of abdominal problems, such as nausea, may point to a diagnosis. Pleurisy does not cause a shadow on an x-ray, so this is of little value.

What are the treatment options?

The underlying infection has to be treated. Painkillers may be prescribed, and wrapping the chest in elastic bandages may offer some relief.

PNEUMONIA

Pneumonia is an infection of the lung tissue in the lower part of the respiratory tract, which includes the bronchi and bronchioles.

Pneumonia is an infection of the lower respiratory tract. Pneumonia causes more deaths than any other infection in the Western world, especially in old age.

What are the causes?

The causes of pneumonia depend on a range of factors including age, the state of the immune system, and exposure to relevant organisms. These organisms vary according to whether the disease is contracted in the community or in the hospital.

- In children, the most common cause is a virus, such as respiratory syncytial virus (RSV) or parainfluenza virus.
- In healthy adults, bacteria such as pneumococcus (the most common), *Streptococcus pneumoniae*, and *Haemophilus influenzae* are the most usual causes. Other organisms causing atypical pneumonias, which do not respond to antibiotics, include *Mycoplasma pneumoniae*, *Legionella pneumophilia*, and *Chlamydia pneumoniae*.

There are 30 separate organisms known to cause pneumonia.

In the hospital, bacteria such as *Klebsiella pneumoniae* and tuberculosis are the most common causes of pneumonia. *Pneumocystis carinii*, a protozoan, is the most common organism causing pneumonia in AIDS patients.

What are the symptoms?

The most obvious symptoms of pneumonia are a cough, fever, and breathlessness.

How is it diagnosed?

Shadowing on the lung shows up on a chest x-ray. Crackles (the sound of fluid in the alveoli) may be heard through a stethoscope. Cultures of sputum and blood samples can help identify the cause, and blood gas analysis can indicate severity by measuring oxygen levels in the blood. *Mycoplasma pneumoniae* often causes initial headaches rather than respiratory symptoms.

What are the treatment options?

Treatment consists of appropriate antibiotics, together with supportive measures such as fluid replacement and oxygen therapy. Mild cases can be treated at home, but hospital treatment is often required. Antiviral drugs are used to treat some viral pneumonias. Chest pain can be treated with analgesics.

PNEUMOTHORAX

Pneumothorax, literally "air chest," refers to the entry of air between the outside of the lung and the chest wall.

What are the causes?

The condition can occur following external trauma such as an accident (traumatic pneumothorax), when air enters from outside, or without trauma (spontaneous pneumothorax), when air enters from the lung itself.

- **Spontaneous pneumothorax** This condition can occur in fit, healthy young people—usually tall, thin men—but it generally affects people with underlying chest disease such as chronic obstructive pulmonary disease (p. 142) or asthma (p. 139). Only one lung is affected in most cases: outside air pushes against the lung, restricting expansion, affecting air entry and oxygen transport into the blood.
- **Tension pneumothorax** When air enters the space outside the lung with each breath but cannot escape, tension pneumothorax results. The pressure on the lung increases until the lung collapses. This is a life-threatening emergency.

What are the symptoms?

Pneumothorax occurs suddenly and may cause a typical pain, which is sharp and occurs when breathing in, often forcing the person to take shallow breaths and hold the affected part of the chest. There is also sudden shortness of breath. Tension pneumothorax may cause a collapse, cyanosis, respiratory failure, and sudden death.

How is it diagnosed?

On the affected side, there is less chest movement, and air entry is quieter when heard through a stethoscope. The extra air outside the lung may cause greater resonance than normal, or hyperresonance, when the chest is tapped with a finger. Tension pneumothorax causes the affected side to expand, pushing the trachea away from that side.

The diagnosis is usually confirmed with a chest x-ray. This shows the air outside the lung as a black shadow, with the border of the lung visible.

What are the treatment options?

In mild cases, a needle is inserted to withdraw the air, with the hope that the lung will seal itself. In more severe cases and in traumatic pneumothorax, a chest drain is inserted. The lung's natural pressures release the extra air in a few days. In tension pneumothorax, a needle is inserted to release the high-pressure air, followed by a chest drain.

PULMONARY EDEMA

Pulmonary edema, literally "swelling," is the filling of the alveoli with fluid because of left-sided heart failure.

What is the cause?

When the left side of the heart stops pumping effectively (for a number of possible reasons, including coronary heart disease, high blood pressure, and disease of the heart valves), there is a buildup of fluid in the pulmonary veins. This fluid leaks out into the alveoli and interferes with oxygen uptake. In addition, the blood pressure in the rest of the body drops, which is interpreted by the body as a loss of fluid. A hormonal system known as the renin-angiotensin-aldosterone system inappropriately constricts peripheral blood vessels and causes the kidneys to retain even more fluid, which worsens the situation in the lungs.

What are the symptoms?

The symptoms depend on whether the left ventricular failure occurs suddenly (acute pulmonary edema) or more gradually (chronic heart failure). Acute pulmonary edema can be life-threatening, with sudden onset of breathlessness, sweating, and clamminess, and cyanosis and collapse if it is severe. In chronic heart failure, breathlessness increases gradually, initially with exertion and eventually at rest, too. It also occurs when lying down and at night, which may wake the patient up. Fatigue is also common.

What are the treatment options?

In acute pulmonary edema, the patient is resuscitated with oxygen. Morphine is given intravenously to dilate the body's arteries, reducing the strain on the heart. Diuretics are given intravenously to allow the body to excrete fluid through the kidneys. The patient is cared for in a coronary care unit, where continuous monitoring is available.

The treatment of chronic heart failure includes oral diuretics and angiotensin-converting enzyme (ACE) inhibitors, which inhibit the renin-angiotensin-aldosterone system. Treatment is also directed at the underlying cause, such as drugs for coronary heart disease and high blood pressure and attention to lifestyle factors such as smoking, diet, and exercise.

What is the outlook?

Unfortunately, despite treatment, the prognosis for patients with heart failure is still poor—as bad as most cancers.

PULMONARY EMBOLISM

A blockage of a blood vessel in the lung, commonly by a thrombus—a clot made up of a mass of cells.

A thrombus can occur anywhere and travel anywhere in the body. It can break off from the blood vessel wall where it formed and travel in the circulation until it becomes stuck. If one forms in a vein, it can travel to the heart and be propelled into the lung, causing a pulmonary embolus.

What are the causes?

Most pulmonary emboli arise from a thrombus in the deep veins of the leg. Their formation is promoted by sluggish blood in the veins. This occurs when a person is immobile, perhaps after surgery or illness. Other predisposing factors include oral contraceptive pills and cancer. A deep vein thrombosis might cause pain and swelling in the calf, but it can go unnoticed. Once the thrombus reaches the lung, it sits in a pulmonary artery. Part of the lung is damaged as it is starved of oxygen, putting the heart under strain.

What are the symptoms?

Symptoms depend on the extent of the blockage. In mild cases, patients may complain of slight breathlessness. Some may experience chest pain, typically worse when breathing in. Larger emboli can cause severe chest pain, and the patient will be pale, sweaty, and in shock; these emboli put serious pressure on the heart, which can lead to cardiac arrest.

How is it diagnosed?

A special lung scan helps with diagnosis: a radioactive dye is injected into the patient, and this can reveal areas of the lung that are receiving enough oxygen from respiration but that are not well supplied with blood.

What are the treatment options?

The purpose of treatment is to halt the movement of the thrombus and avoid further pulmonary emboli. The drug heparin, injected into a vein or under the skin, is used to stop the process of clot formation. Warfarin is a similar-acting drug that can be taken orally. Often, patients are discharged with warfarin to take for at least 6 months.

PULMONARY FIBROSIS

This is not a single disease but a pathological process characterized by irregular scarring of the lungs.

In pulmonary fibrosis, the affected parts of the lung do not function efficiently, and the condition can cause respiratory failure. It may be referred to as honeycomb lung because of the characteristic appearance of the lung: its structure is distorted by shrinkage and scarring, leaving air spaces separated by strands of fibrous tissue, like a honeycomb.

What are the causes?

There are many causes of the syndrome, including the following:

- cryptogenic fibrosing alveolitis (p. 144);
- occupational lung disease (p. 147);
- autoimmune diseases, in which the body produces antibodies that attack itself, such as rheumatoid arthritis, systemic lupus erythematosus, systemic sclerosis, and ankylosing spondylitis;
- allergic bronchopulmonary aspergillosis, an allergic lung response to aspergillus, a common fungus, often seen in patients with asthma;
- hypersensitivity pneumonitis (p. 146);
- certain medications such as the heart drug amiodarone, the immuno-suppressant methotrexate, and some anticancer drugs.

TALKING POINT

Do the health risks of obesity outweigh those of pulmonary hypertension?

Researchers have argued that certain appetite-suppressing drugs known to cause pulmonary hypertension may have a place in a managed weight loss program if used for less than a year. Obesity is a major risk factor for diabetes and heart disease; it is second only to smoking as a cause of preventable death. Studies have shown that women with a body mass index (BMI)—a ratio obtained by dividing weight in kilos by height in meters squared—between 29 and 32 were up to 70 percent more likely to die early than those whose BMI was between 25 and 27, resulting in 1,260 preventable deaths per million women every year. They estimated that appetite-suppressant drugs, by contrast, caused 14 deaths per million patients treated.

What are the symptoms?

Common symptoms include breathlessness and a dry cough. Cyanosis (blueness around the lips and fingertips) may develop as a result of lack of oxygen in the blood. Eventually, the lack of oxygen forces the heart to work too hard, and heart failure develops.

How is it diagnosed?

Diagnosis is usually confirmed with a chest x-ray, a computed tomography (CT) scan, and an open lung biopsy. If possible, the cause is identified from the patient's history (for instance, a relevant occupation or use of a causative drug) and blood tests.

It is hoped that drugs with a similar effect to prostacyclin will soon be available in inhaled or oral form.

What are the treatment options?

Treatment varies according to the underlying condition but may include oxygen therapy (p. 120) and diuretics.

PULMONARY HYPERTENSION AND VASCULAR SCLEROSIS

A syndrome of increased blood pressure in the pulmonary vessels because of their constriction.

Pulmonary hypertension can lead to right-sided heart failure because this side of the heart has to work harder with the increased pressure in the pulmonary vessels.

What are the causes?

It can occur, for no apparent reason, in otherwise healthy young people; in these cases, it is known as primary pulmonary hypertension. More commonly, it is an effect of other heart or lung diseases (when it is called secondary pulmonary hypertension), such as chronic obstructive pulmonary disease (p. 142), pulmonary fibrosis, and chronic pulmonary embolism. It has also occurred because of certain appetite-suppressing drugs used as weight loss aids.

What are the symptoms?

Primary pulmonary hypertension is a rare but serious disease that affects mostly women, typically in their 20s or 30s. Breathlessness is the main symptom. Without treatment, the disease is progressive and may be fatal. If it is identified early, treatment can be successful. Apart from the symptoms of the underlying problem, the symptoms of secondary pulmonary hypertension are predominantly breathlessness and swelling of the legs caused by right-sided heart failure.

How is it diagnosed?

Sophisticated tests of heart and lung function are required to make the diagnosis. An echocardiogram allows measurement of the heart's chambers and main pulmonary vessels. In addition, a fine tube can be inserted in the groin and advanced into the heart, then short-acting dyes and drugs are injected to give detailed information about the heart.

What are the treatment options?

Currently, treatment of primary pulmonary hypertension consists of a substance called prostacyclin, which is naturally produced by the body and has the effect of dilating, or relaxing, the constricted vessels. It is given as a continuous infusion into the skin, which involves wearing a pump about the size of a personal cassette player. This drug has minor side effects but improves symptoms and also prolongs survival.

Treatment of secondary pulmonary hypertension is directed at the underlying cause, often with diuretics for the leg swelling. In chronic obstructive pulmonary disease (p. 142), oxygen therapy is effective in delaying the progression of pulmonary hypertension. Heart–lung or lung transplant may be offered.

PULMONARY INFARCTION

The death of lung tissue as a result of blockage of the arteries supplying the affected tissue.

Pulmonary infarction is relatively uncommon compared with myocardial infarction (heart attack). This is because the lungs have a rich blood supply from large arteries that are not easily blocked, unlike the heart, which is supplied by three small arteries, all susceptible to blockage.

What are the causes?

The most common cause is pulmonary embolism. If large pulmonary emboli block major arteries supplying the lungs with oxygenated blood, areas of lung beyond the blockage are starved of oxygen and die.

Other causes are inflammatory disorders affecting blood vessels (vasculitis). These are autoimmune diseases, in which the body manufactures antibodies against some of its own common cell components. They include Wegener's granulomatosis, polyarteritis nodosa and Goodpasture's syndrome. These diseases strike suddenly and for unknown reasons, causing inflammation and blockage of arteries, which results in pulmonary infarction.

What are the symptoms?

In addition to the symptoms of pulmonary embolism (breathlessness, chest pain, and collapse if severe), there may be hemoptysis (coughing up blood) when infarction is a major factor. The autoimmune diseases also affect other organs, particularly the kidneys, leading to hematuria (blood in the urine) and renal failure.

How is it diagnosed?

The lack of oxygen to the tissues causes a buildup of acid, which lowers the pH of the blood (a metabolic acidosis); this is measurable by a blood test. A chest x-ray may show characteristic wedge-shaped shadows at the edges of the lung where the tissue is most vulnerable to infarction.

What are the treatment options?

The treatment is, first, to support the function of the lungs and circulation with an oxygen mask, and if the infarction is severe enough to cause respiratory failure, with mechanical ventilation on a life-support machine. The underlying cause must then be addressed, for instance with blood-thinning medication for pulmonary embolism or immune-suppressing drugs for vasculitis.

SARCOIDOSIS

An uncommon disease that can affect many different organs, most frequently the eyes, skin, and lungs, where it causes scarring that often results in breathlessness.

Most often affecting people between the ages of 20 and 40, sarcoidosis is more persistent in black people than white (for unknown reasons). The cause remains obscure, but it does not appear to be an infection. When diseased tissue is examined under the microscope, it exhibits granuloma. This is a cluster of cells that has taken part in an inflammatory reaction toward an as yet unidentified agent. A similar pattern is seen in tuberculosis.

What are the symptoms?

Lung disease includes enlargement of the glands at the center of the lung and scarring, causing breathlessness. The eyes become inflamed, causing pain and redness; this is known as uveitis. The skin, commonly on the shins, may develop a nodular, purple rash (erythema nodosum), which can be painful. Sarcoidosis may involve the nervous system, causing paralysis of the facial nerve and a form of non-infectious meningitis. It can also affect bone, dissolving the calcium and raising the level of calcium in the blood. This can cause such symptoms as confusion and abdominal pain.

How is it diagnosed?

In the absence of a known cause, sarcoidosis is diagnosed only when other conditions are excluded. The symptoms are not specific, and there are no diagnostic blood tests. To help with the diagnosis, it is necessary to take a biopsy sample from the most accessible organ with disease, usually the lung.

What are the treatment options?

The disease often resolves spontaneously without requiring treatment, and all that may be necessary is regular follow-up and x-rays. However, there are particular situations where treatment with steroid tablets is necessary. These include lung disease causing severe shortness of breath, eye disease threatening sight, and involvement of vital organs such as the heart or nervous system. In most cases a 6-month course is required, and during this period dosages will be gradually reduced to minimize side effects.

TUBERCULOSIS (TB)

A highly infectious disease that can affect any organ, but most commonly the lungs; formerly known as consumption.

In the U.S. during the 19th century, TB caused more deaths than any other disease. There was a dramatic decline in this number in the first half of the 20th century, probably because of improved nutrition and sanitation, followed up with the discovery of effective antibiotics. From an all-time low of about 22,000 cases in 1985, however, TB started to reemerge, although rates in the U.S. are generally declining again. The disease is more prevalent in some parts of the world and among certain sectors of society.

What is the cause?

TB is caused by the bacterium *Mycobacterium tuberculosis*. The recent rise in cases is mainly fueled by the increased number of HIV-infected people, in whom tuberculosis is a common complication. Well-recognized at-risk populations include the elderly, immigrants from the Indian subcontinent and Far East, hospital employees, and people with other diseases that are damaging the body's defenses, for example diabetes and alcoholism, and those undergoing certain treatments, such as steroids or chemotherapy. In addition, homelessness, overcrowding, poor ventilation, and malnutrition all contribute.

What is being done to control TB worldwide?

Part of the World Health Organization strategy to reduce the spread of TB and the number of deaths caused is known as DOTS—directly observed treatment, short course. There are five main elements to DOTS. First, there has to be political commitment to TB control in the country concerned. Second, individuals suspected of having the disease are diagnosed as quickly as possible by sputum analysis. Third, drug treatment is begun: for the first 2 months (of the 6–8 months necessary for treatment), health-care workers and public health officials support the patient to ensure that the correct drugs are taken at the right time. Knowing the number of patients being treated enables the fourth part of the plan—ensuring an adequate supply of drugs—to be followed. Finally, health-care workers record and evaluate whether patients are being cured and therefore whether the number of cases is falling.

ASK THE EXPERT

What are the symptoms?

There are three stages of infection. Primary TB is the first infection, usually occurring in childhood, and is normally without symptoms. An inflammatory reaction around the bacteria breaks down to form a cheeselike nodule (caseation), then heals (fibrosis) and calcifies. This calcification is often evident on a chest x-ray. The bacteria have the ability to survive within the walls of the inflammatory reaction without causing symptoms. At this stage the disease is known as latent TB, until a causal factor (listed earlier) leads to reactivation of the disease as postprimary TB. This secondary stage of infection can heal and calcify, but it can also rupture into the lung airways, causing pneumonia. The patient may initially feel tired and experience weight loss. More specifically, there may be a cough, sometimes containing blood (hemoptysis), pain in the chest, and breathlessness. The infection may also spread via the blood to the liver, spleen, bone, and the lining of the brain. This is called miliary TB because the organs look as if they are full of millet grains. The widespread infection is serious.

How is it diagnosed?

The most reliable way of confirming the diagnosis is by isolating the bacteria in the sputum and performing a stain test in a laboratory. Sometimes sputum is not available, and a bronchoscopy or even a biopsy of the affected organ needs to be performed. Chest x-rays can help in the diagnosis, showing characteristic features such as shadowing in the upper lobes of the lung and calcification.

What are the treatment options?

TB is curable, but several antibiotics must be taken daily for at least 6 months. Drug resistance has become a problem, and additional antibiotics may be needed.

There is evidence that malnutrition lowers resistance to TB, so a good diet is essential. Smoking and alcohol reduce the body's defenses to the bacteria, too. Contact tracing allows identification of all people in close contact to an infected person. These people need to be tested to see whether they have the disease, and they may then be fully treated or given a short course of antibiotics if they are at high risk of developing the disease.

Advances in immunology mean that the prospect of improved TB vaccines in the future is high.

UPPER RESPIRATORY TRACT INFECTIONS (URTIs)

Infections of the upper respiratory tract are the most common infections known in humans.

URTIs include colds, sore throats (pharyngitis), tonsillitis, ear infections (otitis), sinusitis, laryngitis, and bronchitis. The types of organisms responsible include viruses, bacteria, and fungi. Many of these, such as cold viruses, influenza, and streptococci, possess properties that allow them to infect healthy people, but others (such as *Candida* fungi) only flourish if the immune system of the host is impaired.

ACUTE PHARYNGITIS

Pharyngitis can either occur alone or in association with a cold or because of immune responses and inflammation in the lymphatic tissue known as Waldeyer's ring, which includes the tonsils and adenoids.

What is the cause?

More than 70 percent of cases are caused by viruses such as the Epstein-Barr virus (which causes glandular fever) and adenoviruses. The most common bacterial infection is with *Streptococcus pyogenes* group A.

What are the symptoms?

As well as a red, sore throat, the patient may have a raised temperature and headache and feel chilly. Glands in the neck may be swollen, and there may be a dry cough.

How is it diagnosed?

A throat swab is taken to help identify if bacterial infection is present.

What are the treatment options?

Painkillers such as acetaminophen or aspirin will help to relieve the soreness, as will drinking plenty of fluids. If bacterial infection is present, antibiotics may be prescribed, but overuse of antibiotics for viral sore throats may encourage bacterial resistance.

What is the outlook?

Potentially serious complications of infection with *Streptococcus* include scarlatina (a widespread red skin rash) and renal disease. These complications are, however, much less common since the advent of penicillin.

COMMON COLD

The common cold is the most frequent infection of the upper respiratory tract.

What is the cause?

Colds may be caused by many different strains of virus, although more than 50 percent of them are caused by two main groups: the rhinoviruses and coronaviruses. These have the ability to stick to cells lining the nasopharynx (the nose and throat), despite the attempts of the cilia (minute hairs on the outside of the cells) to brush them away. They then enter the cells and force them to divert their energies to making new virus copies.

What are the symptoms?

The viruses stimulate secretion of large amounts of fluid, which causes the sneezing and coughing reflex. This high-speed aerosol successfully spreads millions of viruses to other humans. At the same time, the immune system produces chemicals, such as interferon, which raise body temperature, producing lethargy, fever, sweating, and loss of appetite. These effects all help the body to concentrate on the fight against the virus. This usually takes several days.

What are the treatment options?

No special treatment is needed beyond measures to alleviate the symptoms and make life more comfortable. These include acetaminophen or aspirin, cough medicines, and nasal sprays or inhalation to help clear blocked nasal and sinus passages. Additional fluids and rest may be needed.

INFLUENZA

There is an outbreak of influenza virtually every winter, and although they vary in their severity and extent, many vulnerable people die in each outbreak. Widespread outbreaks, known as epidemics, occur every 1–3 years on average. Once every 10–15 years, a global epidemic, or pandemic, occurs.

What are the causes?

Of the three groups of influenza viruses (A, B, and C), influenza A is the one responsible for most severe cases of human illness.

HELP YOUR DOCTOR TO HELP YOU

Common sense and the flu

The influenza vaccine is made up each year from the most common strains and is very effective. It has to be repeated every year. You can help your doctor by taking the following steps:

- *If you are in a group for whom vaccination is recommended (p. 47), see your doctor in September for an injection.*
- *The elderly and those with underlying chest or heart disease are most at risk of complications. Influenza may progress to pneumonia, with breathlessness, wheezing, and a cough producing phlegm. See your doctor as soon as possible if you experience any of these symptoms.*
- *If you are in good general health, you do not need to see your doctor if you have the flu. To alleviate symptoms, rest, take painkillers, and drink plenty of fluids.*

What are the symptoms?

In healthy adults and children, influenza is more of a nuisance than a severe illness. The onset is often sudden, and headaches, high fever with chills, weakness, muscle ache, cough, and sore throat are the main symptoms.

What are the treatment options?

Rest, high fluid intake, and acetaminophen or aspirin for fever and muscle ache are all that is required (aspirin should be avoided for children). The inhaled antiviral drug zanamivir may be given to those most at risk of complications. Usually, the illness lasts about a week.

WHOOPING COUGH

A serious, highly infectious childhood disease spread by airborne droplets released by coughing or sneezing. Babies are routinely vaccinated against whooping cough.

What is the cause?

Whooping cough is caused by the bacteria *Bordetella pertussis*. The bacteria attaches itself to the cilia of cells lining the upper respiratory tract and releases toxins that impair the structure and function of these cells.

What are the symptoms?

The disease starts with the symptoms of a cold. After a few days a characteristic cough develops, worse at night and producing much mucus. Coughing spasms are so severe that the child may become red or blue in the face, ending in a desperate inward gasp of air causing a "whoop" sound.

How is it diagnosed?

The characteristic whooping cough is the easiest way to recognize the illness.

What are the treatment options?

Because of the increased risk of complications, children younger than 1 are usually admitted to the hospital and isolated. Older children are kept at home unless very sick. Treatment with the antibiotic erythromycin helps to some extent, and reduces the spread of the disease.

What is the outlook?

Most children recover fully, although some remain prone to bacterial infection. In severe cases, blood flow to the brain may be impaired, causing seizures, which can lead to brain damage. Secondary bacterial pneumonia may occur.

Index

Acknowledgments

Carroll & Brown Limited would also like to thank:

Picture researcher
Sandra Schneider

Production manager
Karol Davies

Production controller
Nigel Reed

Computer management
Paul Stradling

Indexer
Jill Dormon

3-D anatomy
Mirashade/Matt Gould

Illustrators
Andy Baker, Jacey, Kevin Jones Associates, Debbie Maizels, Mikki Rain, John Woodcock, Jurgen Ziewe

Photographers
Jules Selmes, David Murray

Yoga programme demonstrated by
Judi Medhurst (07788 968220)

Photographic sources
7 GCa-CNRI/SPL
8 *(top left)* Dr Linda Stannard, UCT/SPL
(bottom) "Courtesy of Tourism New Zealand"
9 Claude Nuridsany and Marie Perennou/SPL
10 *(top)* Clinical Radiology Dept., Salisbury District Hospital/SPL
(bottom left) Keith/Custom Medical Stock Photo/SPL
10/11 Corbis/Stockmarket
11 *(right)* Pictor
(bottom) CNRI/SPL
12 *(top)* Image Bank
(bottom) Allsport
13 Dr. Linda Stannard, UCT/SPL
14 *(right)* Corbis/Stockmarket
18 *(top right)* GettyOne Stone
24 *(bottom left)* SPL
24/25 Wellcome Trust Medical Photographic Library/Medical Art Service, Munich
31 *(top)* Prof. P. Motta/Dept. of Anatomy/University "La Sapienza," Rome/SPL
35 *(top)* Corbis/Stockmarket
(bottom) Telegraph Colour Library
36 *(center)* Corbis/Stockmarket
38 *(left)* Angela Hampton/Family Life Pictures
47 *(center)* Angela Hampton/Family Life Pictures
51 Mark Clarke/SPL
53 *(center, bottom)* Image Bank
55 *(top)* Dr. Linda Stannard, UCT/SPL
(bottom) Corbis/Stockmarket
57 *(right, second from bottom)* Corbis/Stockmarket
59 Bedfont Scientific Limited
60 *(left)* Bubbles/Chris Rout
61 GettyOne Stone
62 *(center left)* Ruth Jenkinson/ MIDIRS/SPL
(center right) Corbis/Stockmarket
63 *(center right, bottom right)* Corbis/Stockmarket
70 Matthew Munro/SPL
70/1 Corbis/Stockmarket
73 *(top left)* Retna/Jenny Acheson
(top right) Matthew Munro/SPL
(bottom left) Corbis/Stockmarket
74 *(top)* Corbis/Stockmarket
(bottom) Matthew Oldfield/SPL
76 *(center left)* Sandra Schneider
77 *(bottom)* Mauro Fermariello/SPL
78 *(top)* Malcolm Earl/medipics
(bottom) Performing Arts Library
79 *(left)* Pictor
(right top) Ken Biggs/SPL
(second from top) James King-Holmes/SPL
(second from bottom) Dr. Jeremy Burgess/SPL
(bottom) K. H. Kjeldsen/SPL
80 Ken Biggs/SPL
81 *(top)* David Murray
(bottom) Tim Lester/SPL
82 GettyOne Stone
83 James King-Holmes /SPL
85 Dr. Jeremy Burgess/SPL
86 *(top)* Alexander Tsiaras/SPL
88 K. H. Kjeldsen/SPL
89 Pictor
90 *(left)* Dr. Linda Stannard UCT/SPL
(center) Mark Clarke/SPL
91 Salisbury District Hospital/SPL
94 *(top)* CNRI/SPL
(bottom) Wellcome Photo Library/Anthea Sieveking
98 *(top)* Simon Fraser/SPL
(bottom) Mauro Fermariello/SPL
99 Malcolm Earl/medipics
100 Geoff Tompkinson/SPL
101 *(top)* Larry Mulvehill/SPL
(bottom) James Prince/SPL
102 *(top)* Dr. Linda Stannard, UCT/SPL
(bottom) Institut Pasteur/CNRI/ SPL
103 *(top right)* Jurgen Berger, Max-Planck Institute/SPL
104 *(top)* Frederick C. Skvara/medipics
(bottom) Sinclair Stammers
106 *(left)* By kind permission of Dr. Ruth Whitfield, Chest Clinic, Mayday Hospital, Croydon
(bottom) Wellcome Trust Medical Photographic Library
106/7 as 106 *(left)*
107 *(top center)* Wellcome Trust Medical Photographic Library
(top right) BSIP, Laurent/ H. Americain/SPL
(center right) Blair Sietz/SPL
(bottom) Salisbury District Hospital/SPL
109 *(top)* GCa-CNRI/SPL
(bottom) Simon Fraser/SPL
110 *(center)* Volker Steger/SPL
(bottom) Alexander Tsiaras/SPL
111 BSIP, Laurent/H. Americain/SPL
112 NIBSC/SPL
115 *(top)* Mark Clarke/SPL
(bottom) Garry Watson/SPL
120 BSIP, Laurent, Meeus/SPL
121 "Courtesy of BOC, Guildford"
122 *(top)* Simon Fraser/SPL
(bottom) CNRI/SPL
123 Peter Menzel/SPL
124–128 Nick Geddes/medipics
129 Peter Menzel/SPL
130/1 Nick Geddes/medipics

Back cover *(right)* CNRI/SPL

619–004–1